Marine Animals

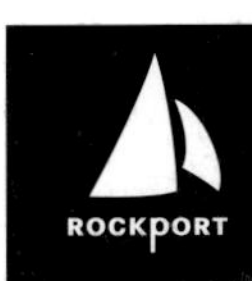

First published in 2011 in the USA by
Rockport Publishers, a member of
Quayside Publishing Group
100 Cummings Center / 406-L
Beverly, Massachusetts 01915
USA
Phone: 987-282-9590
Fax: 978-283-2742
www.rockpub.com

Illustrations for Templates: Curl, Miwa Hirose, Yuki Kobayashi
Illustrations for Components: RYOKEN
Illustrations for Examples In Use: Andrew Pothecary (forbiddencolour)
Art Direction: Katsuya Moriizumi
Design: Andrew Pothecary (forbiddencolour)
Translation: Alma Reyes (ricorico)
Editing: Rico Komanoya (ricorico)

ISBN-13: 978-1-59253-659-7
ISBN-10: 1-59253-659-X

10 9 8 7 6 5 4 3 2 1

Printed in China

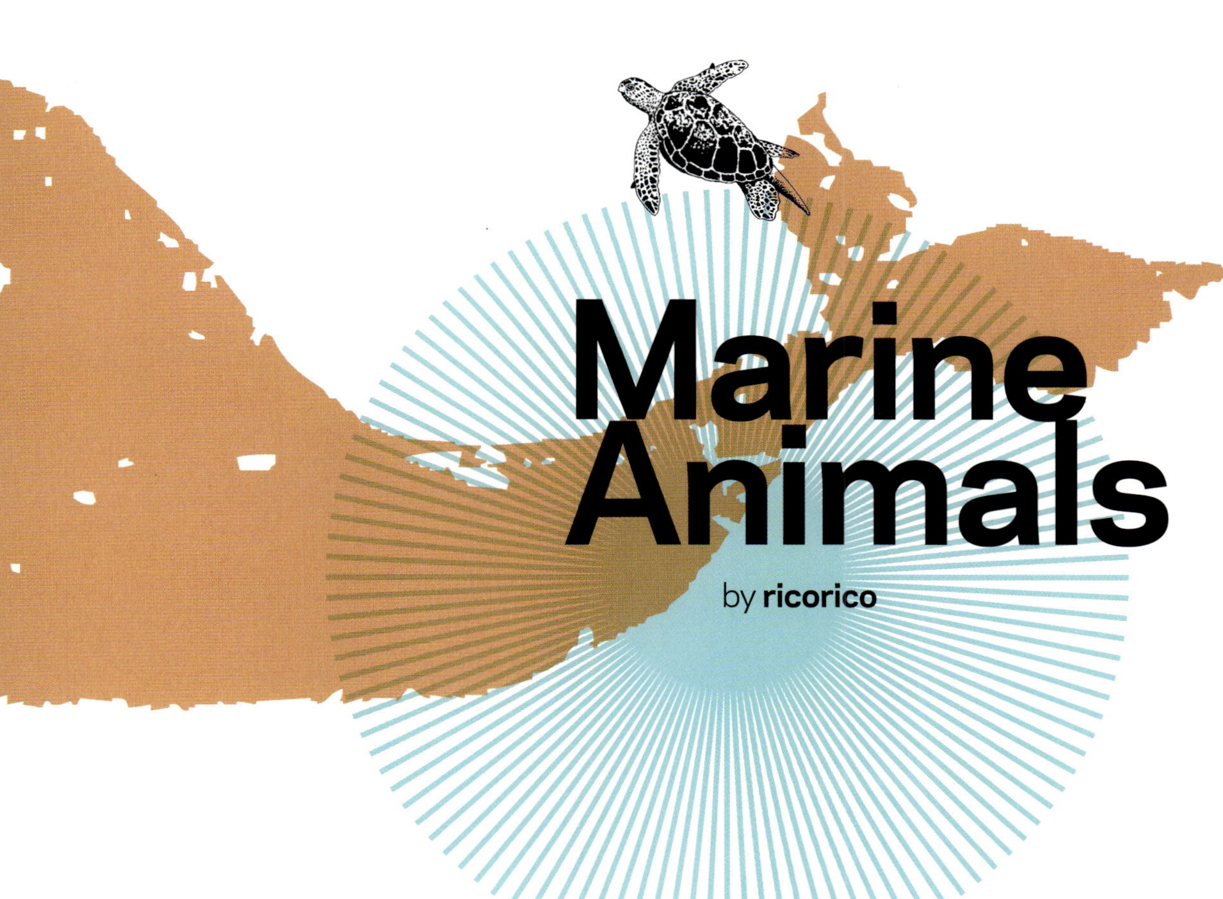

Marine Animals

by **ricorico**

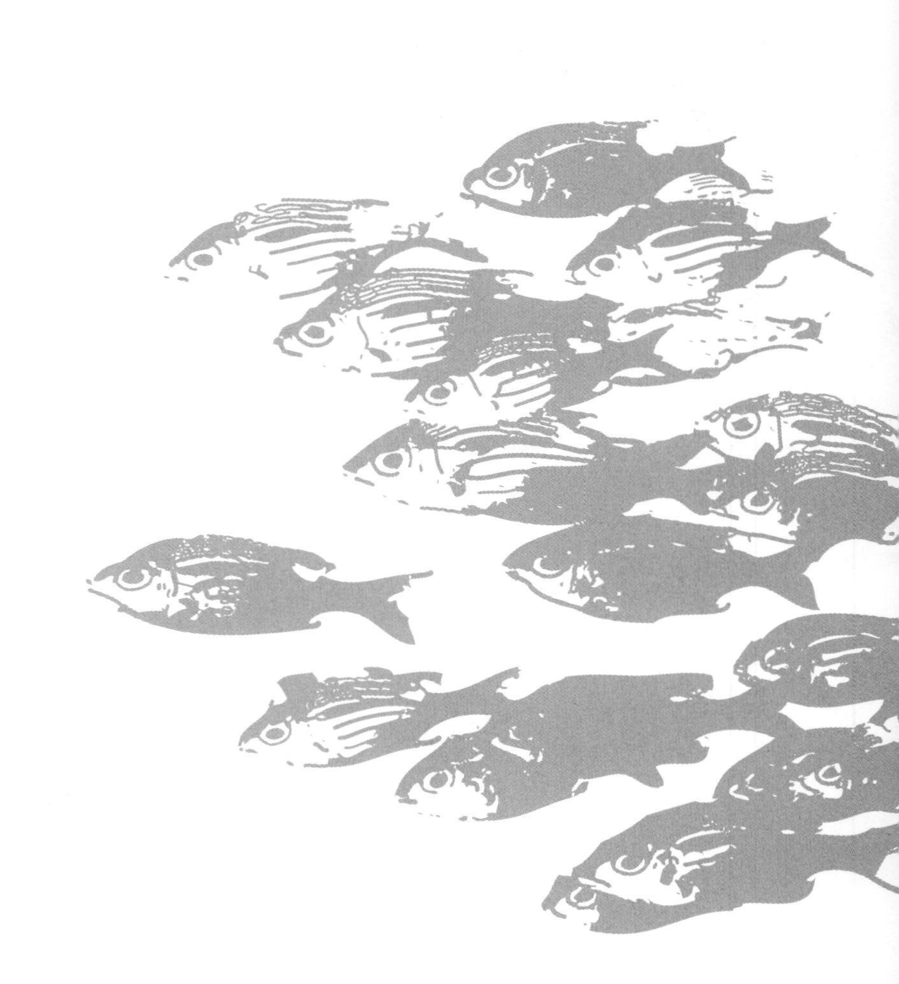

CONTENTS

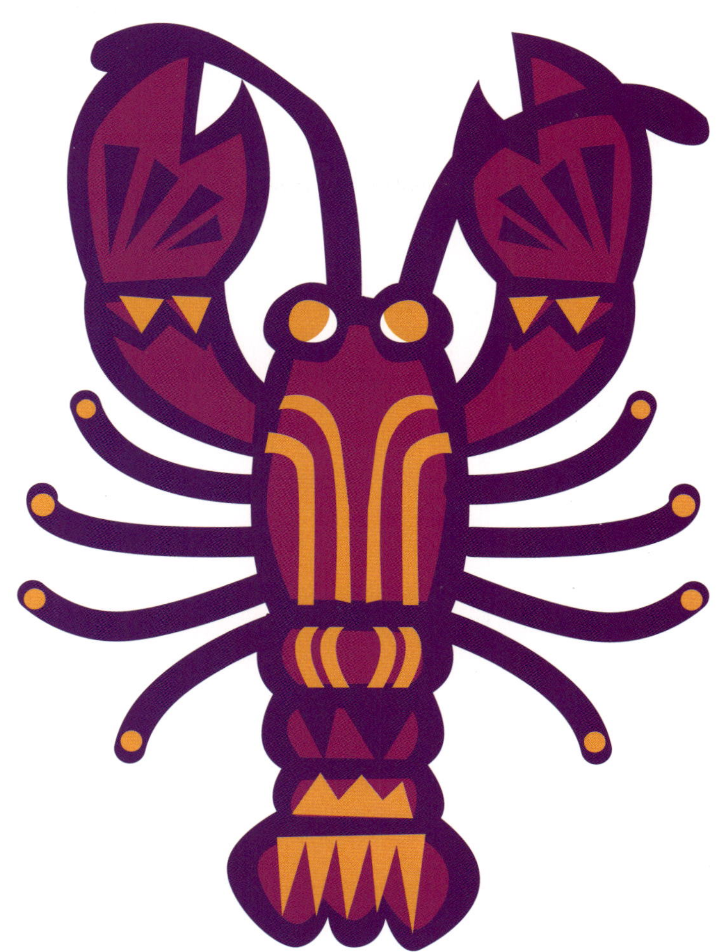

HOW TO USE THIS BOOK AND THE CD-ROM

This volume is a collection of usable artworks for designers and artists that features hundreds of popular and thematic subjects. It is designed to highlight the following categories:

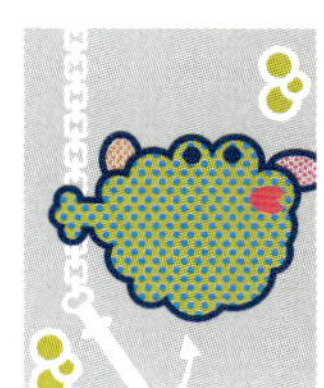

Templates: *These are designed to be used as is, or to be manipulated, edited, and/or modified as preferred, for your personal and professional use. This chapter lies in the middle section of the book, and shows one item per page in order for you to see its details.*

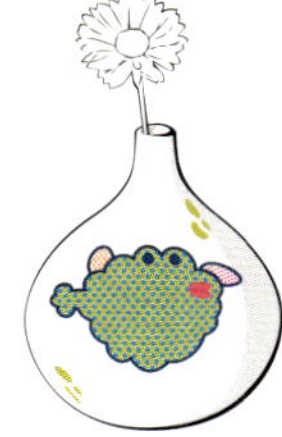

Examples of Applied Templates: *In the following page, and before the Templates chapter begins, there are seventeen variations of examples of the applied templates illustrated in this chapter. From printed materials to interior decoration items, you can see how effectively the entire template drawing or a part of it can be rendered.*

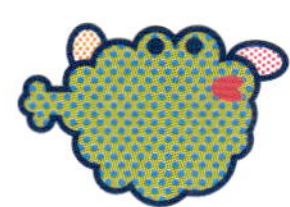

Components: *All templates are made of multiple components introduced in this chapter. These components can be used as single or combined items, or joined with other components from other templates, to create your own unique and original artworks. The file numbers of the components correspond to the page number of the template illustrations.*

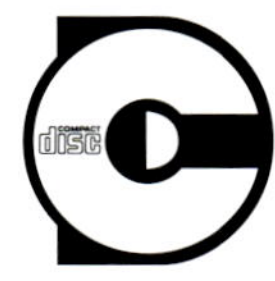

CD-ROM: *All the original files for the templates and components are digitally archived both in JPEG and in Adobe Illustrator vector files in the CD-ROM that is attached at the end of the book.*

EXAMPLES

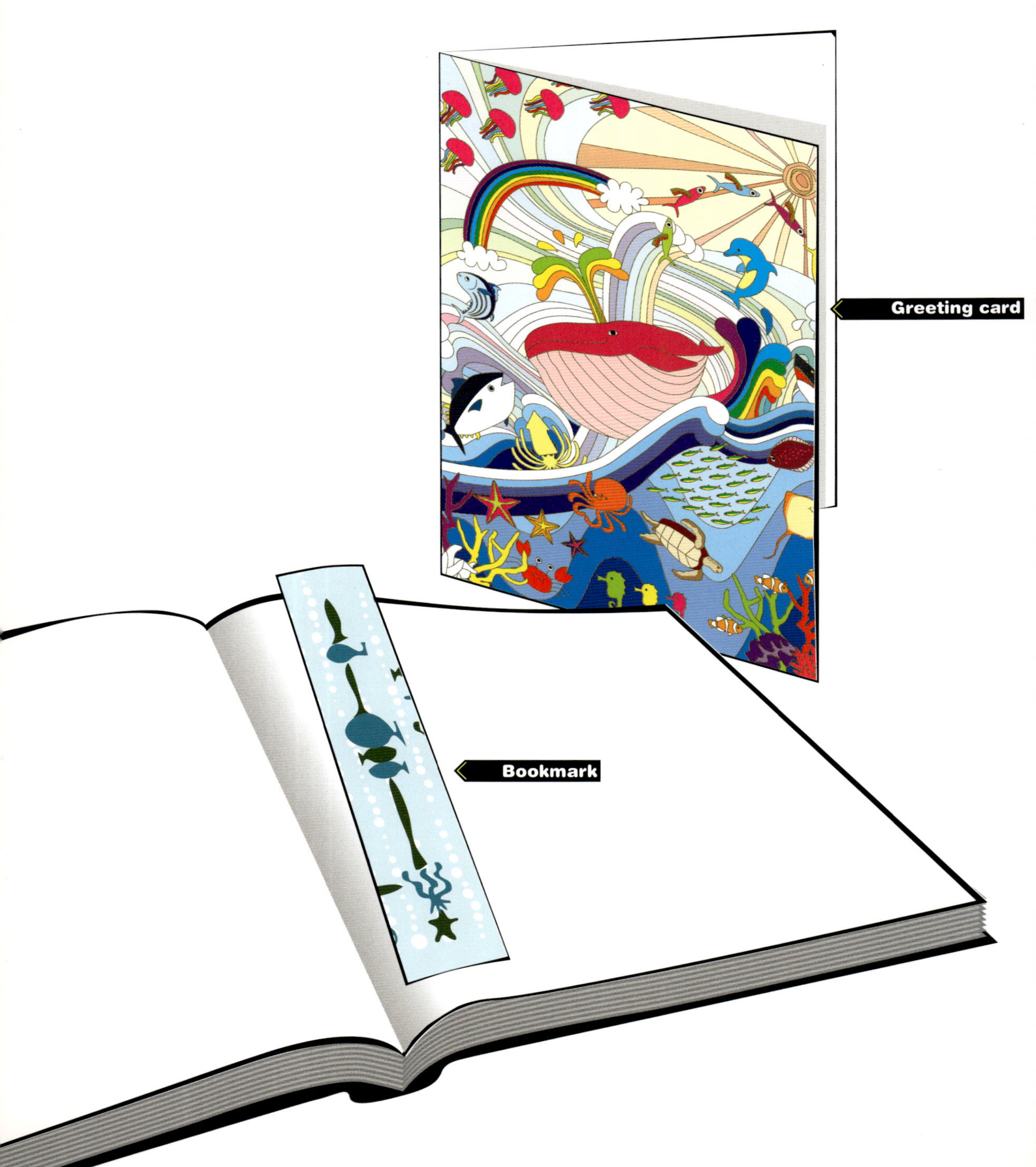

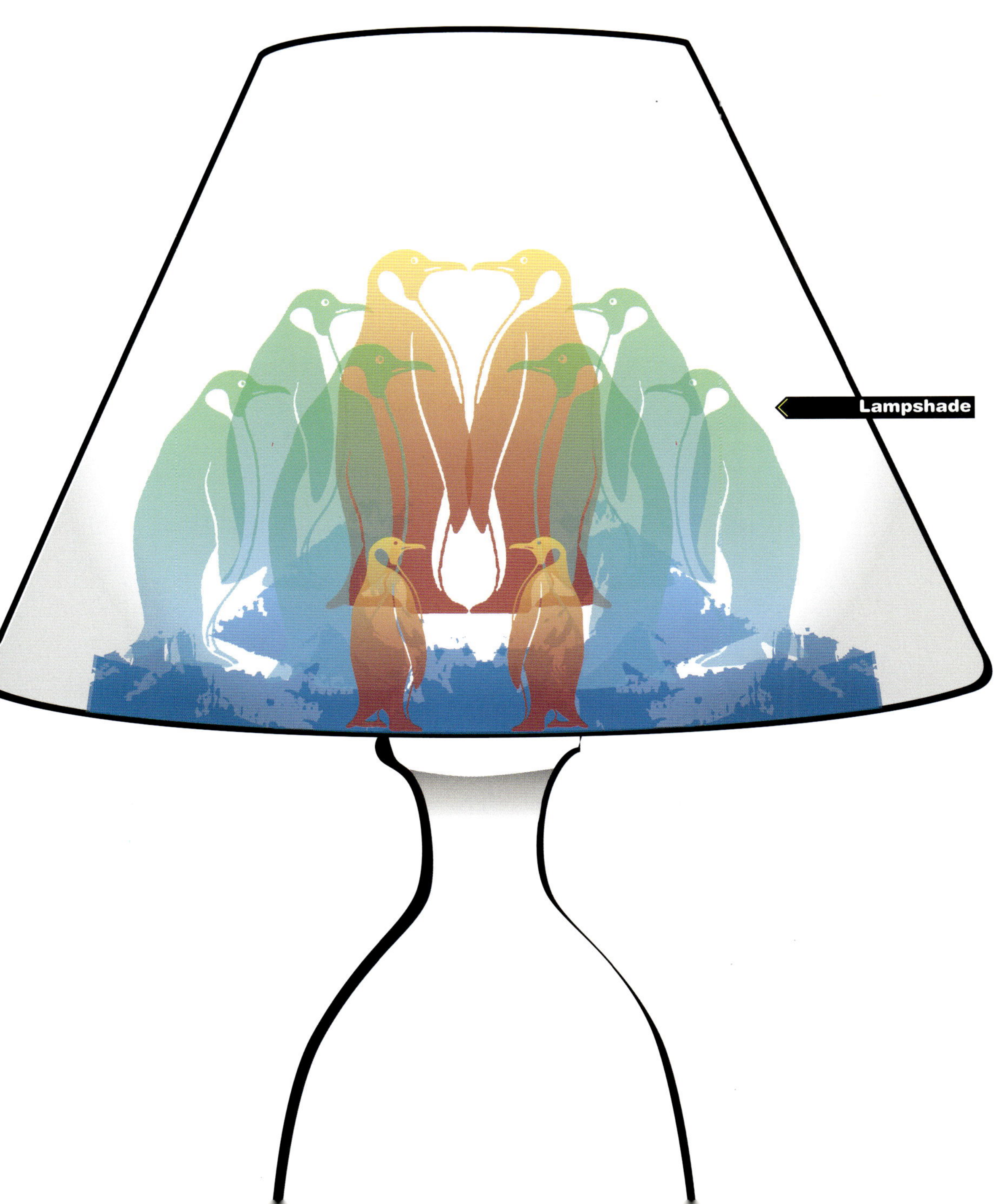
Lampshade

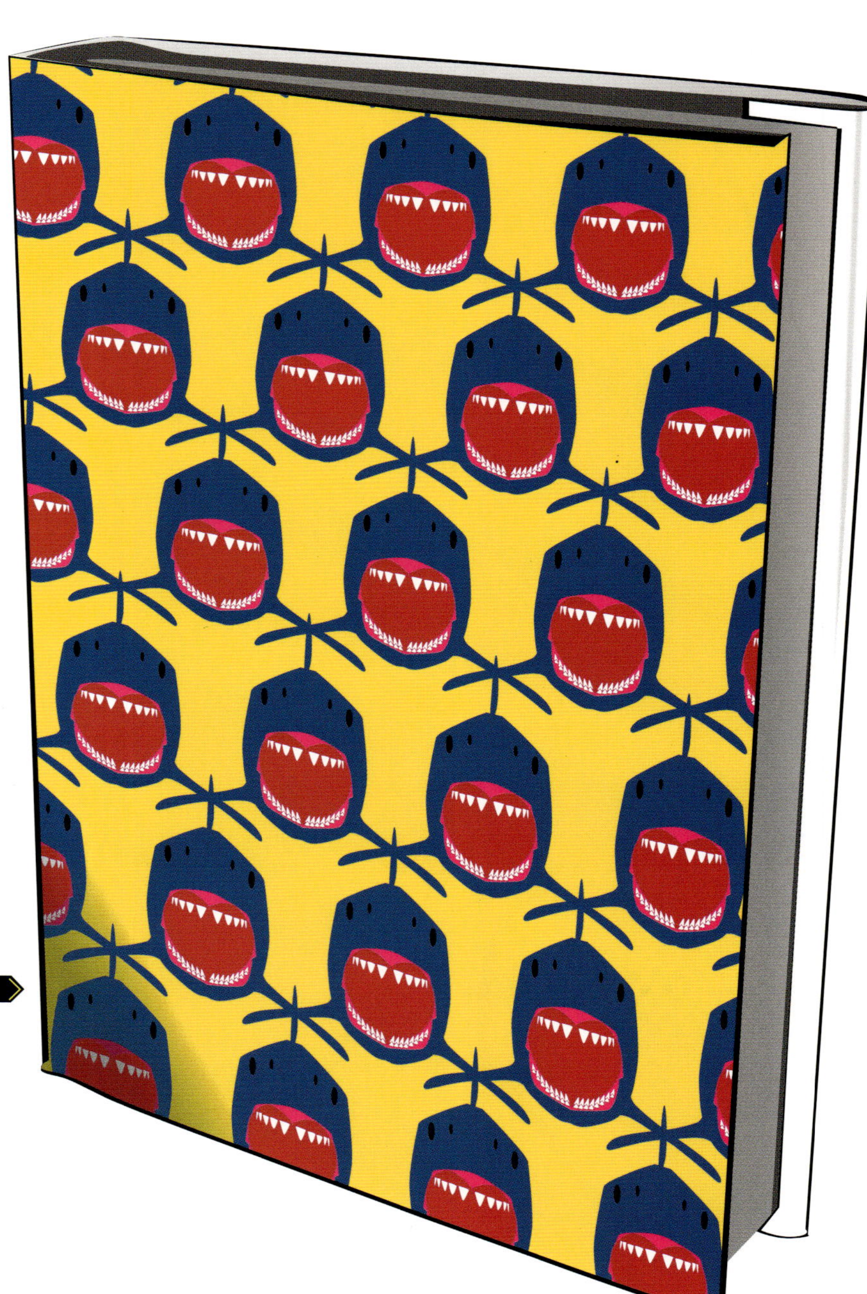

Dust jacket

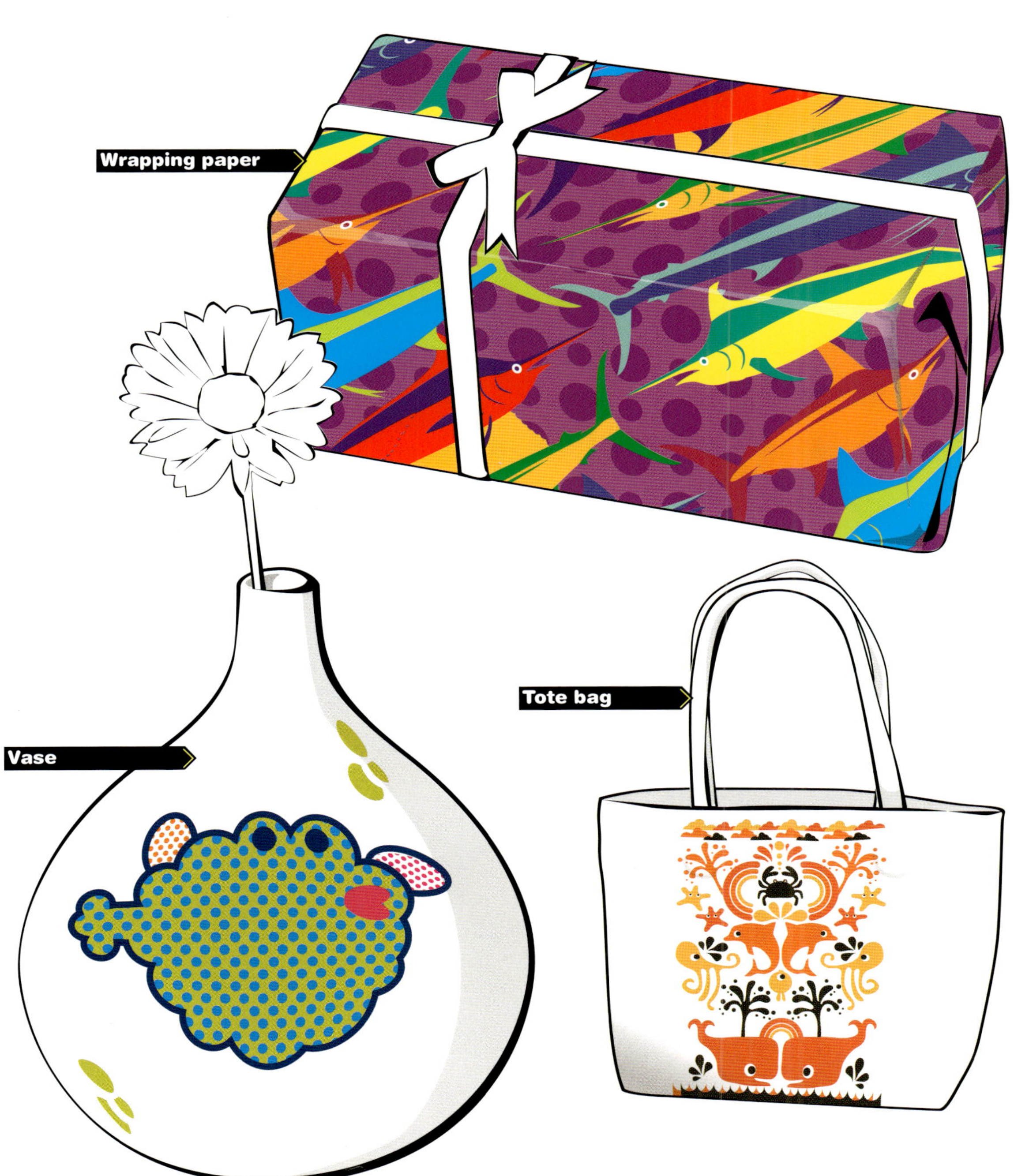
Wrapping paper
Tote bag
Vase

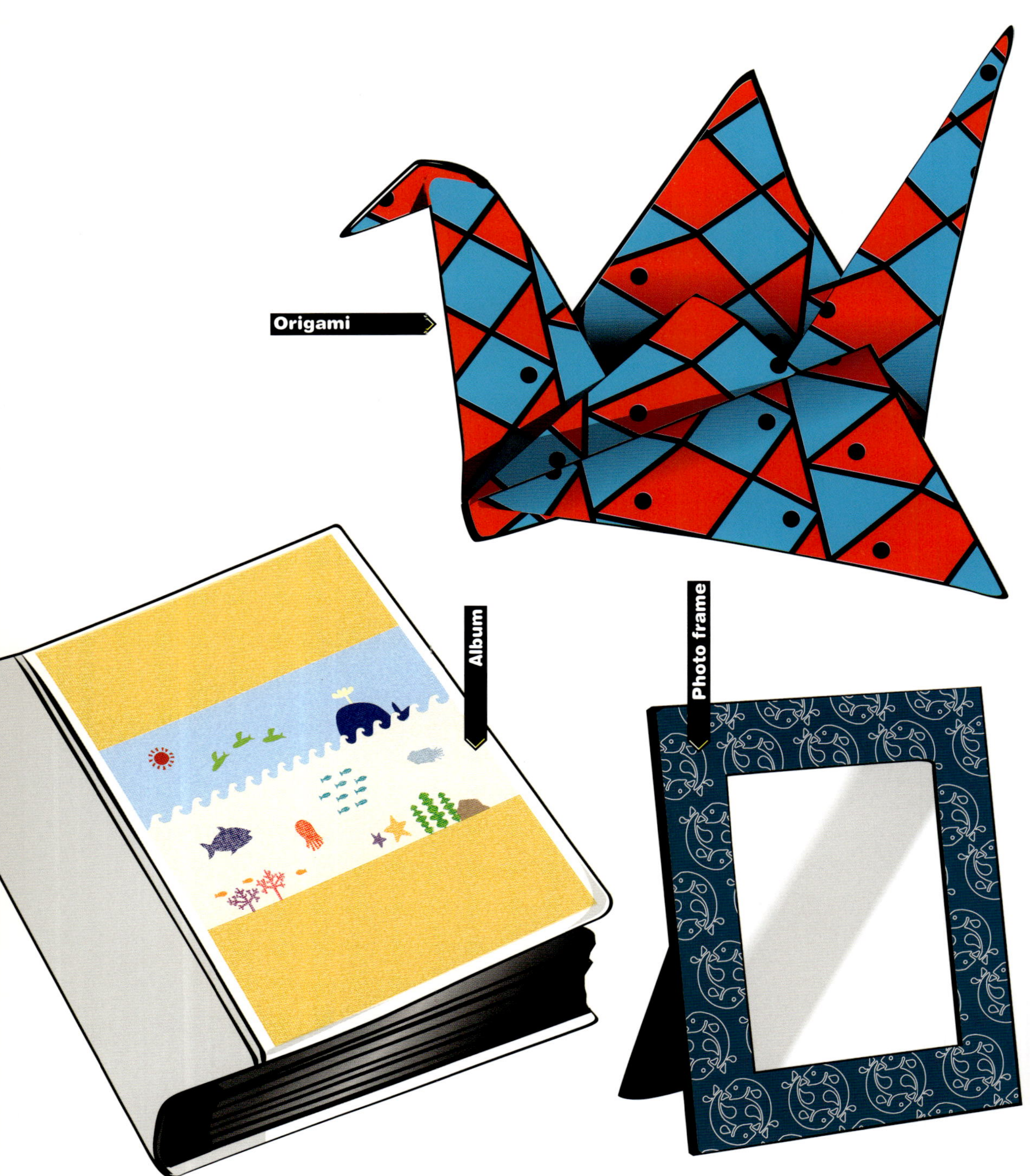
Origami
Album
Photo frame

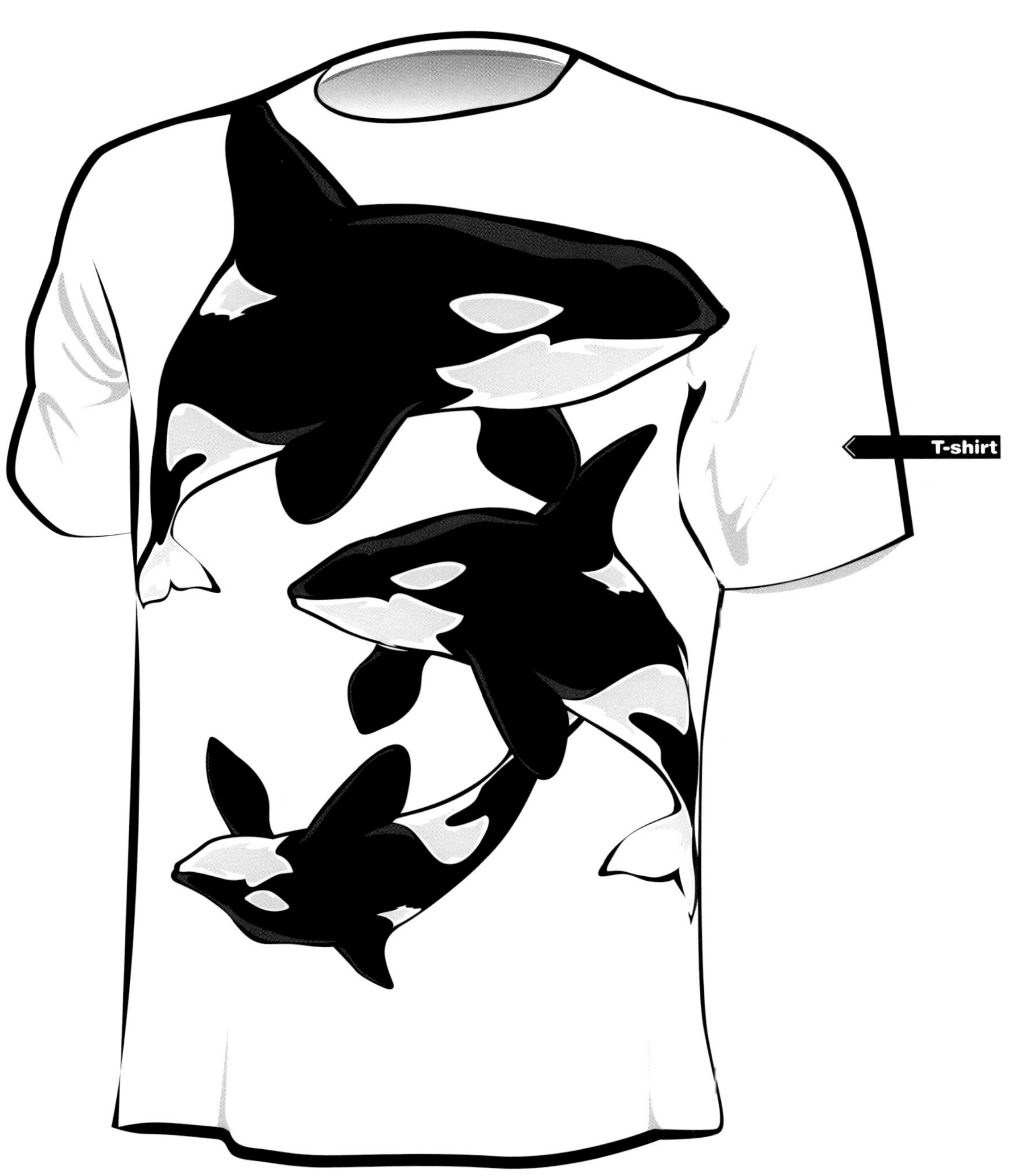
T-shirt

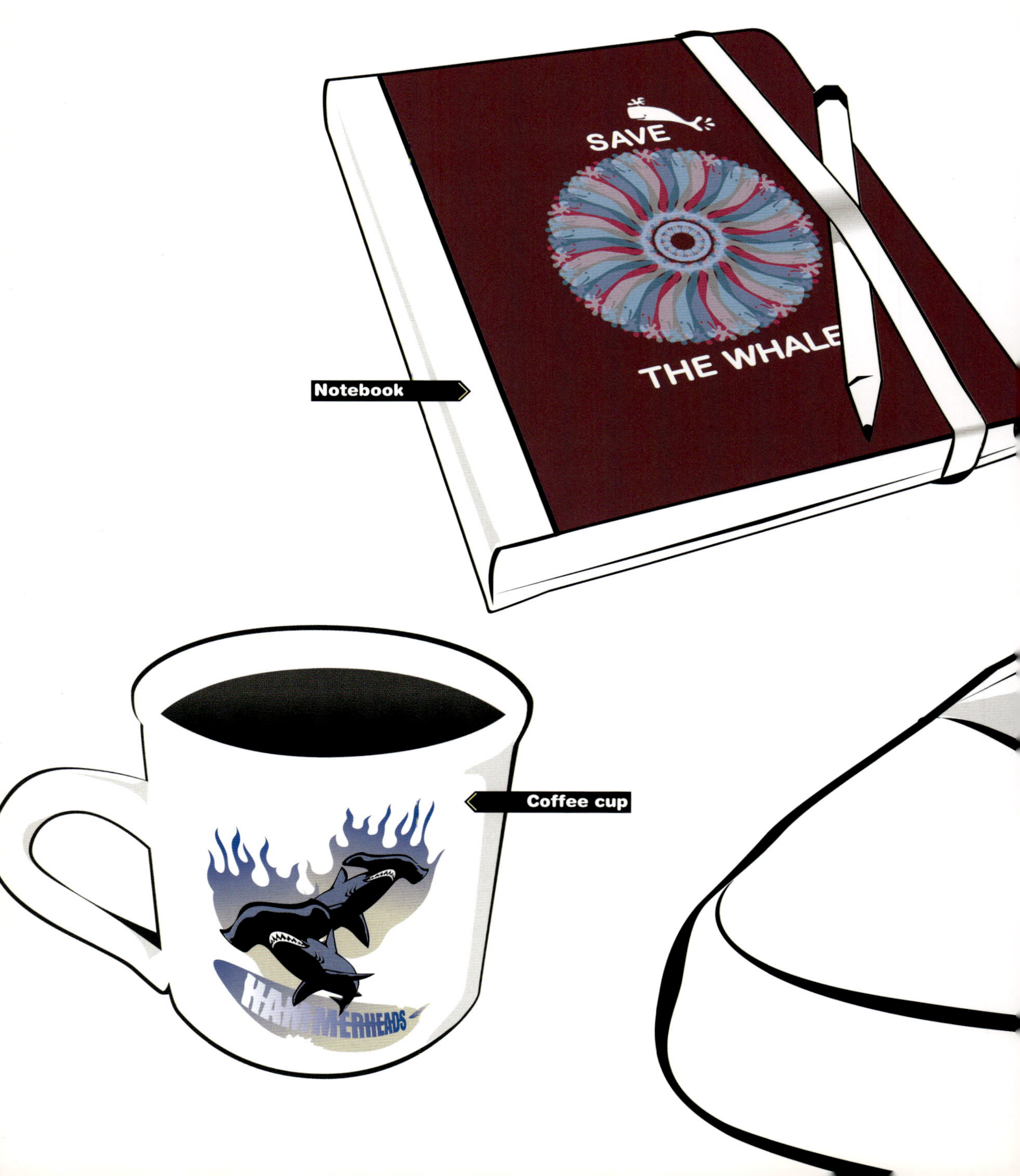
SAVE
THE WHALE
Notebook
Coffee cup
HAMMERHEADS

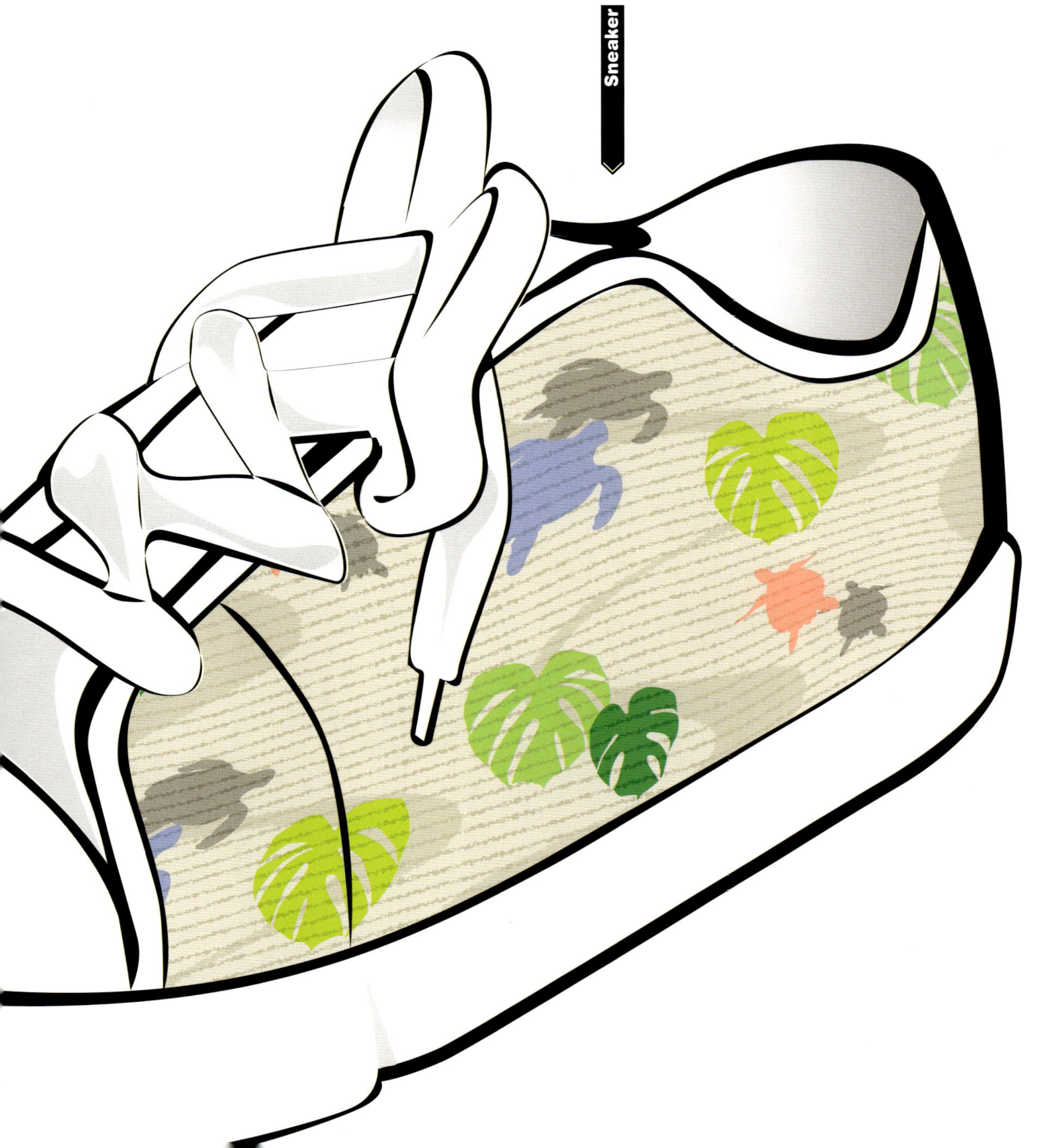
Sneaker

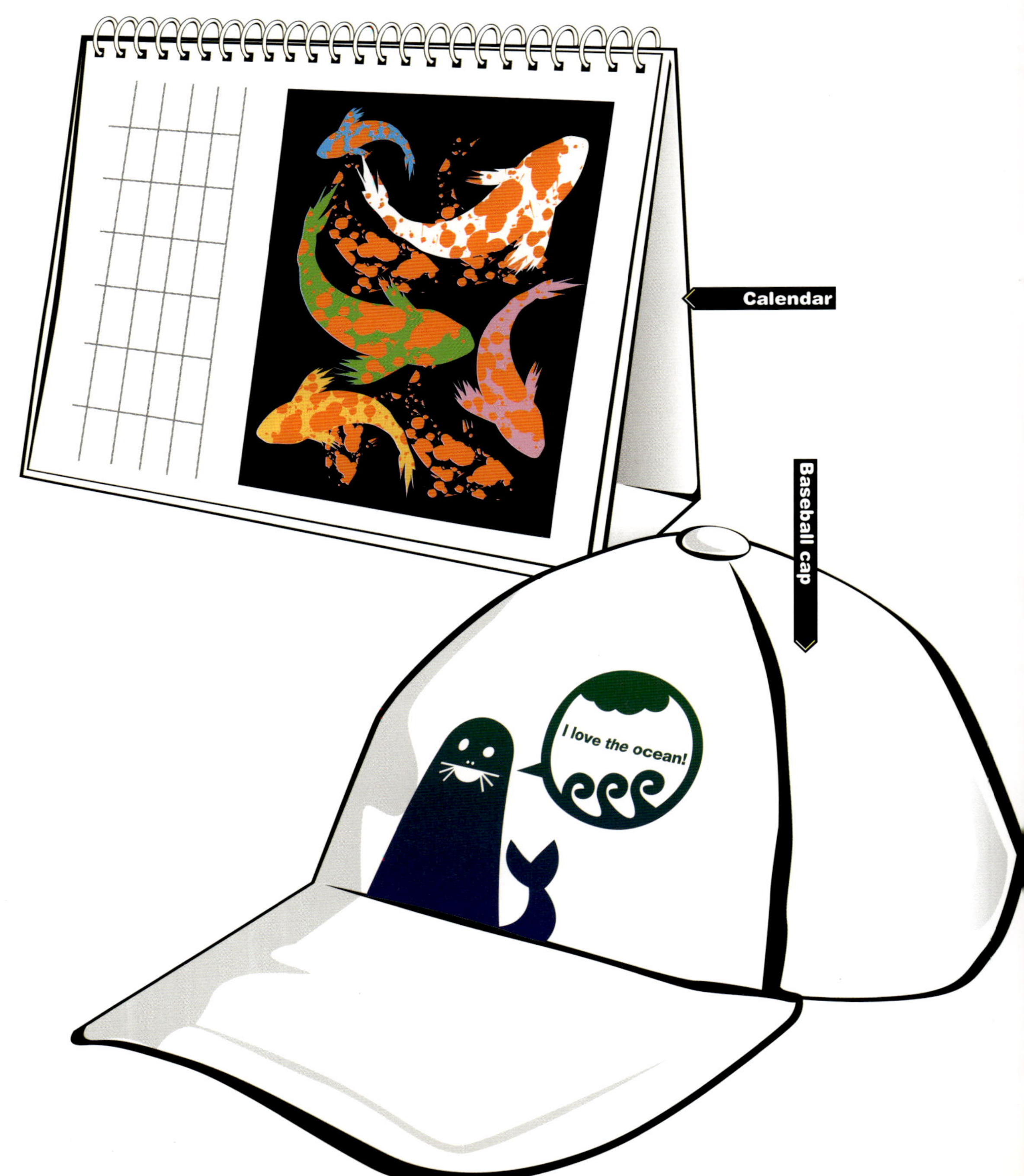
Calendar
Baseball cap
I love the ocean!

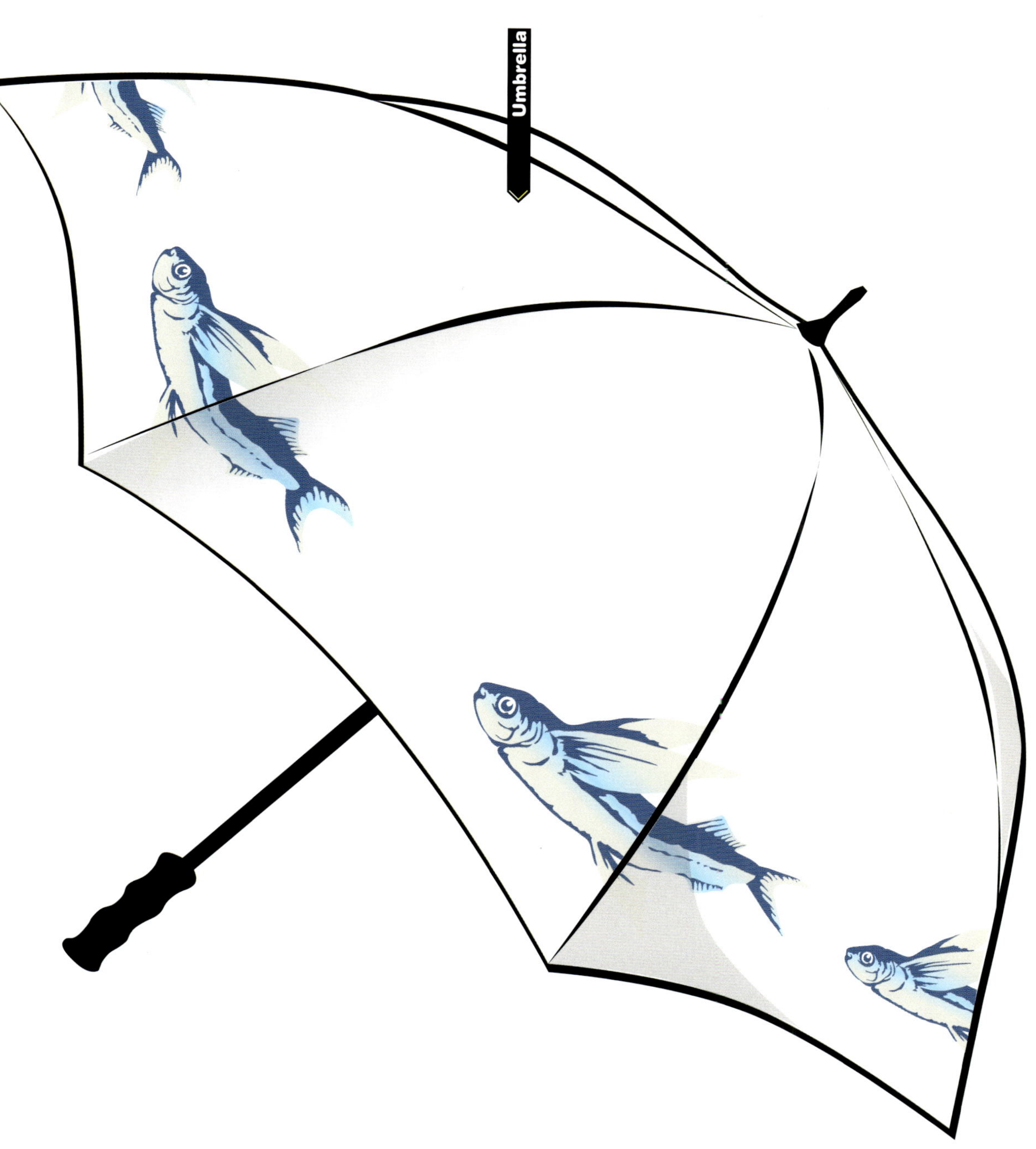
Umbrella

TEMPLATES

MA_T22

TEMPLATES

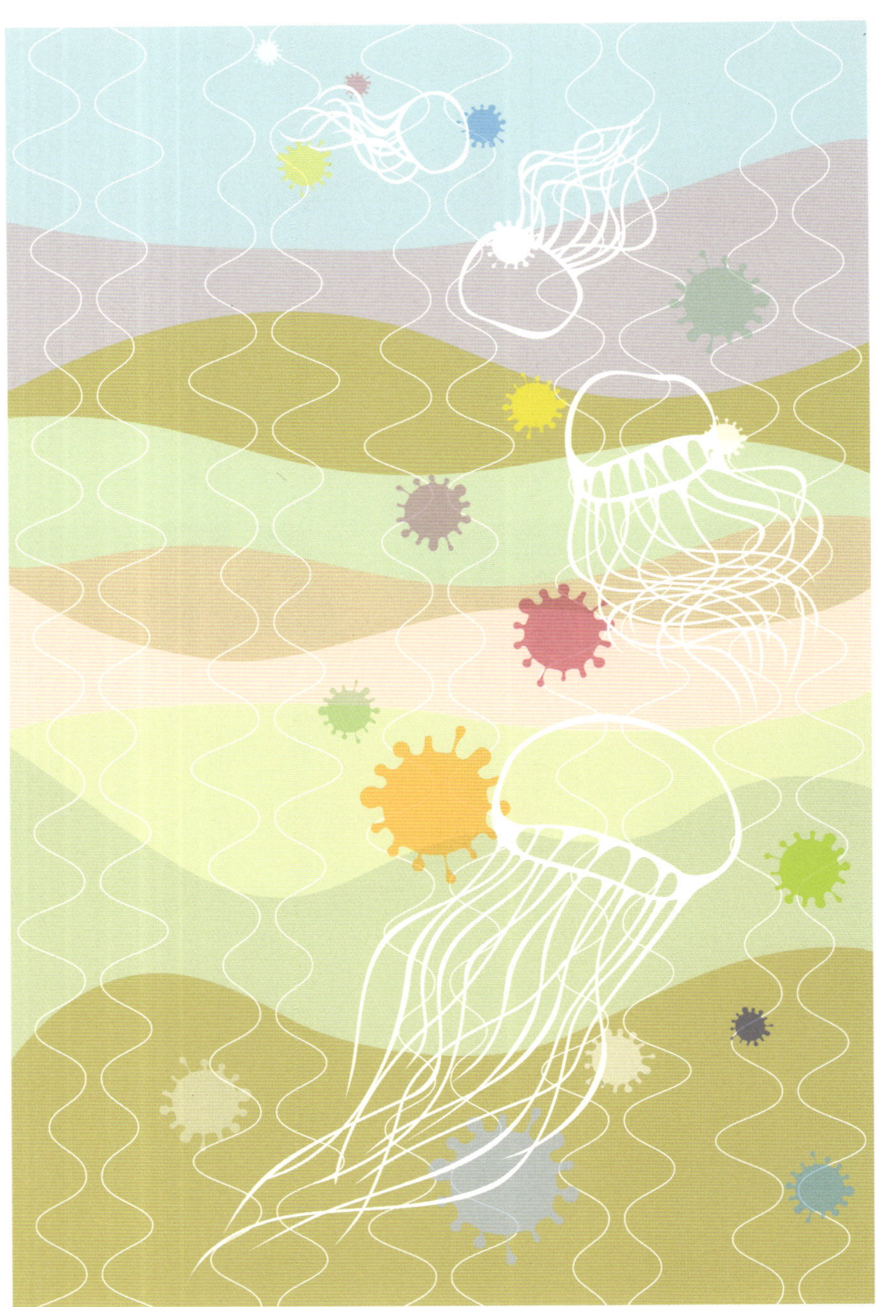

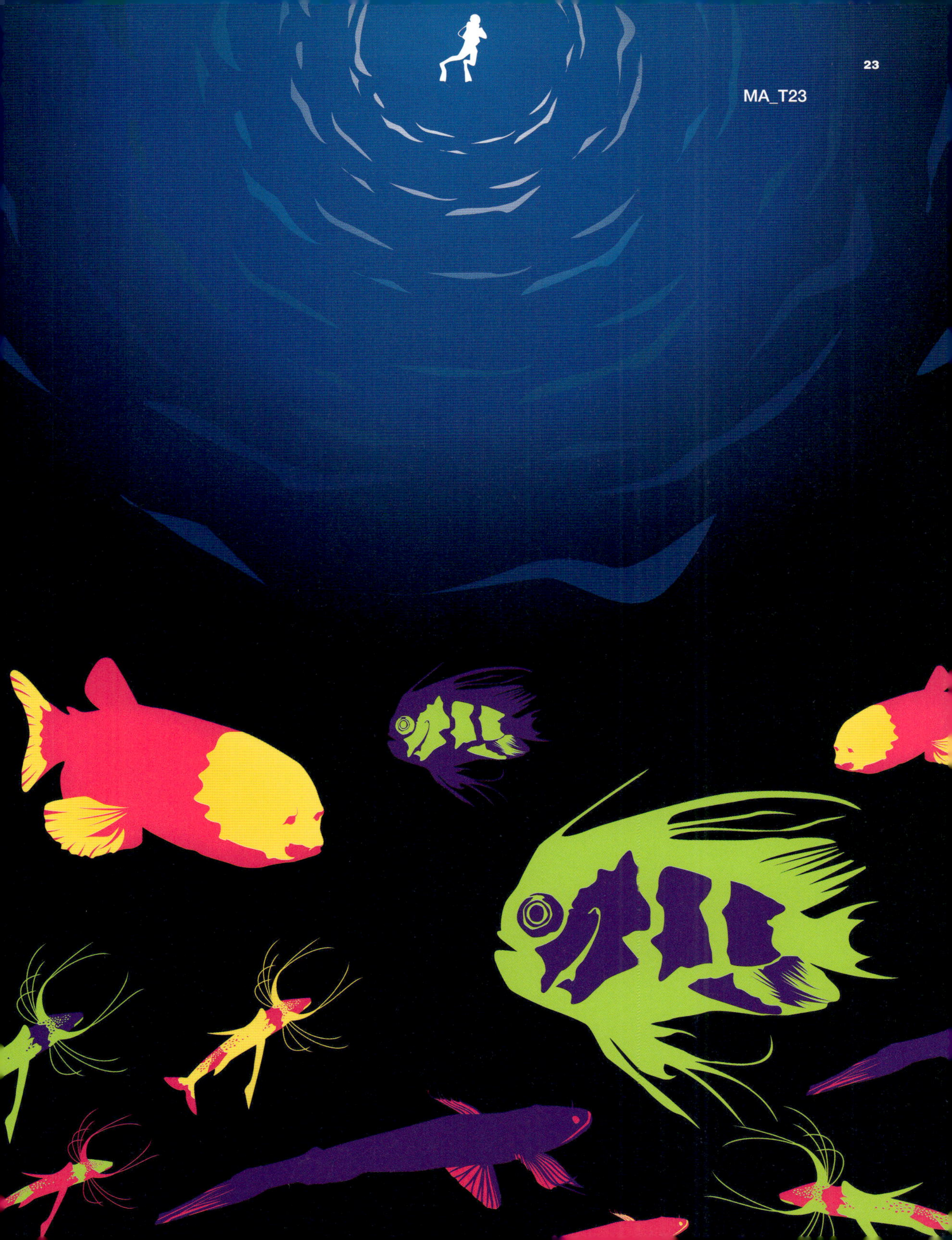
MA_T23

MA_T24

TEMPLATES

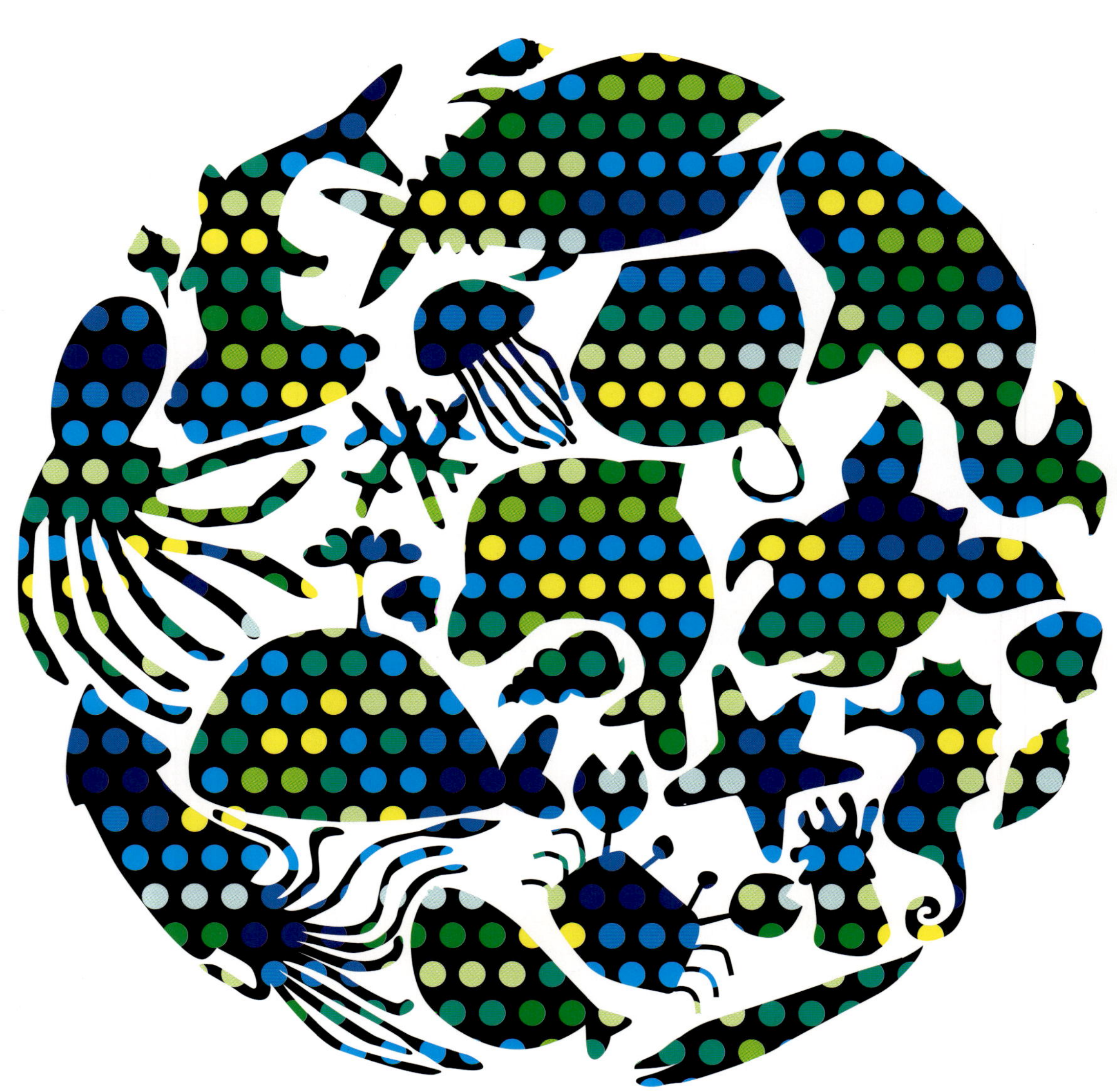

MA_T25

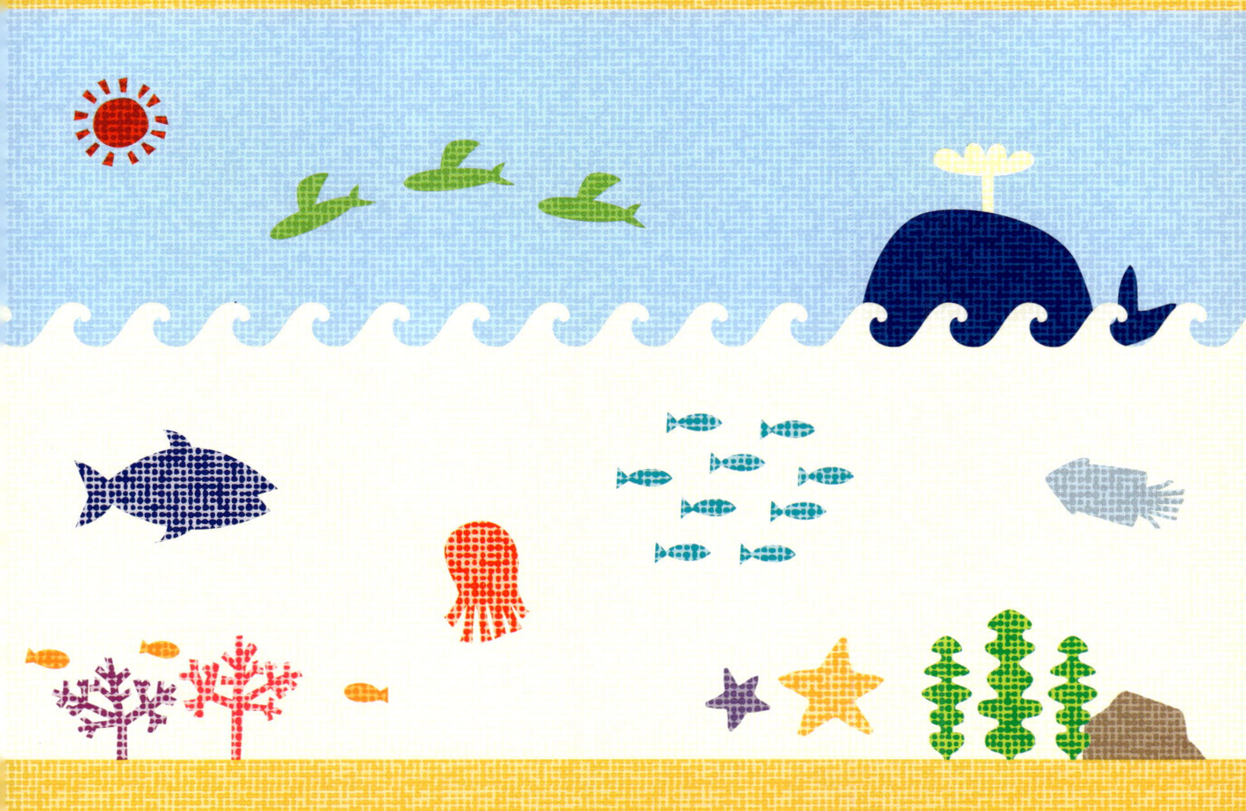

MA_T26

TEMPLATES

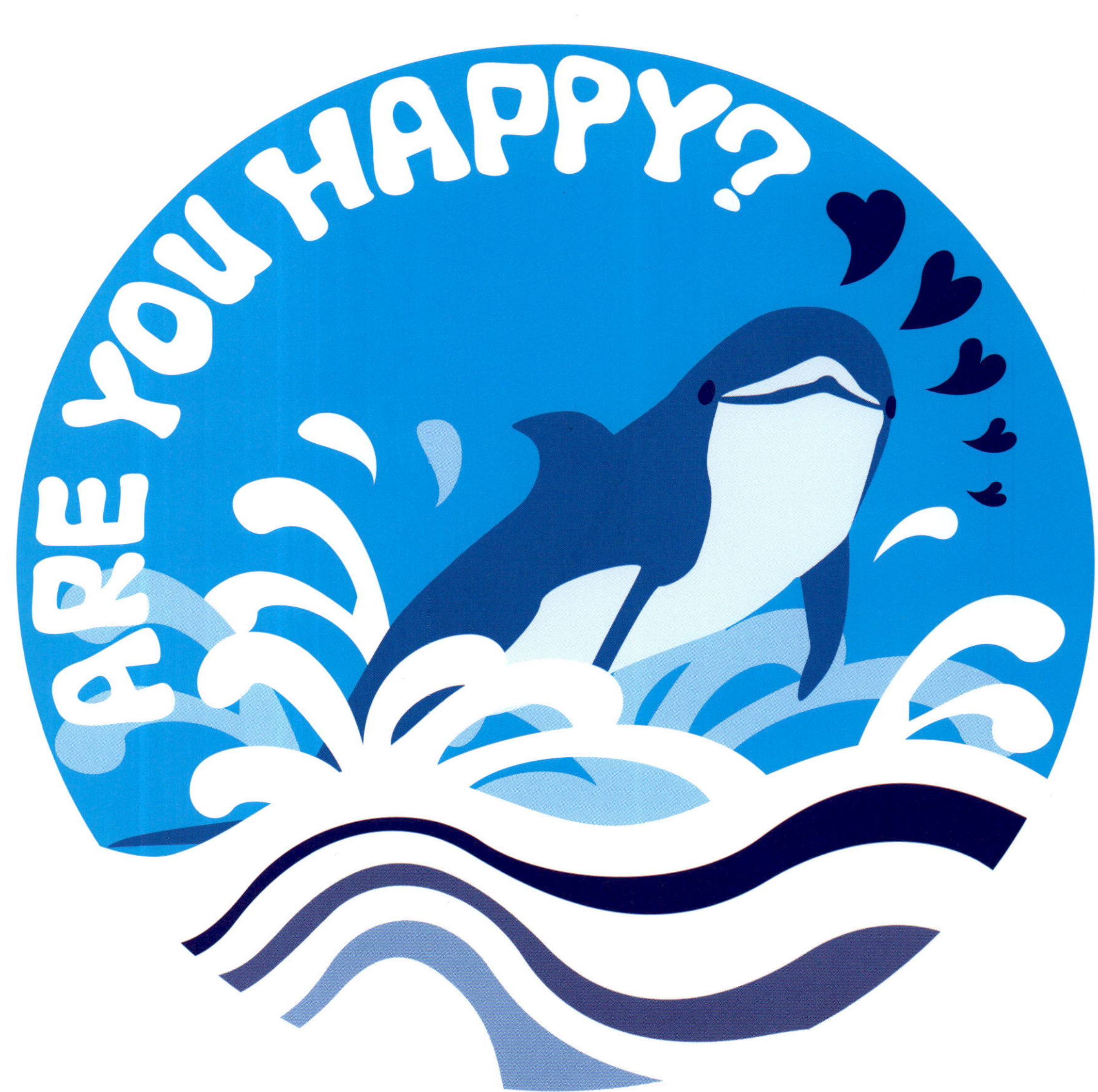

MA_T27

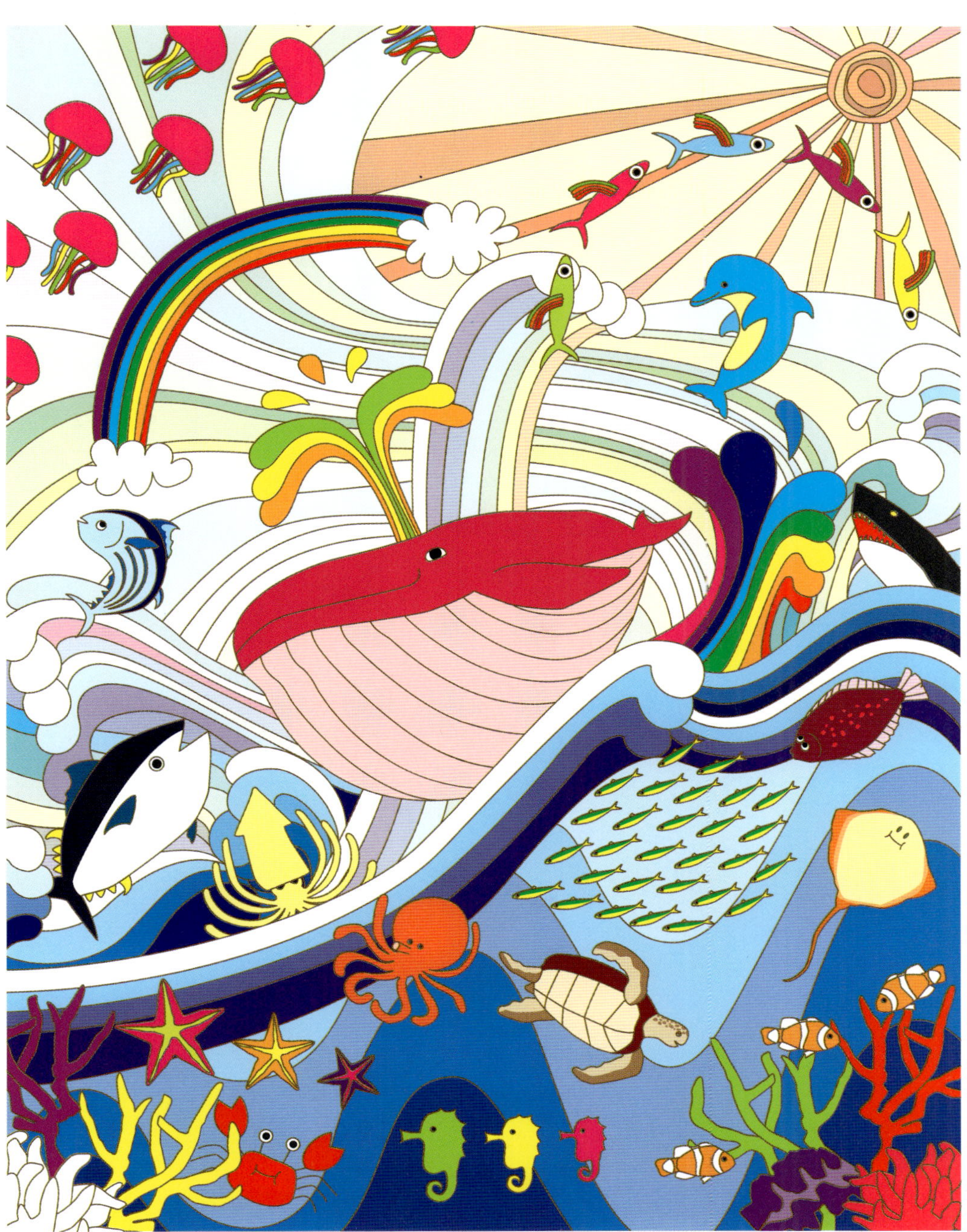

MA_T28

TEMPLATES

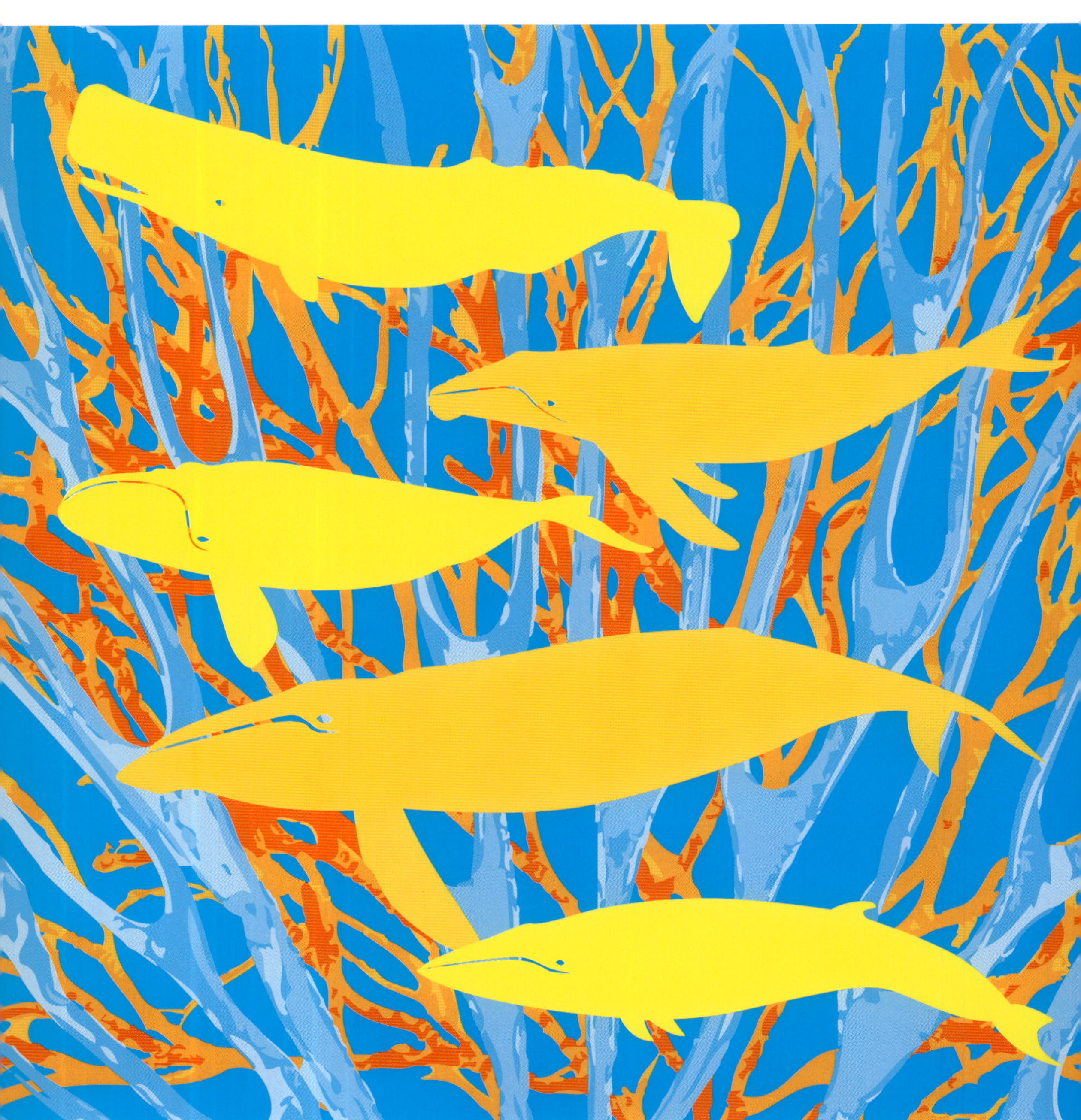

MA_T29

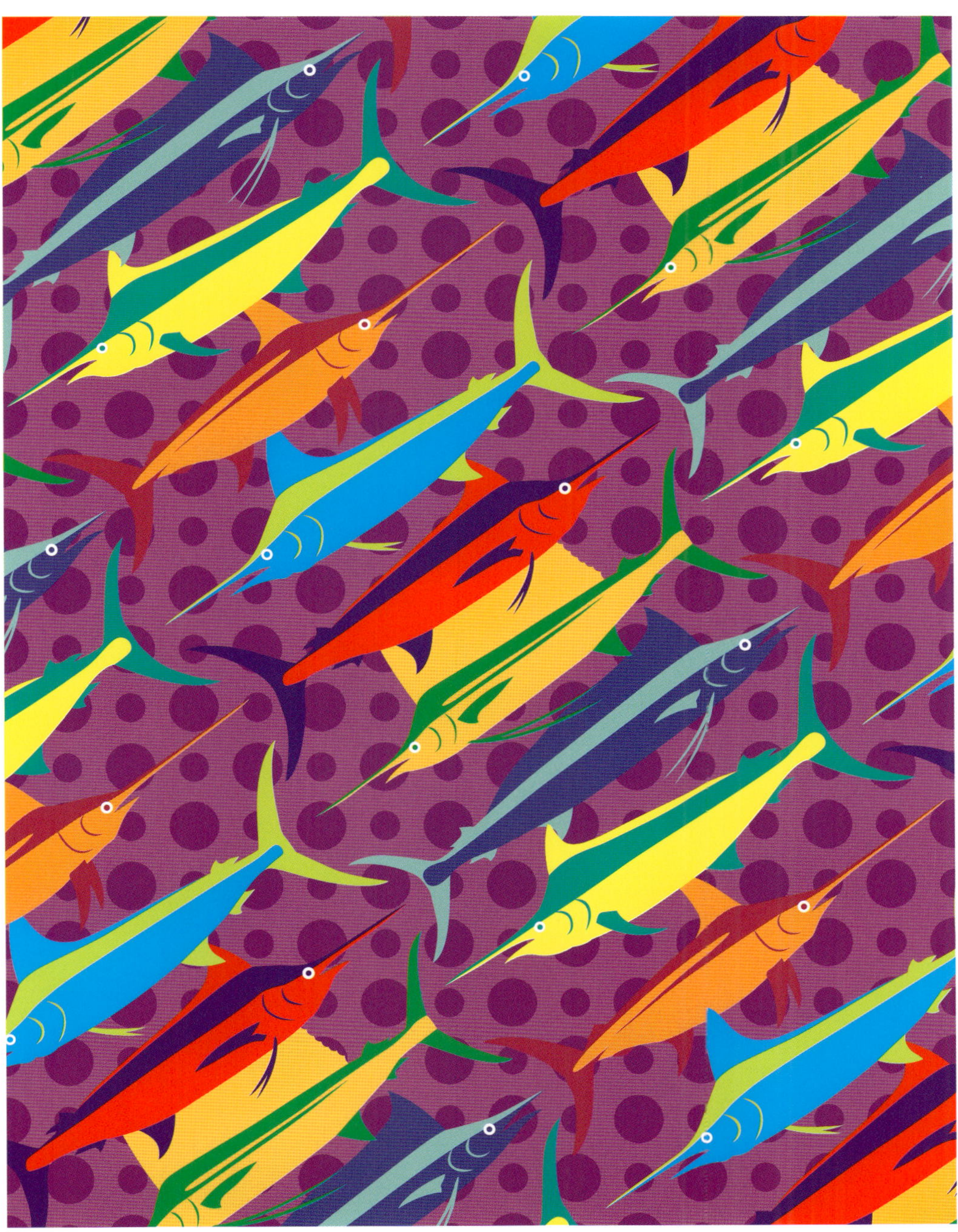

MA_T30

TEMPLATES

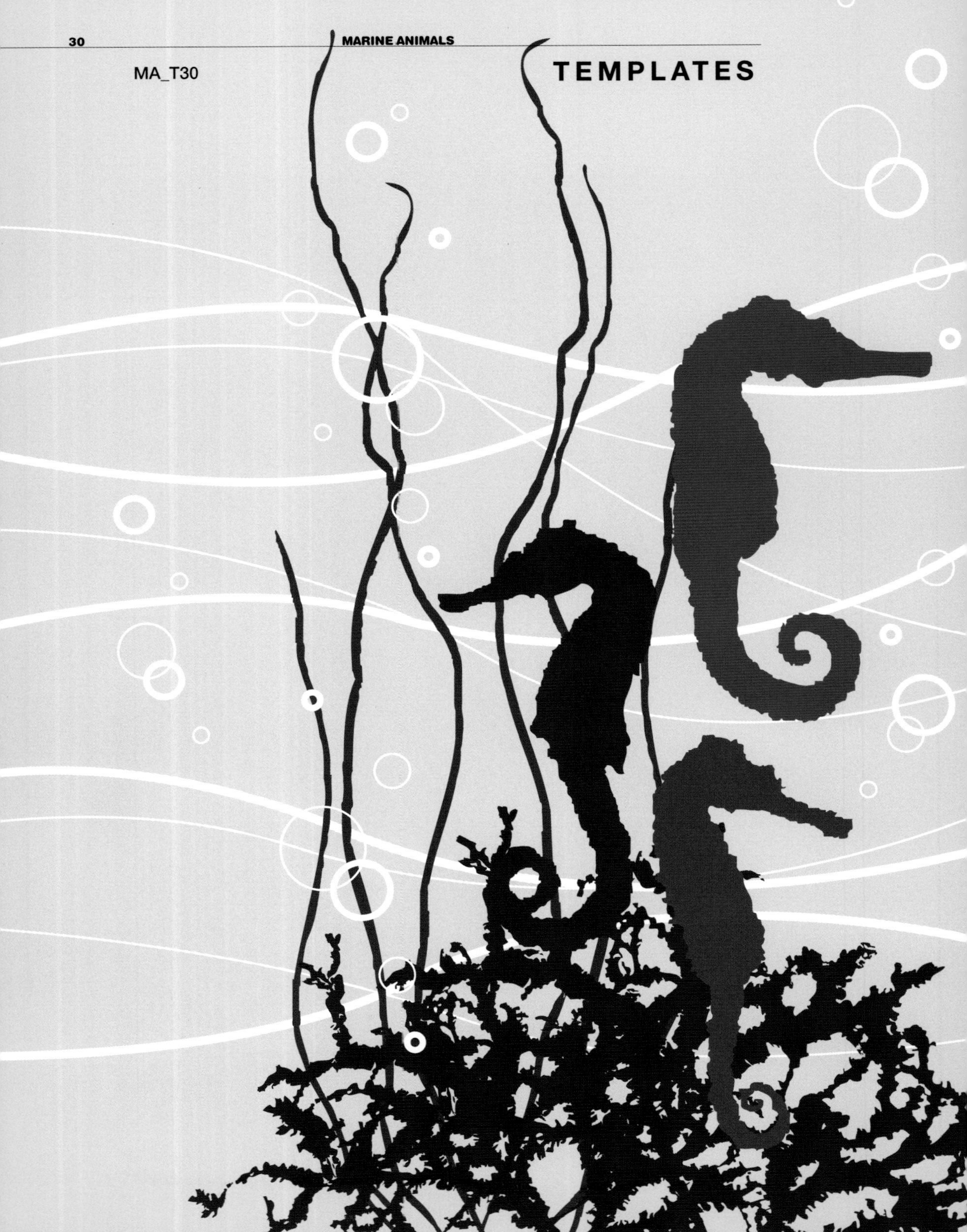

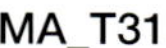
MA_T31

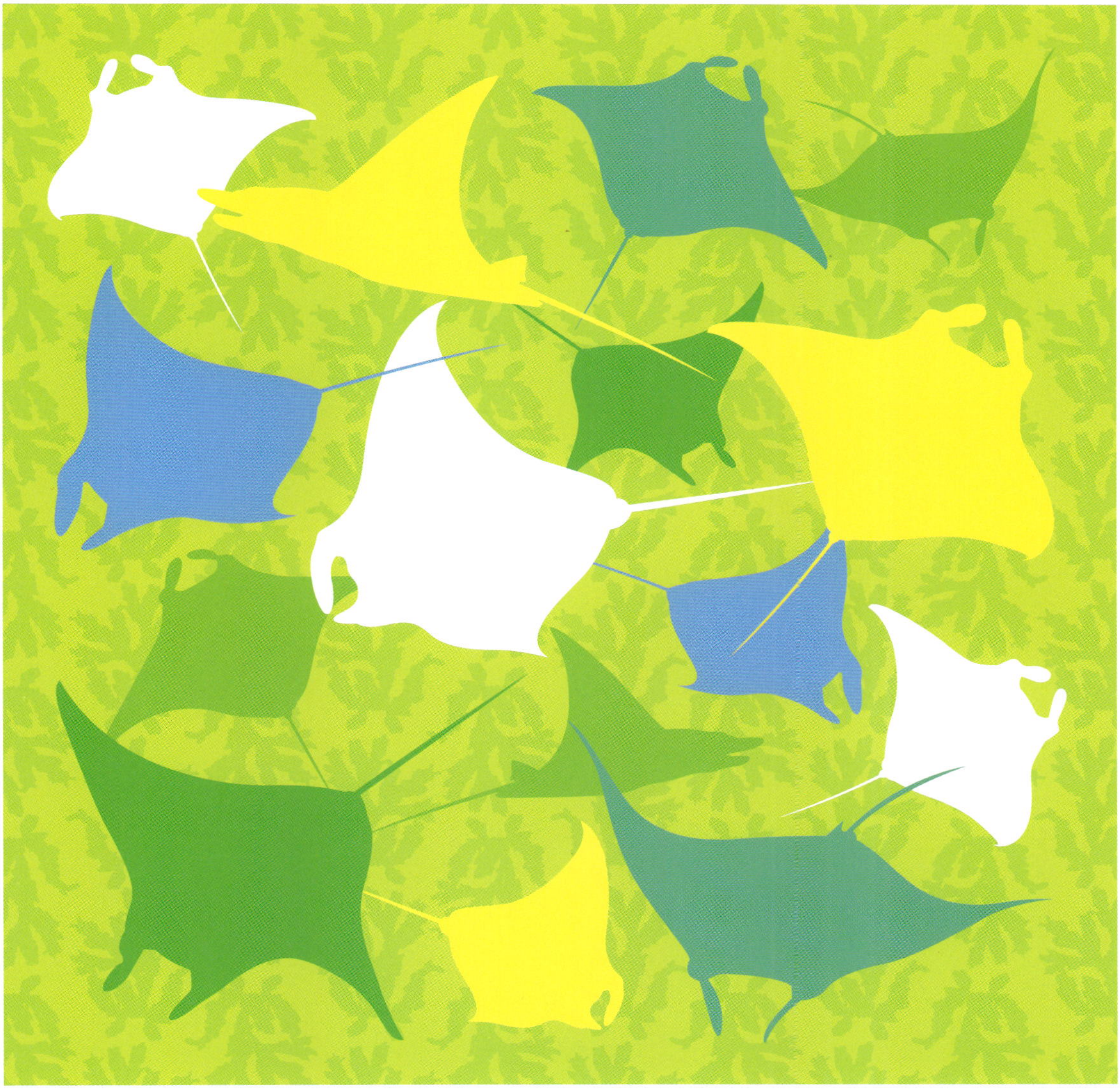

MA_T32

TEMPLATES

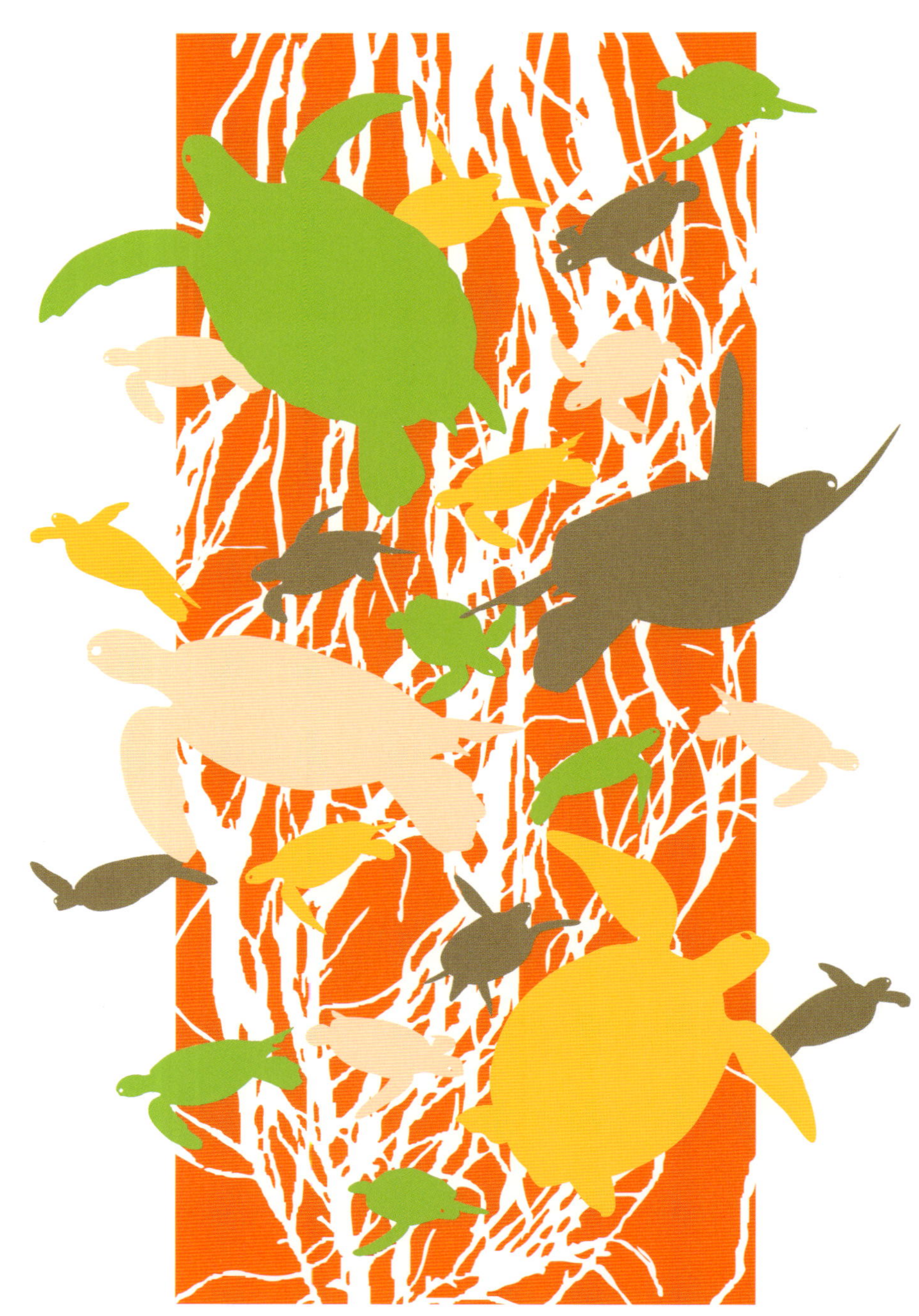

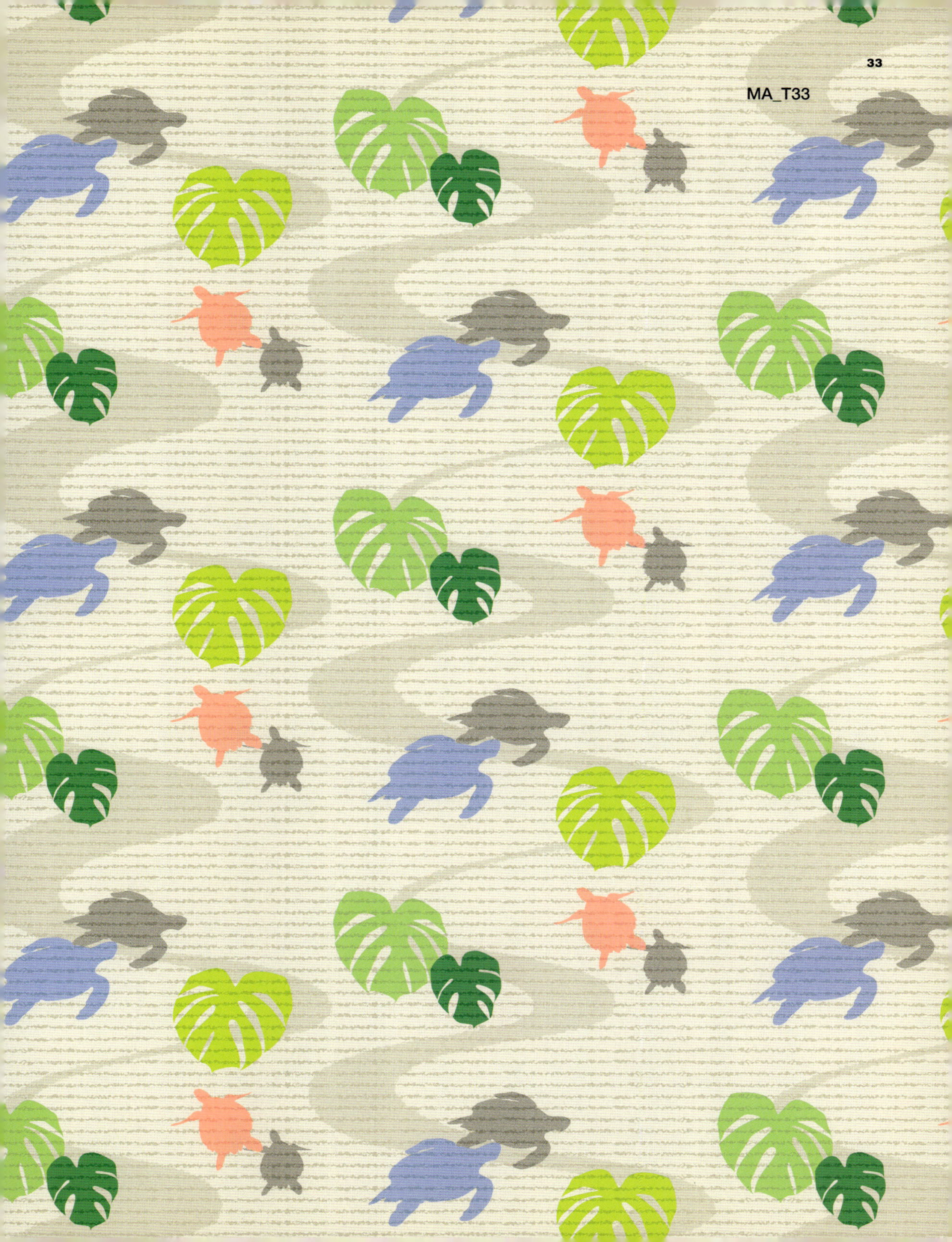
MA_T33

MA_T34

TEMPLATES

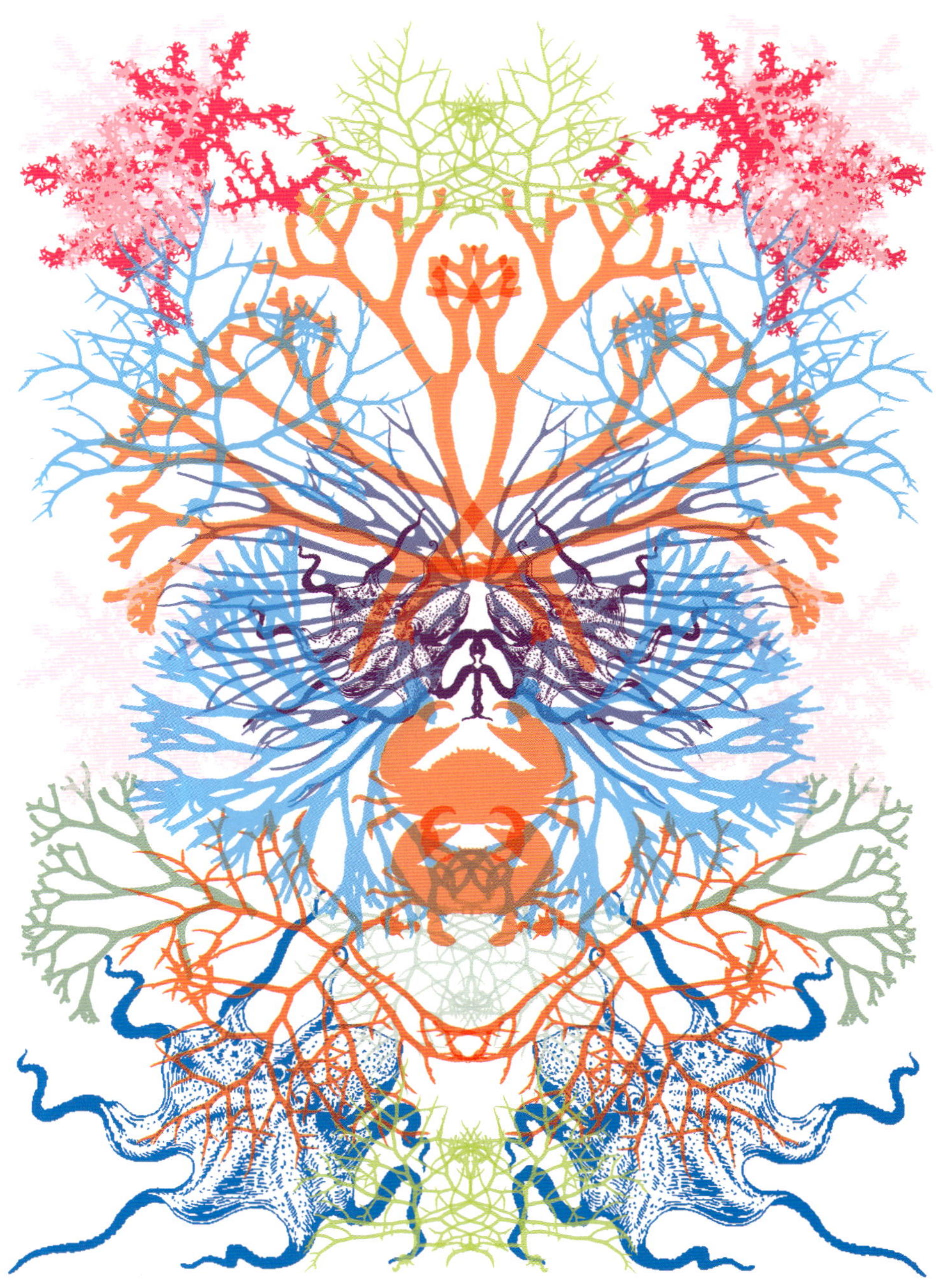

MA_T35

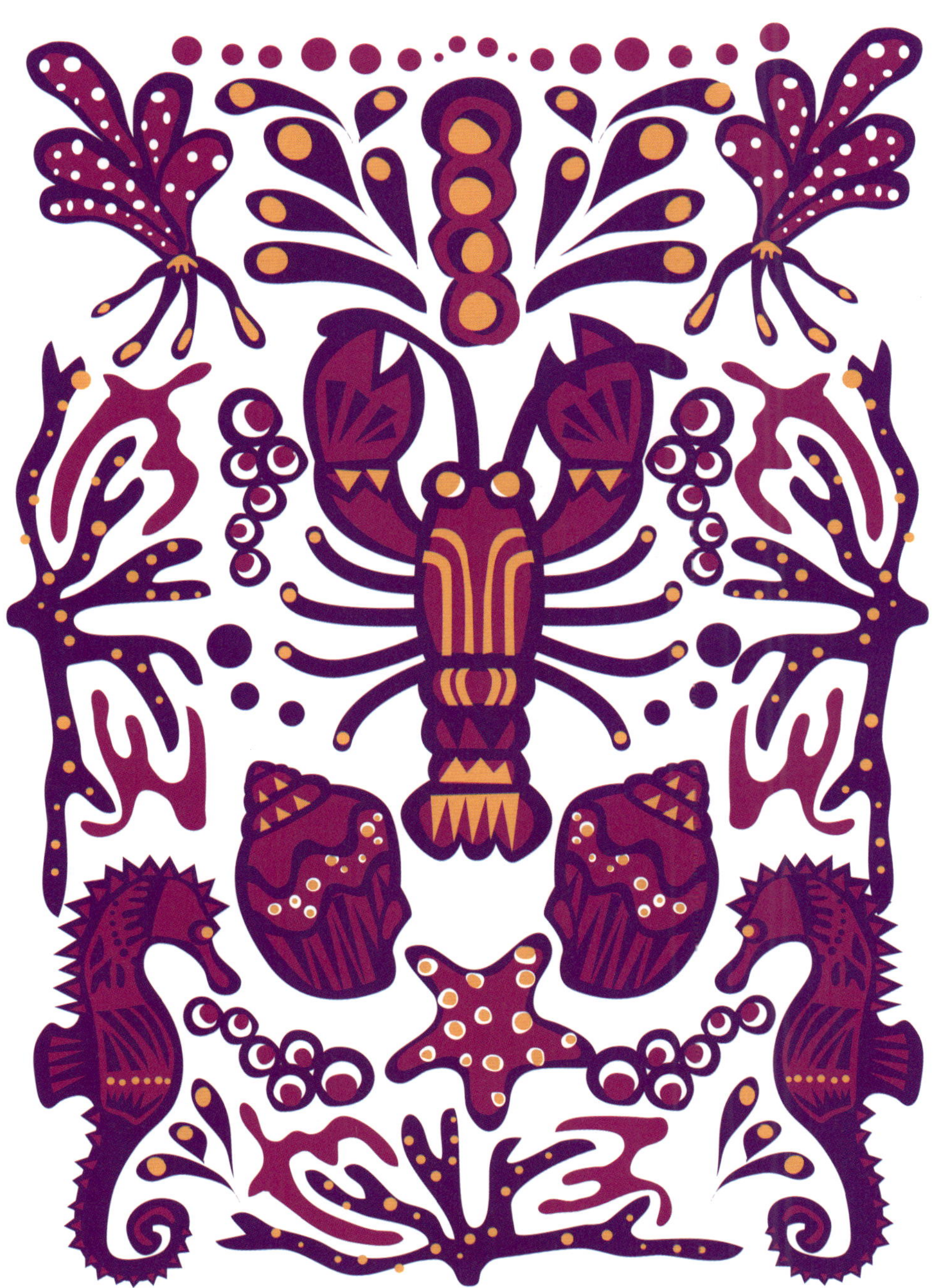

MA_T36

TEMPLATES

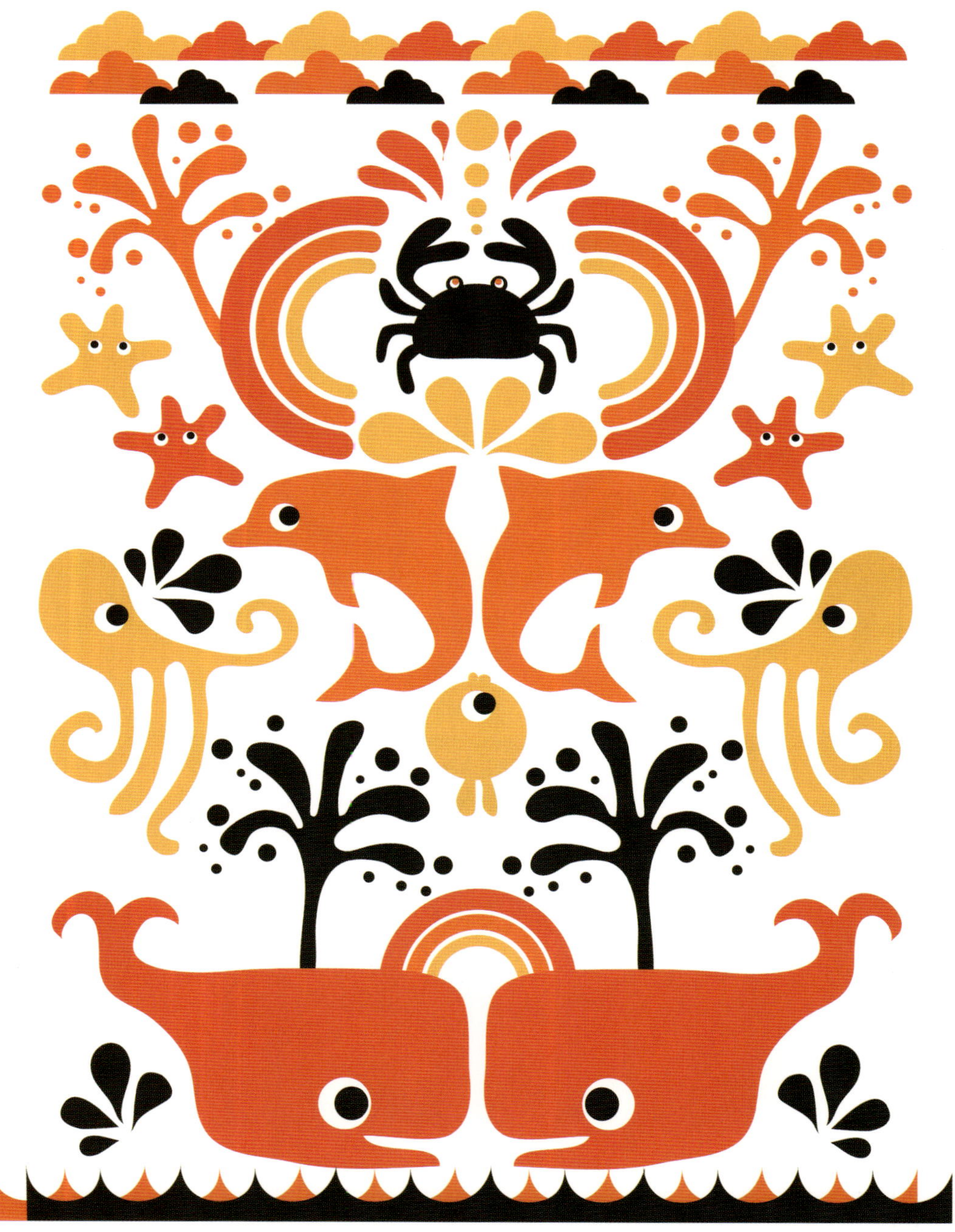

MA_T37

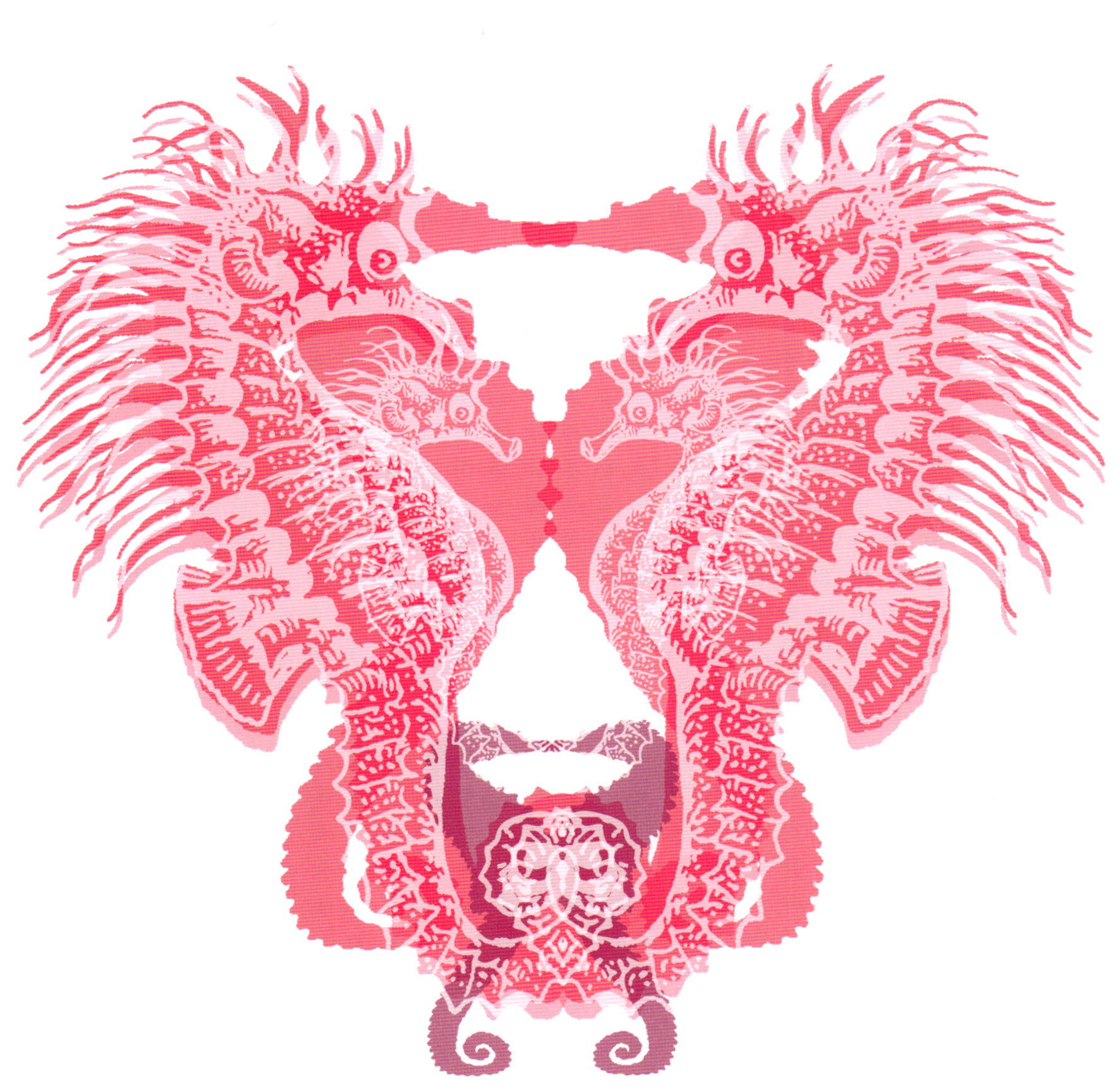

MA_T38

TEMPLATES

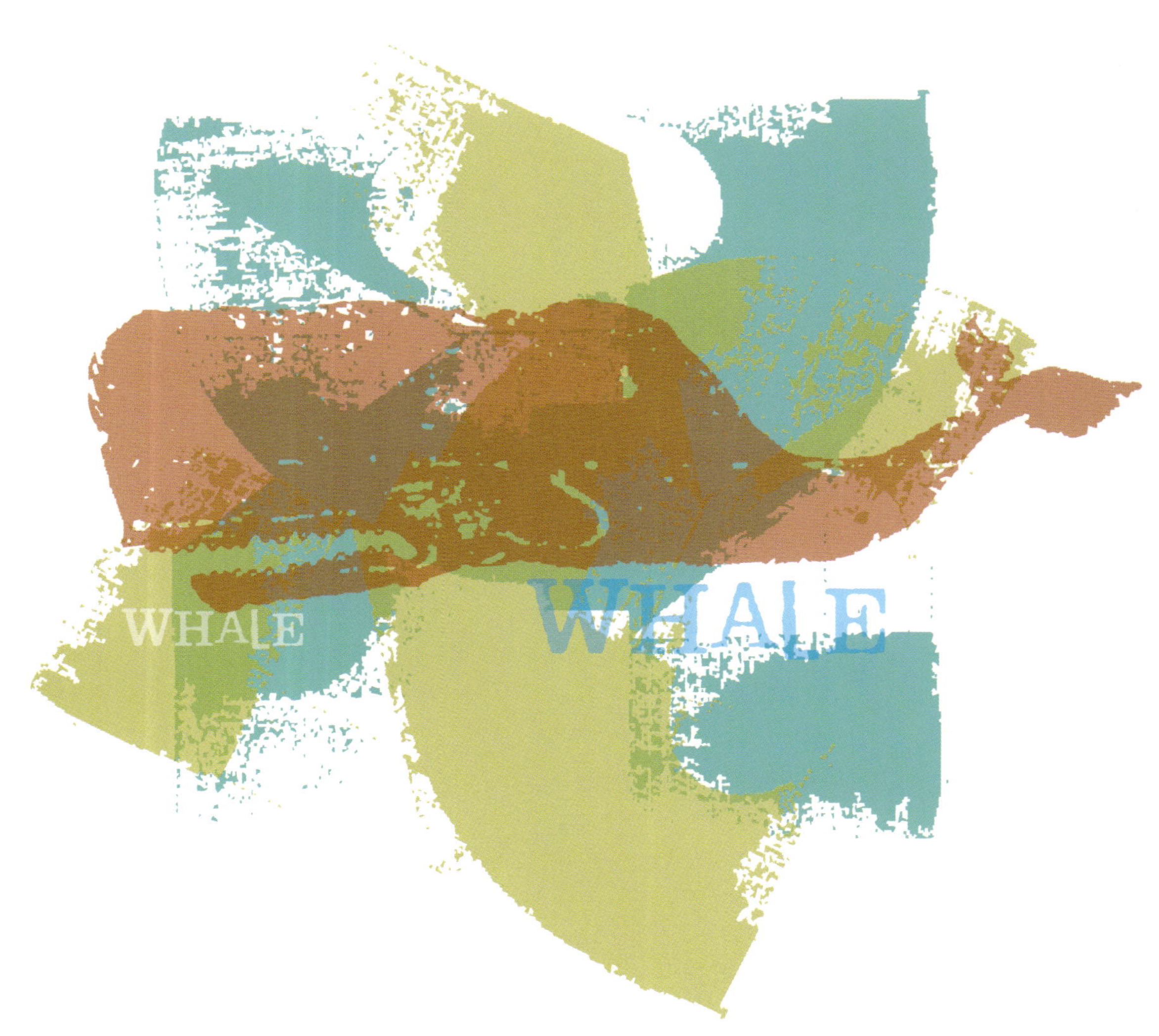

MA_T39

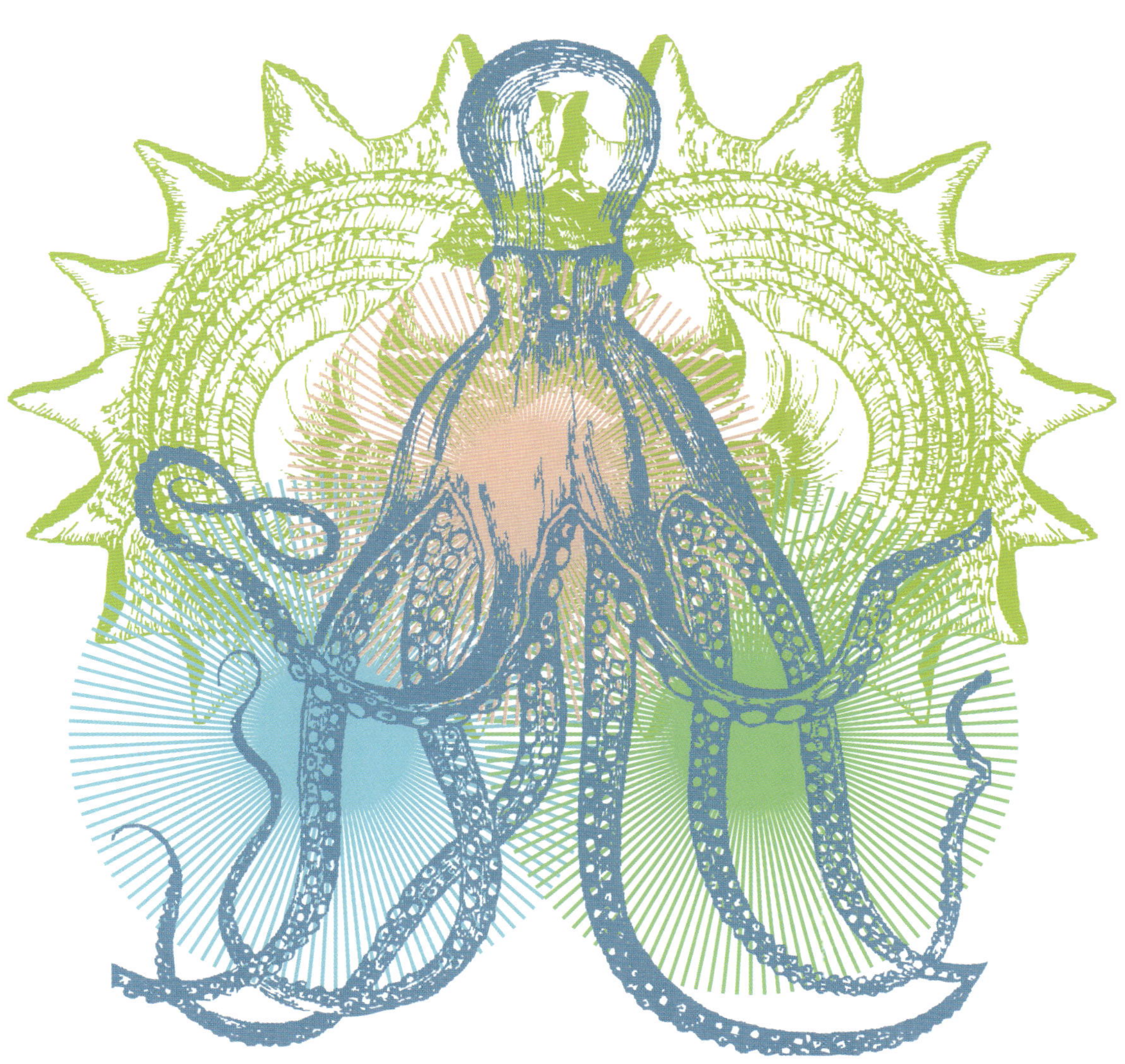

MA_T40

TEMPLATES

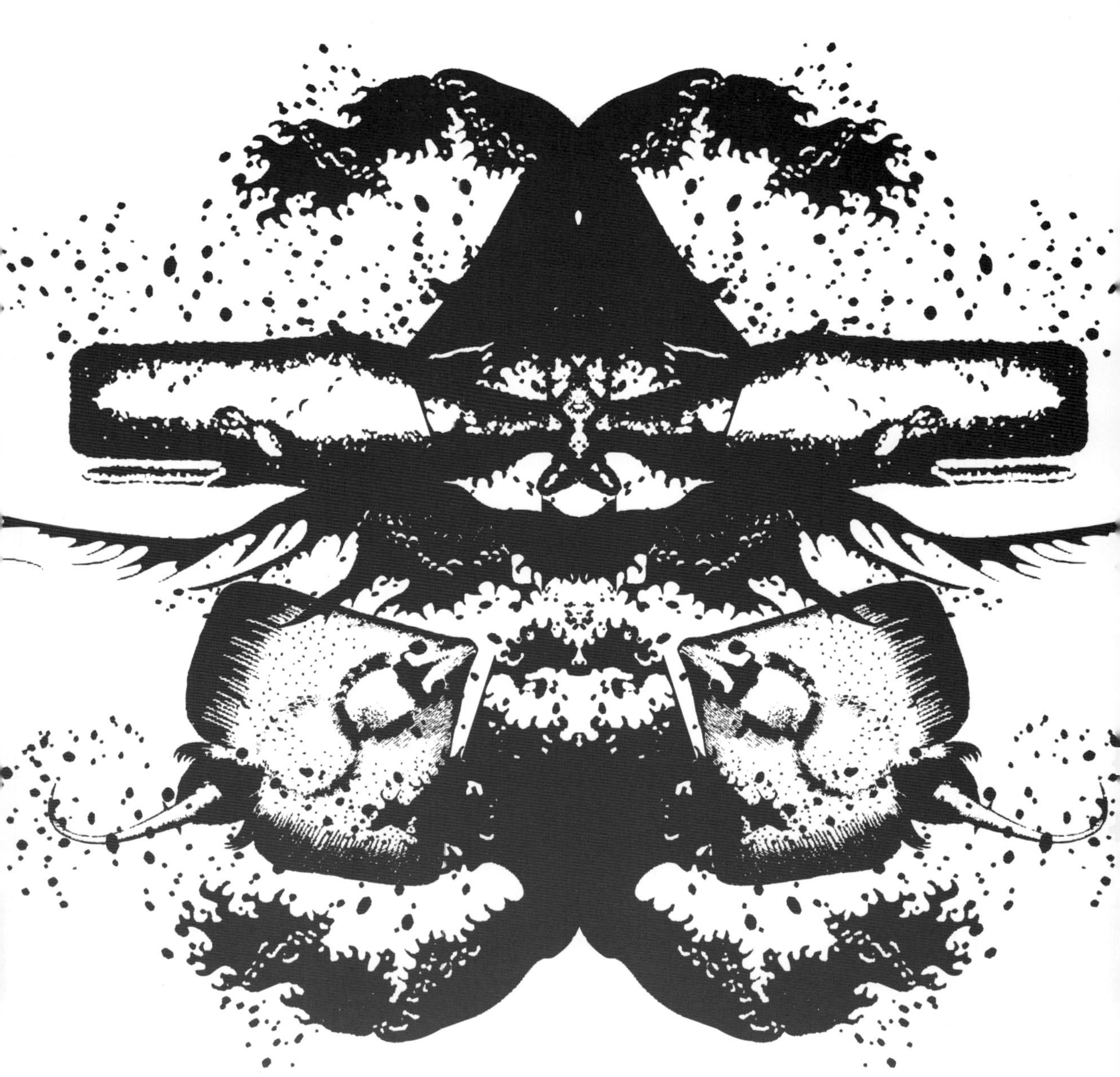

MA_T41

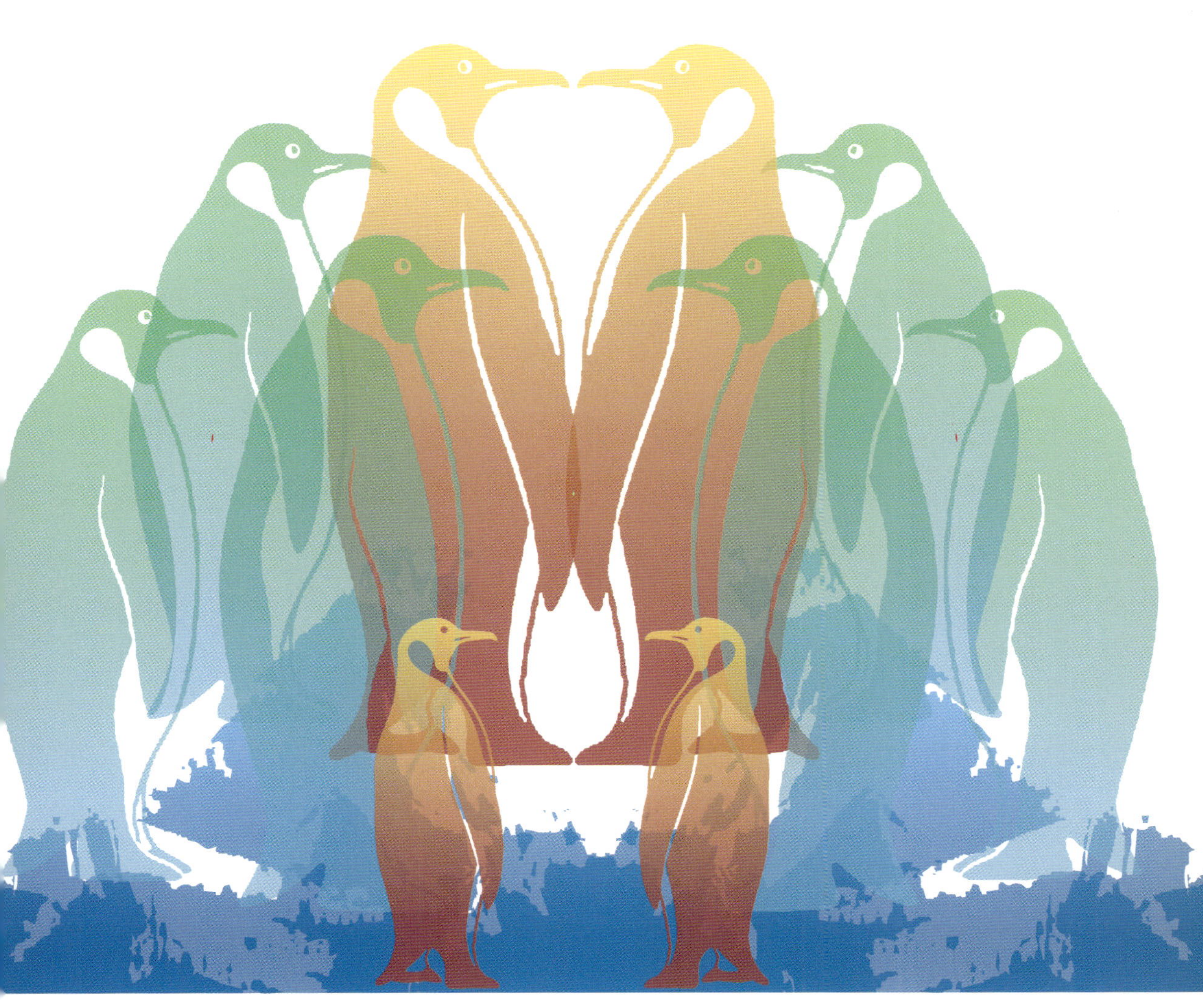

MA_T42

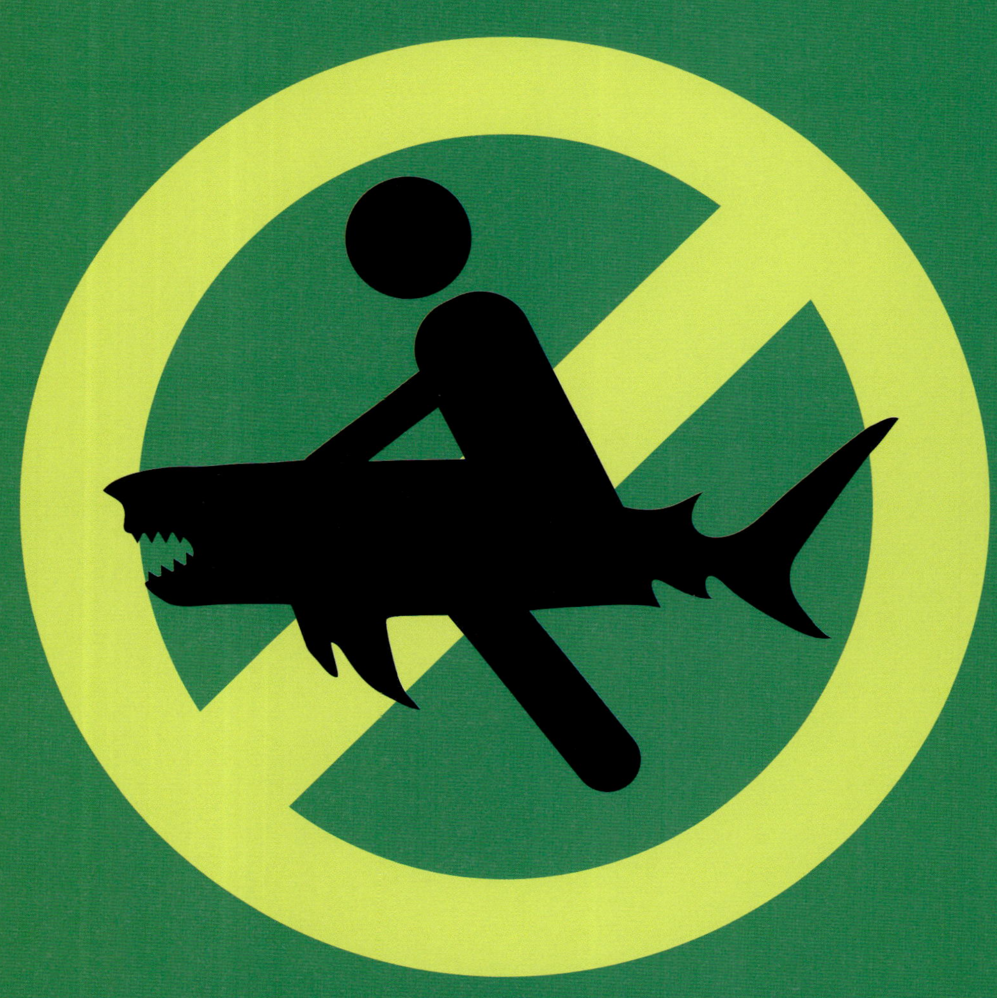

MA_T43

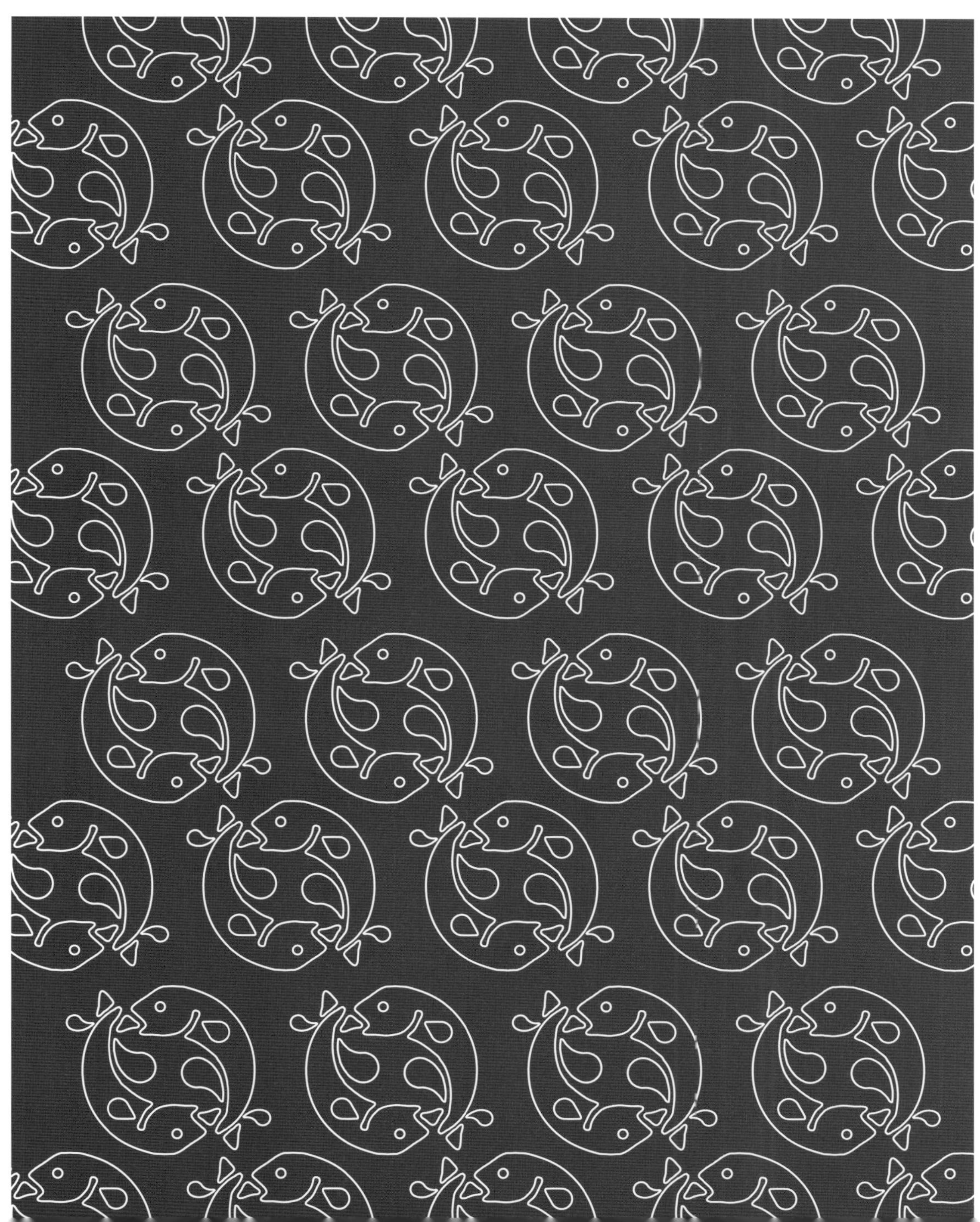

MA_T44

TEMPLATES

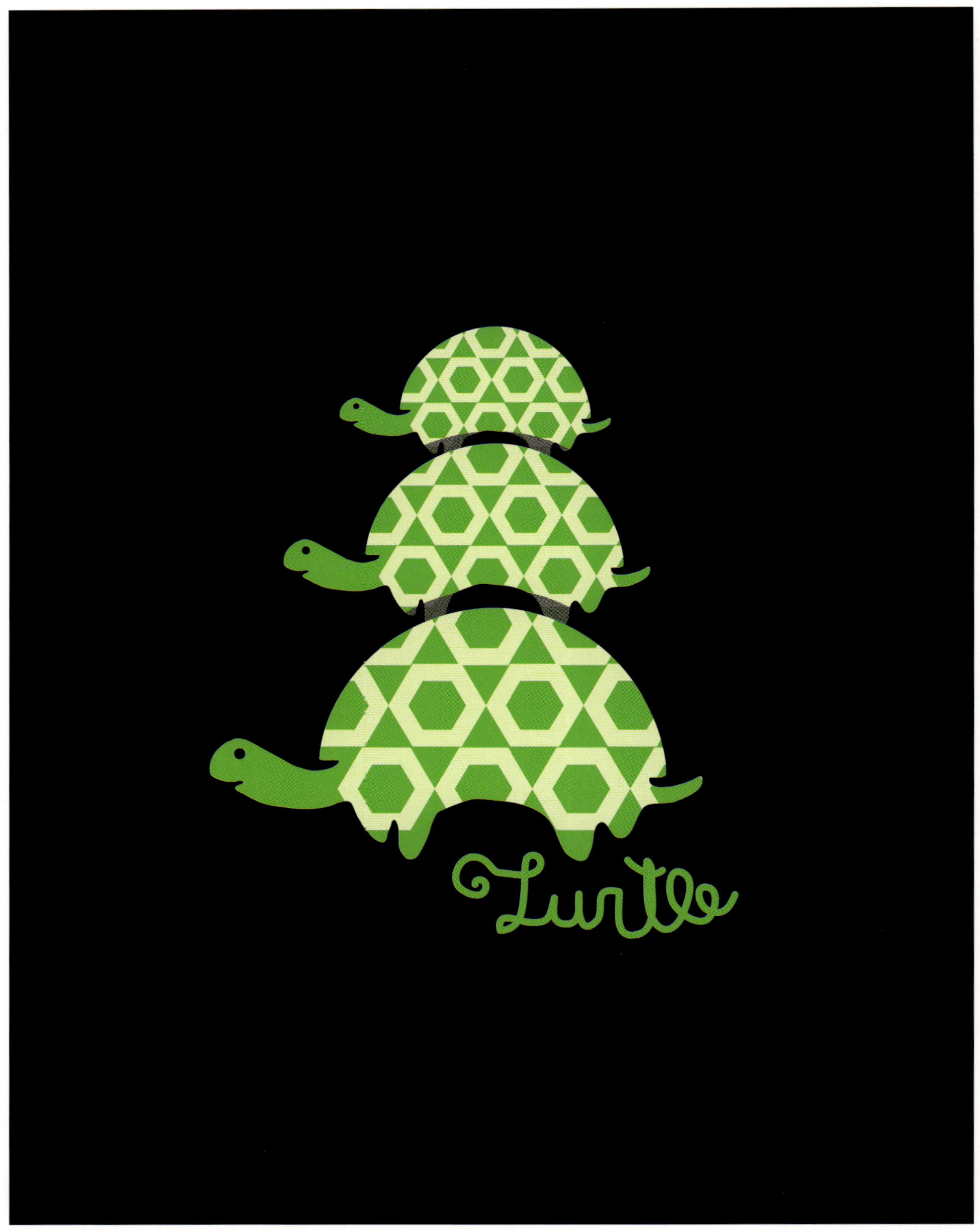

MA_T45

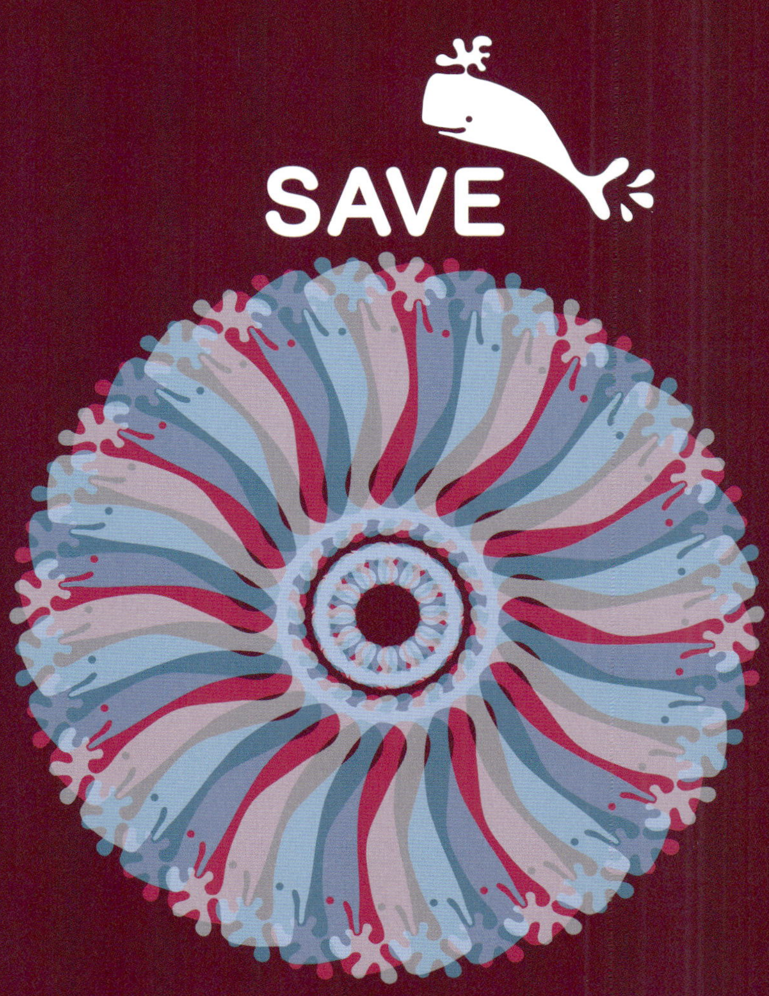

MA_T46

TEMPLATES

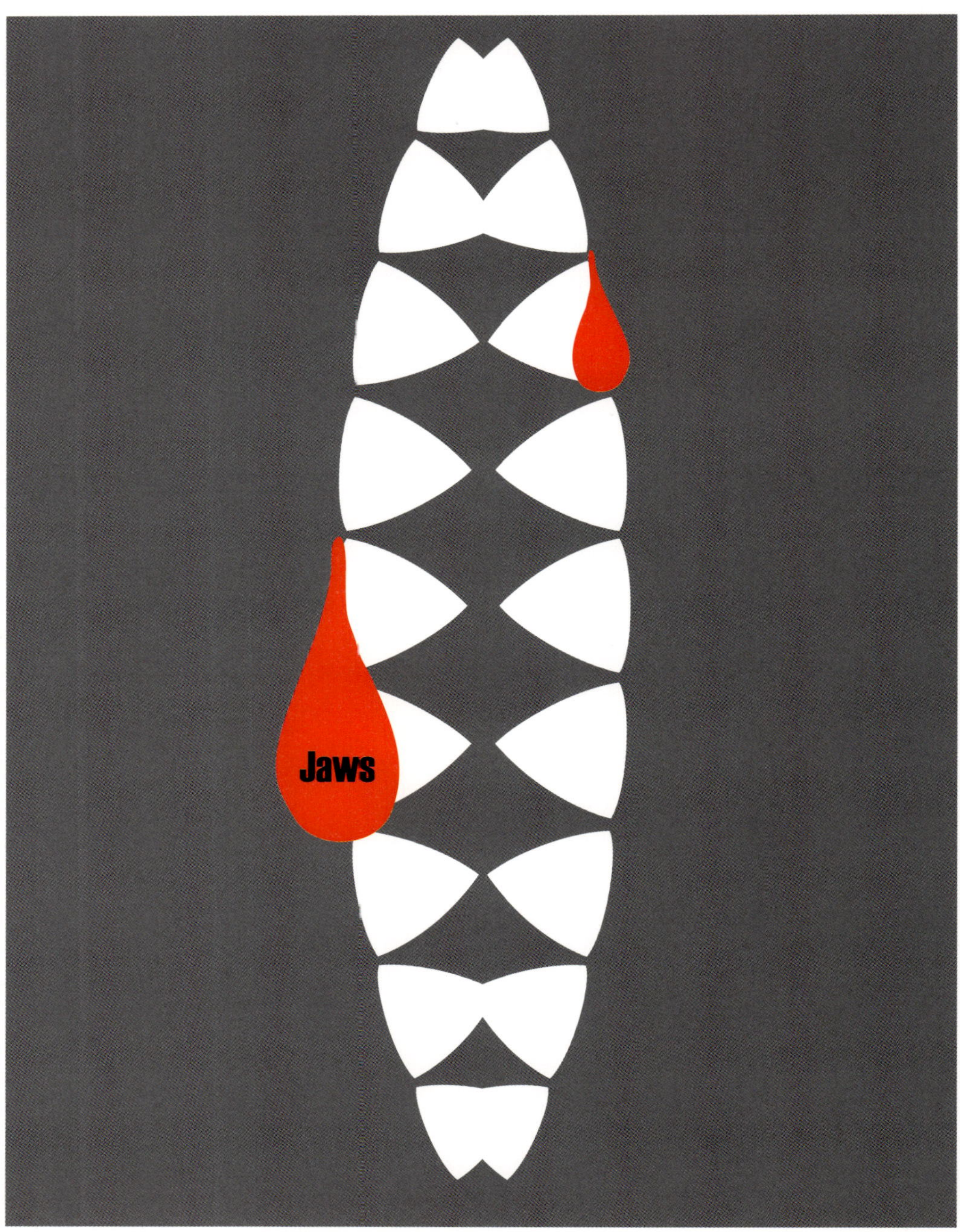

MA_T47

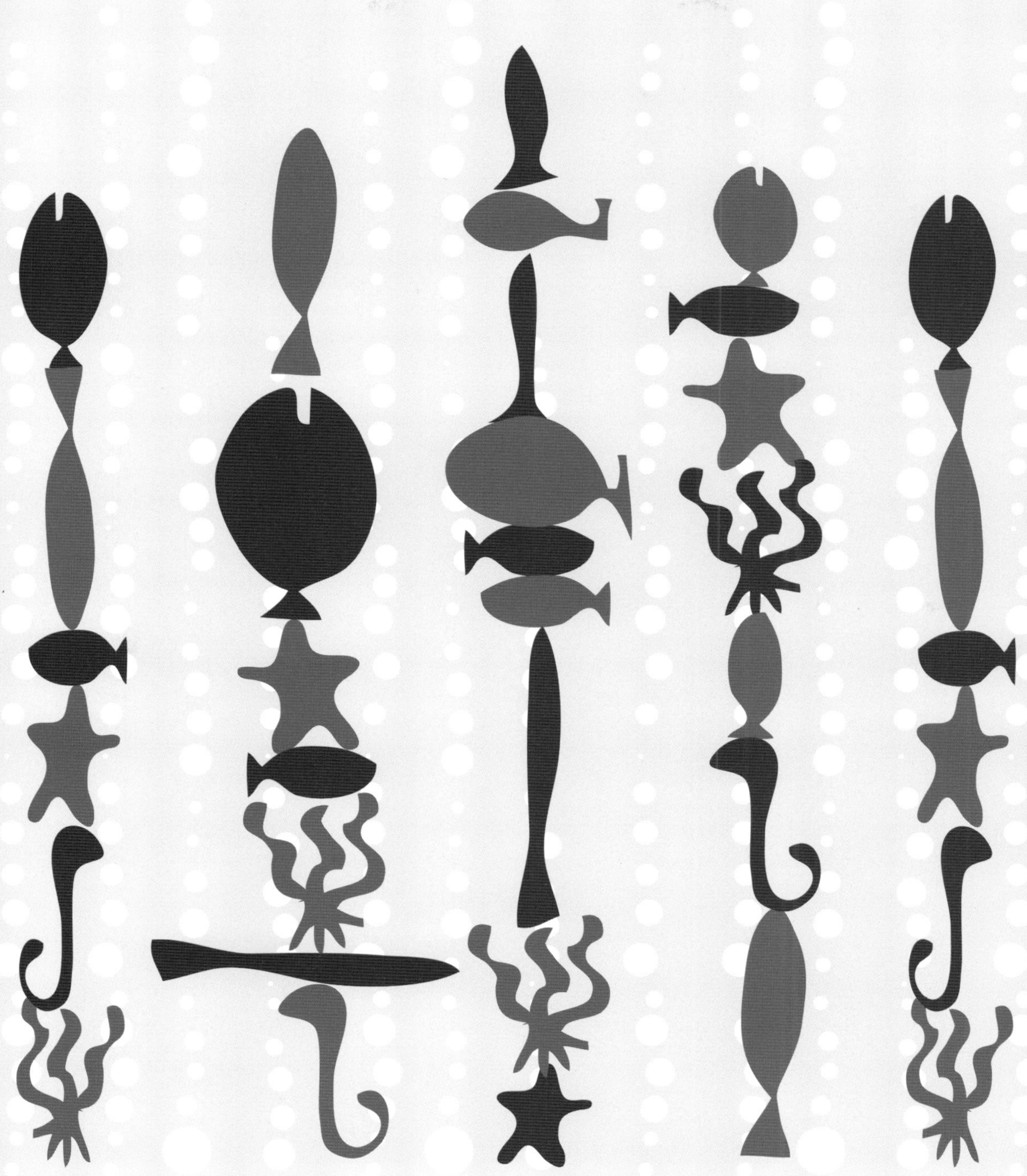

MA_T48

TEMPLATES

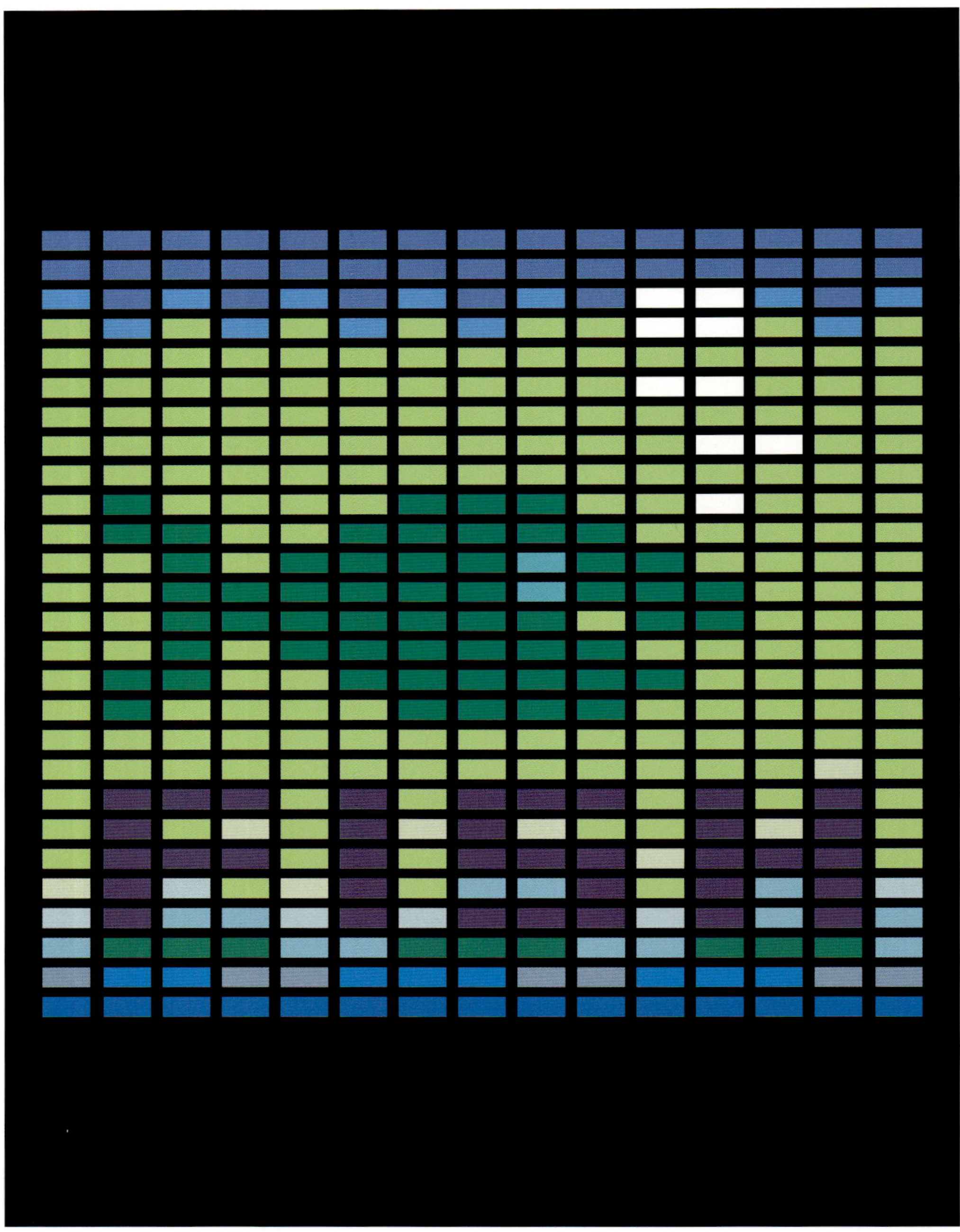

MA_T49

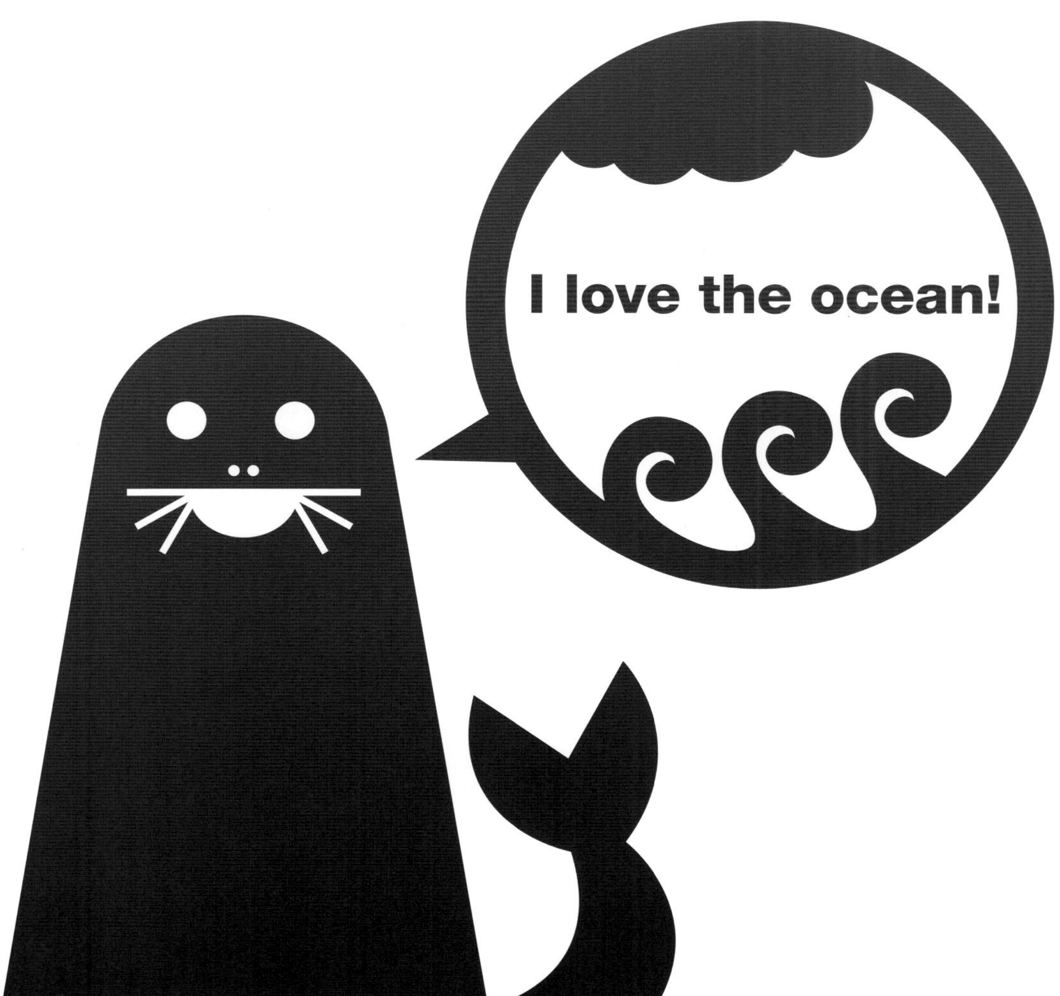

MA_T50

TEMPLATES

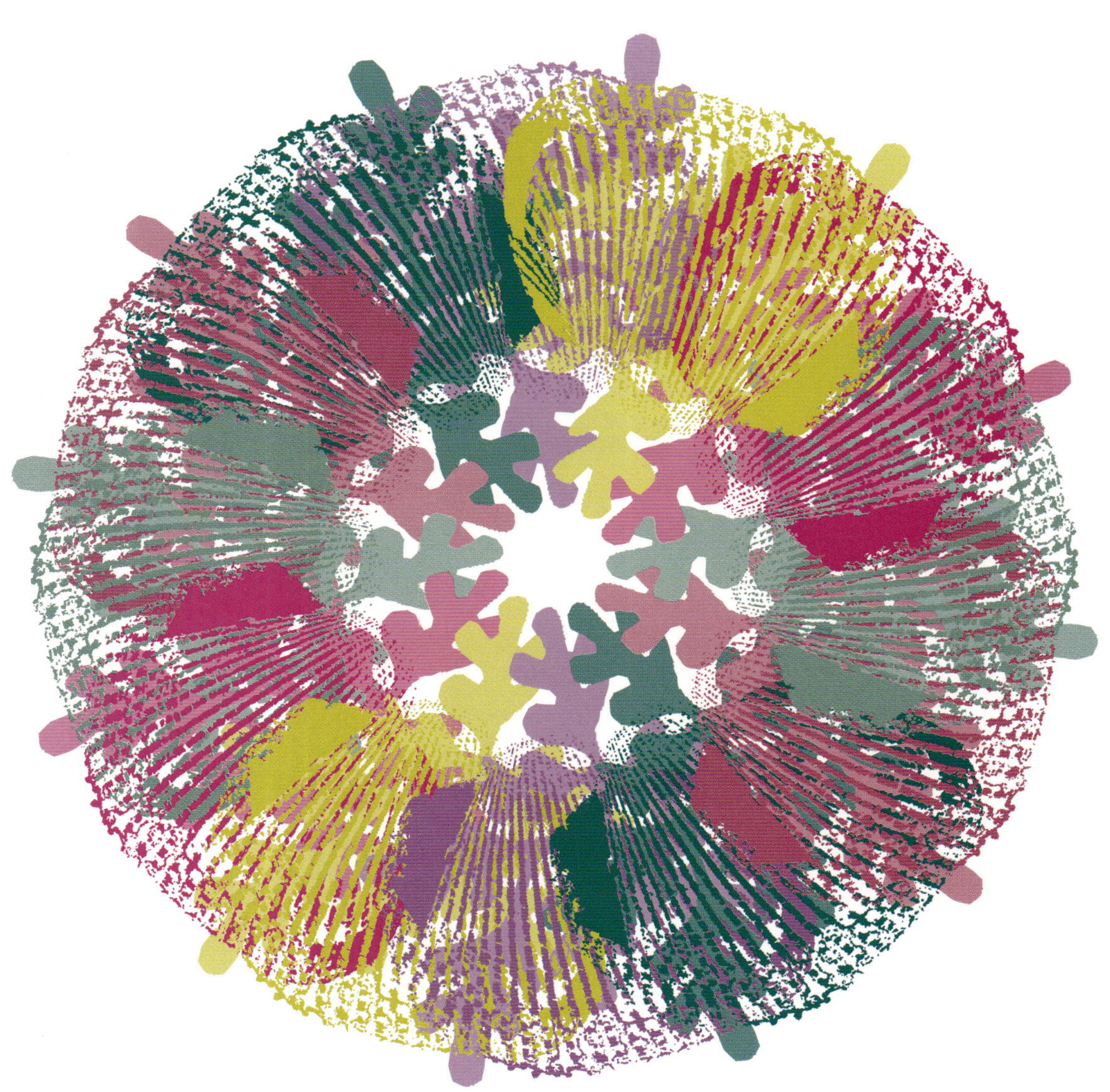

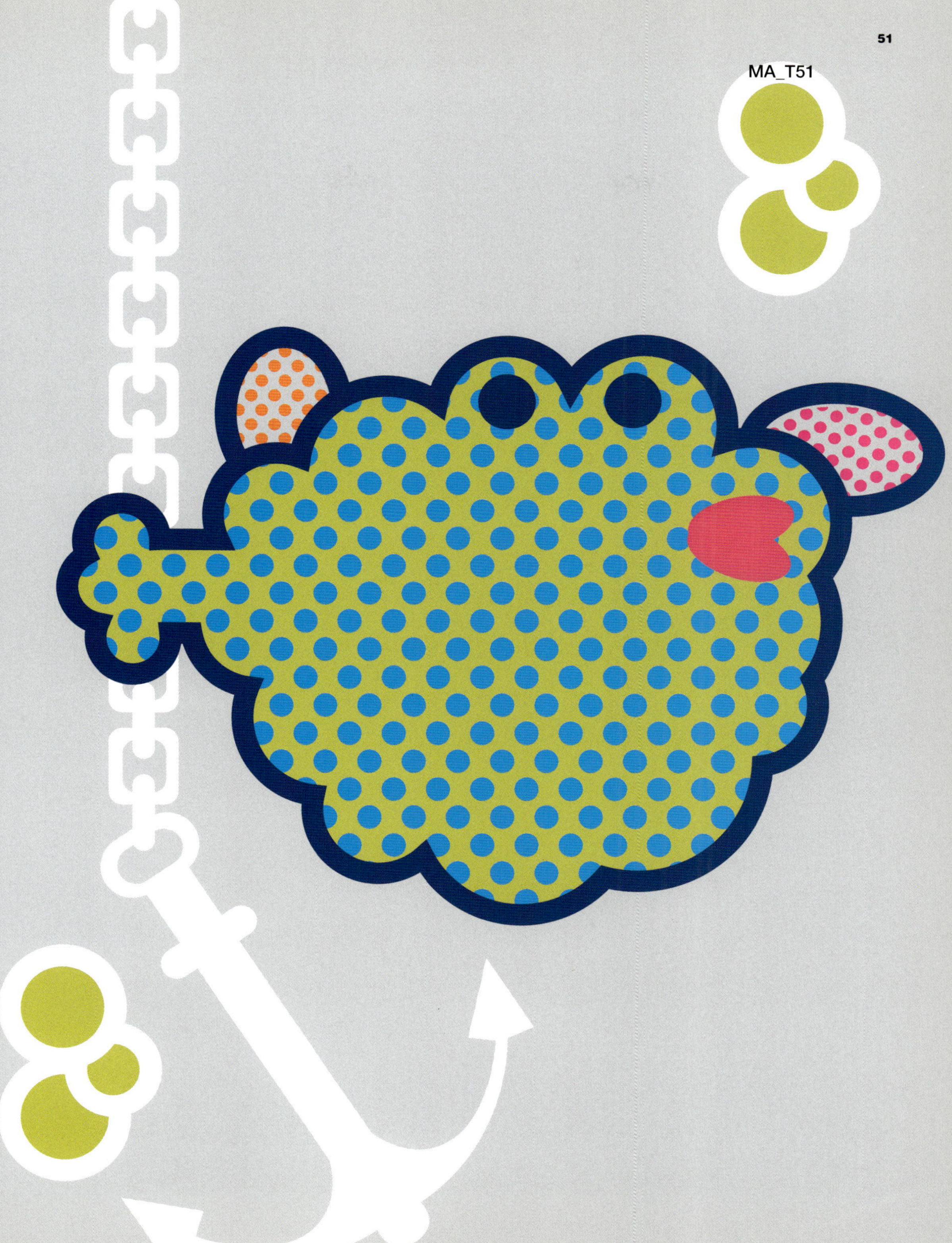
MA_T51

MA_T52

TEMPLATES

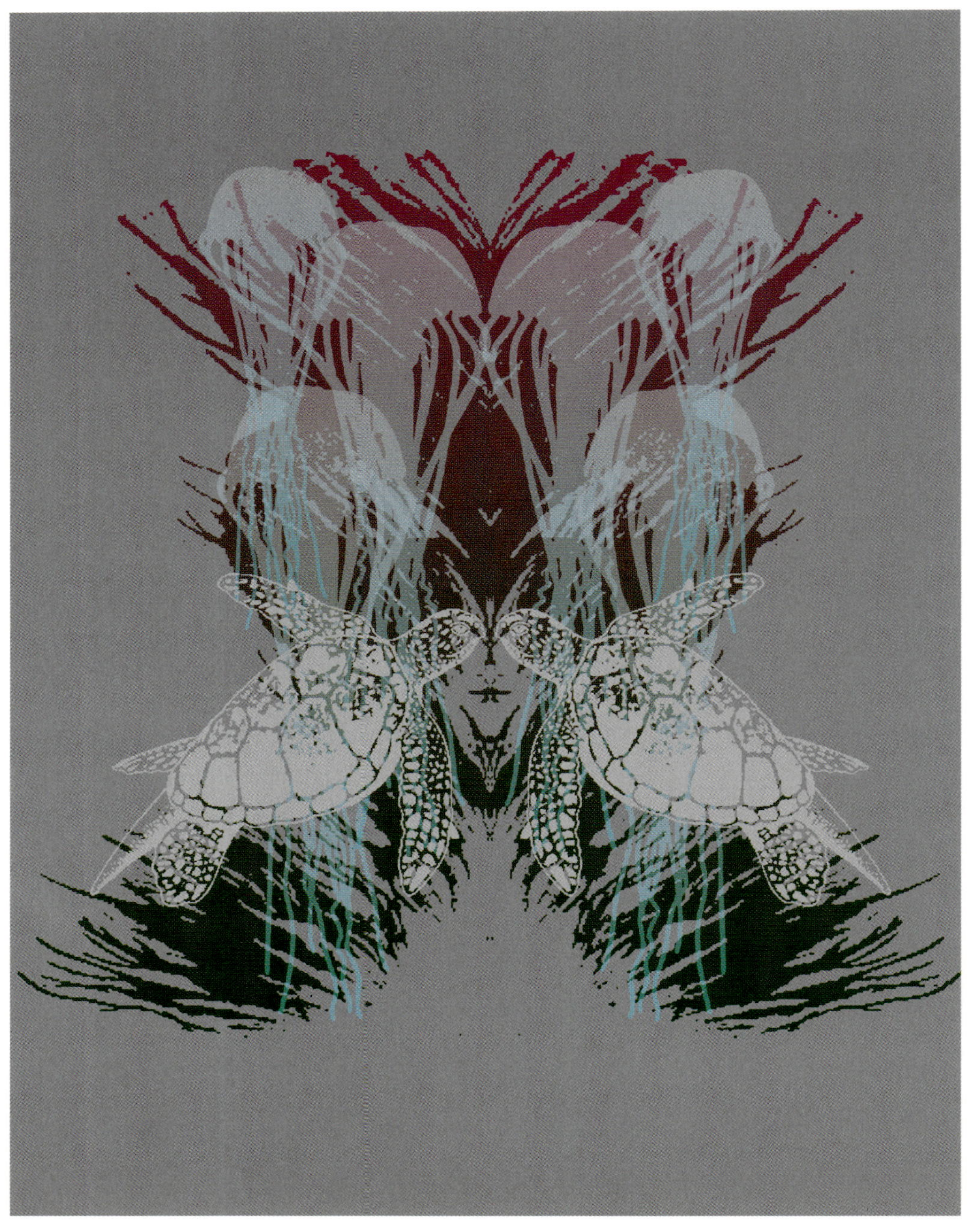

MA_T53

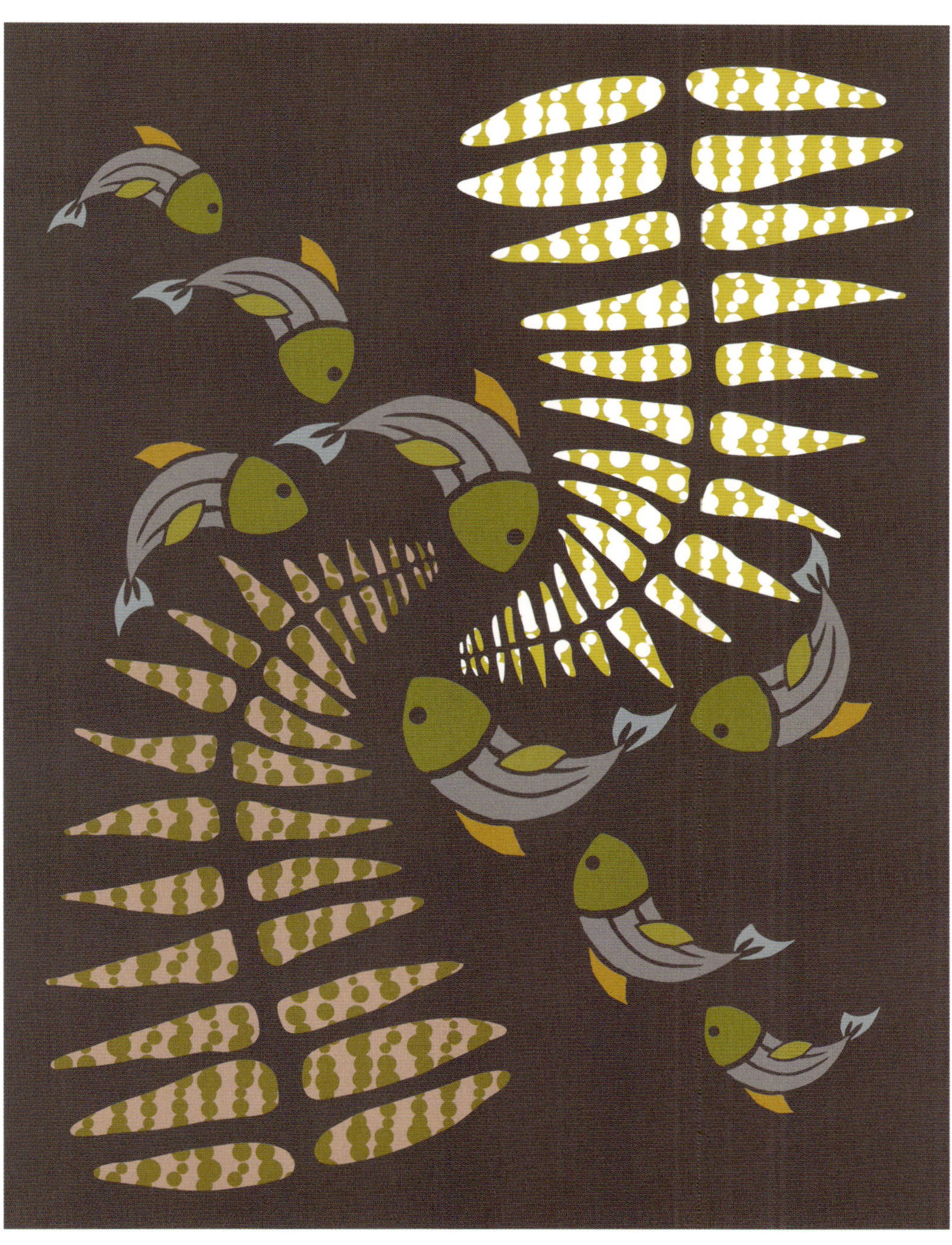

MA_T54

TEMPLATES

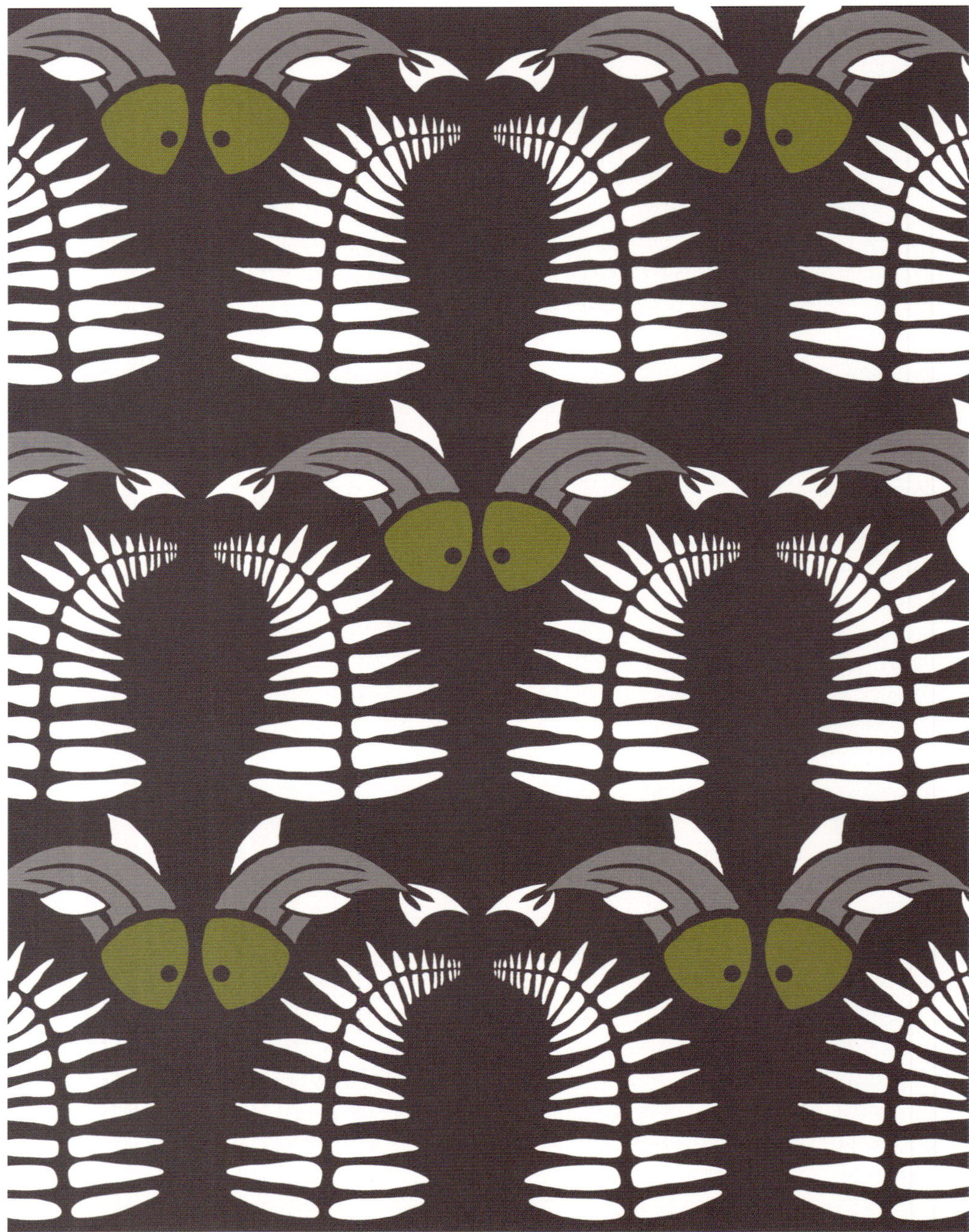

MA_T55

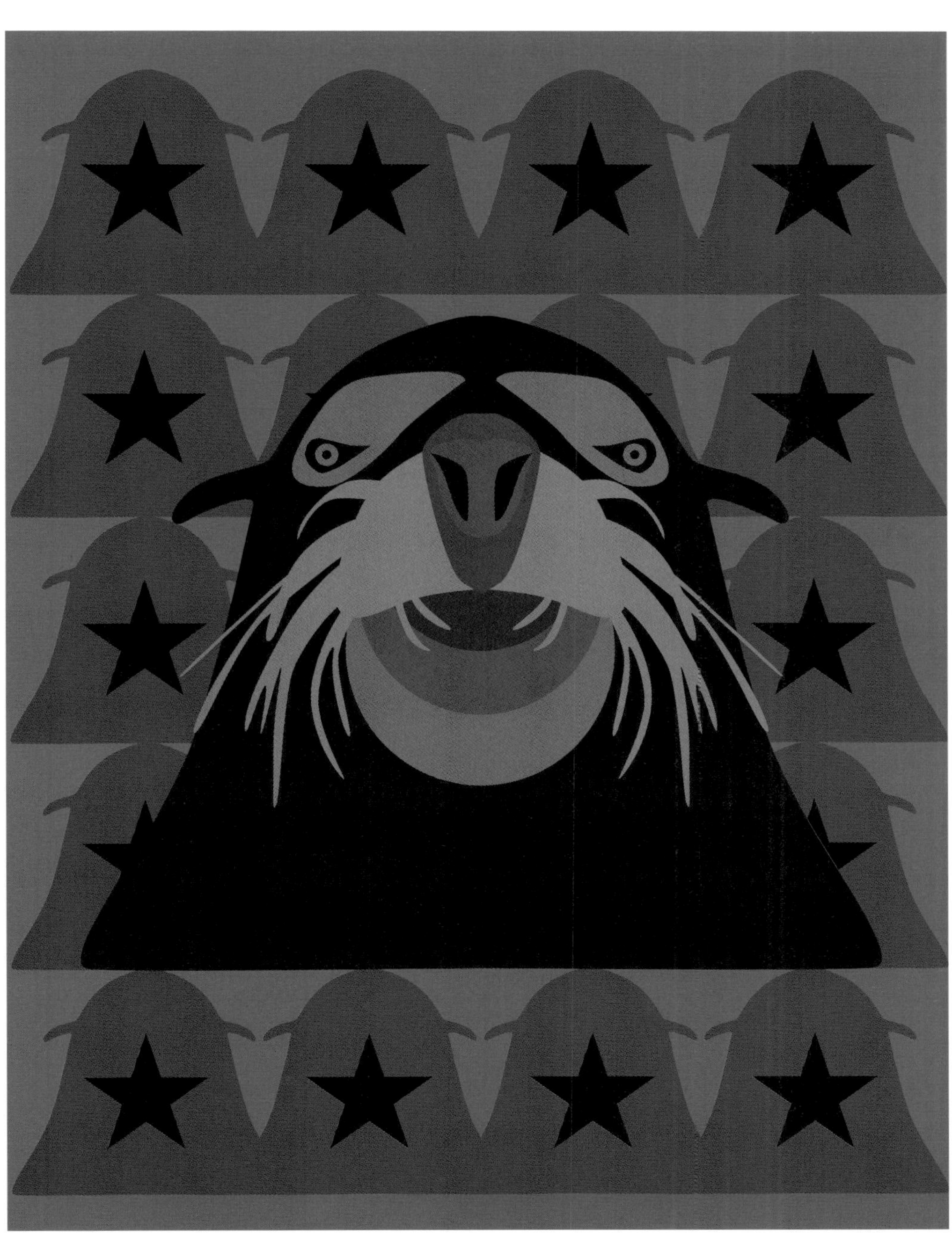

MA_T56

TEMPLATES

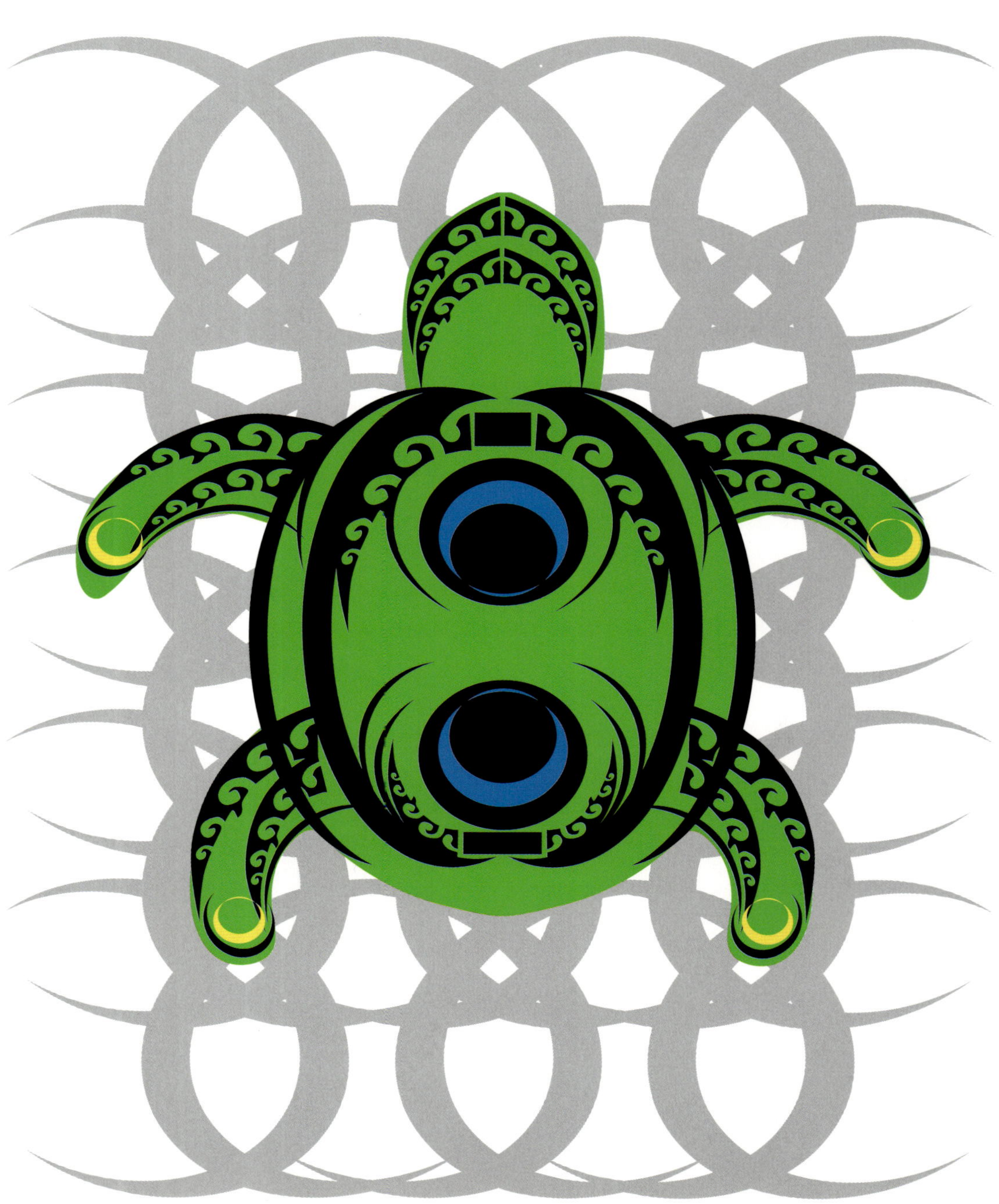

MA_T57

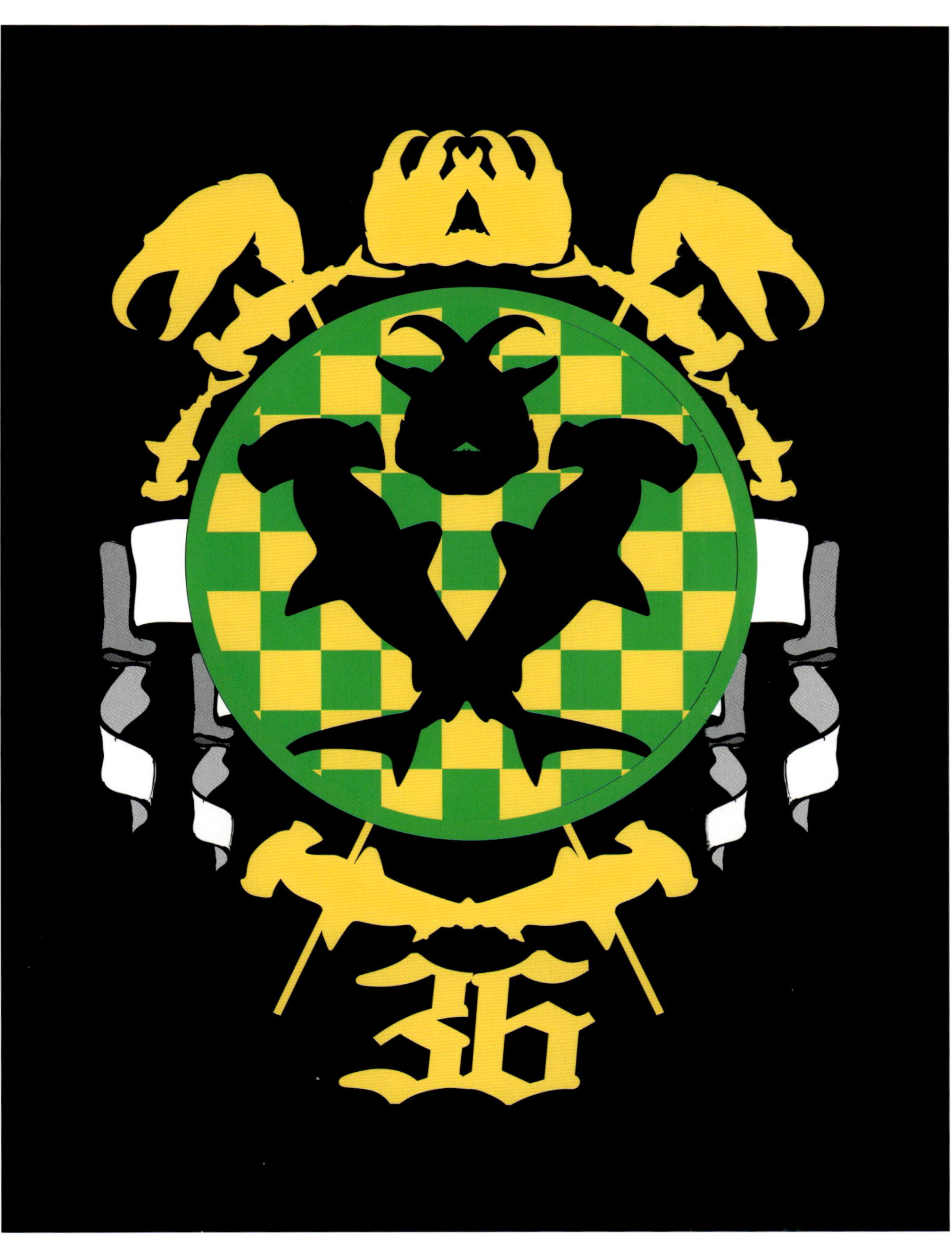

MA_T58

TEMPLATES

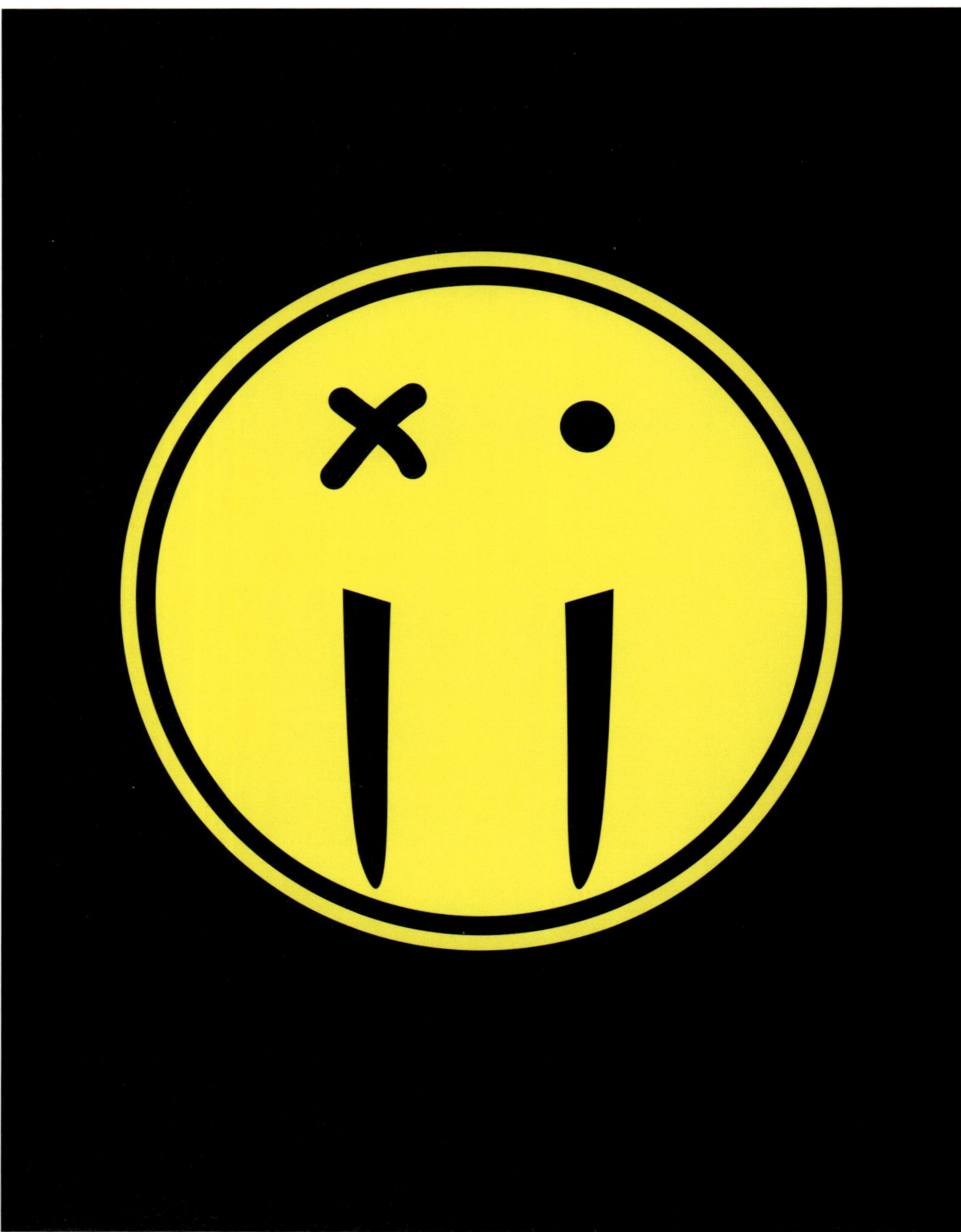

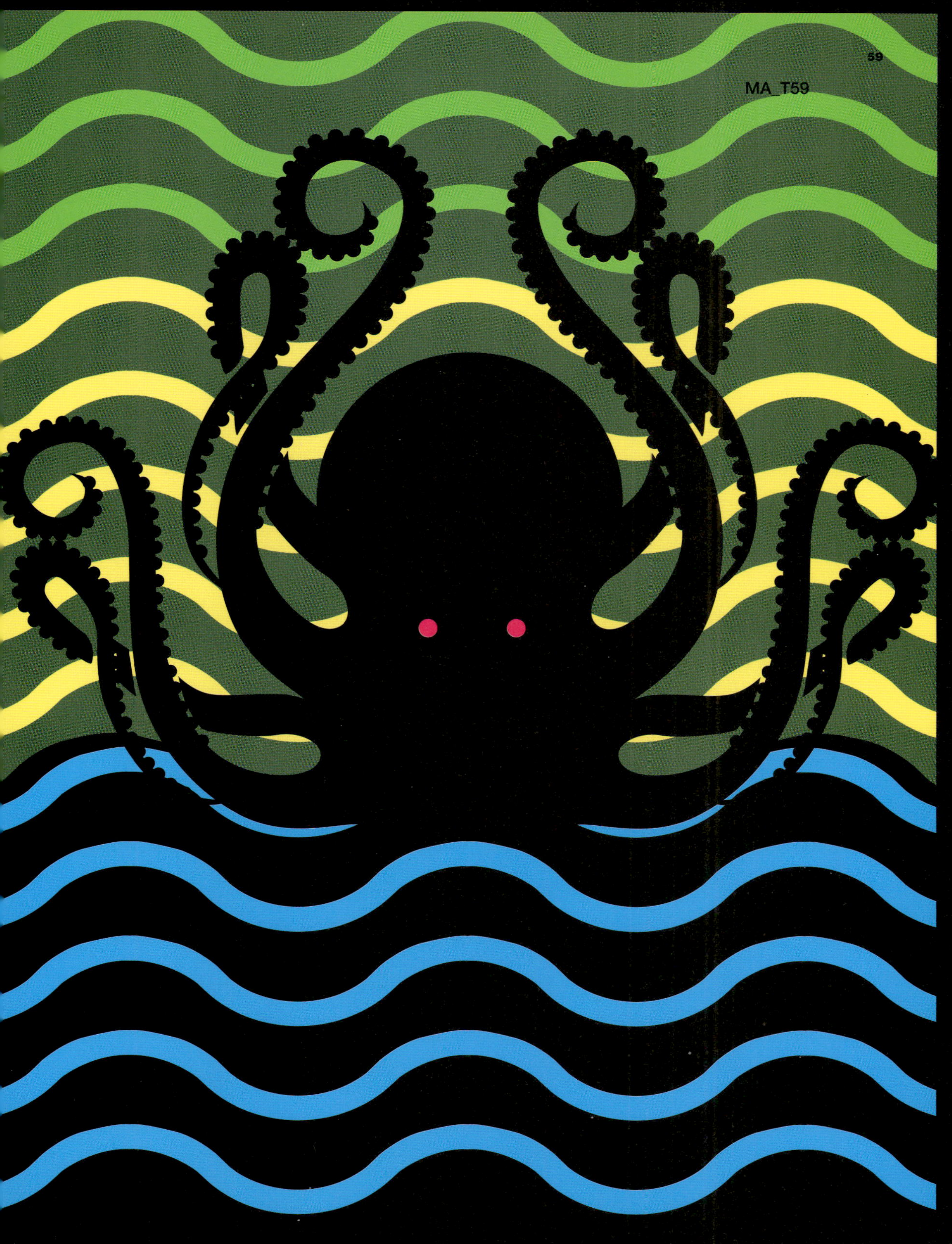
MA_T59

MA_T60

TEMPLATES

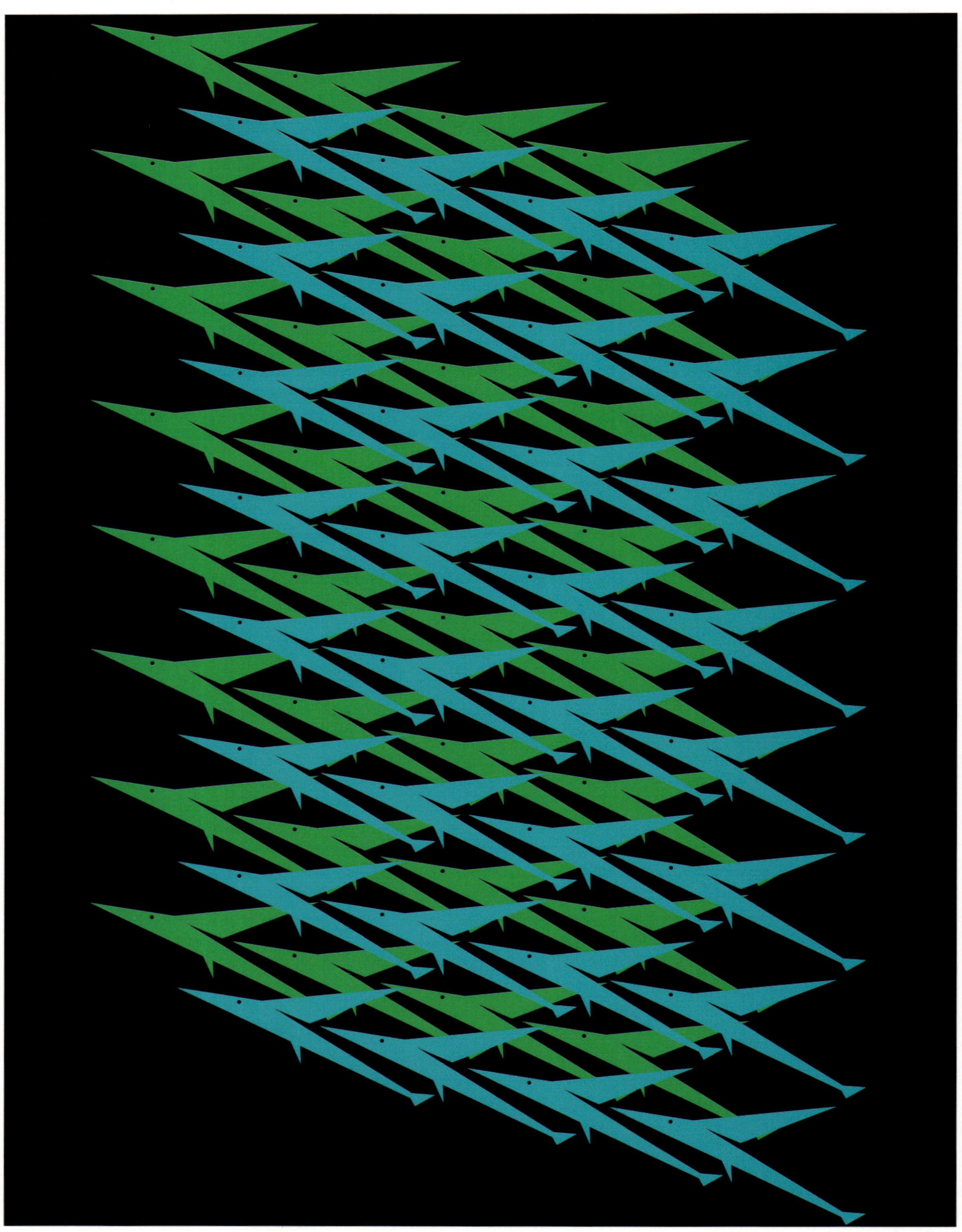

MA_T61

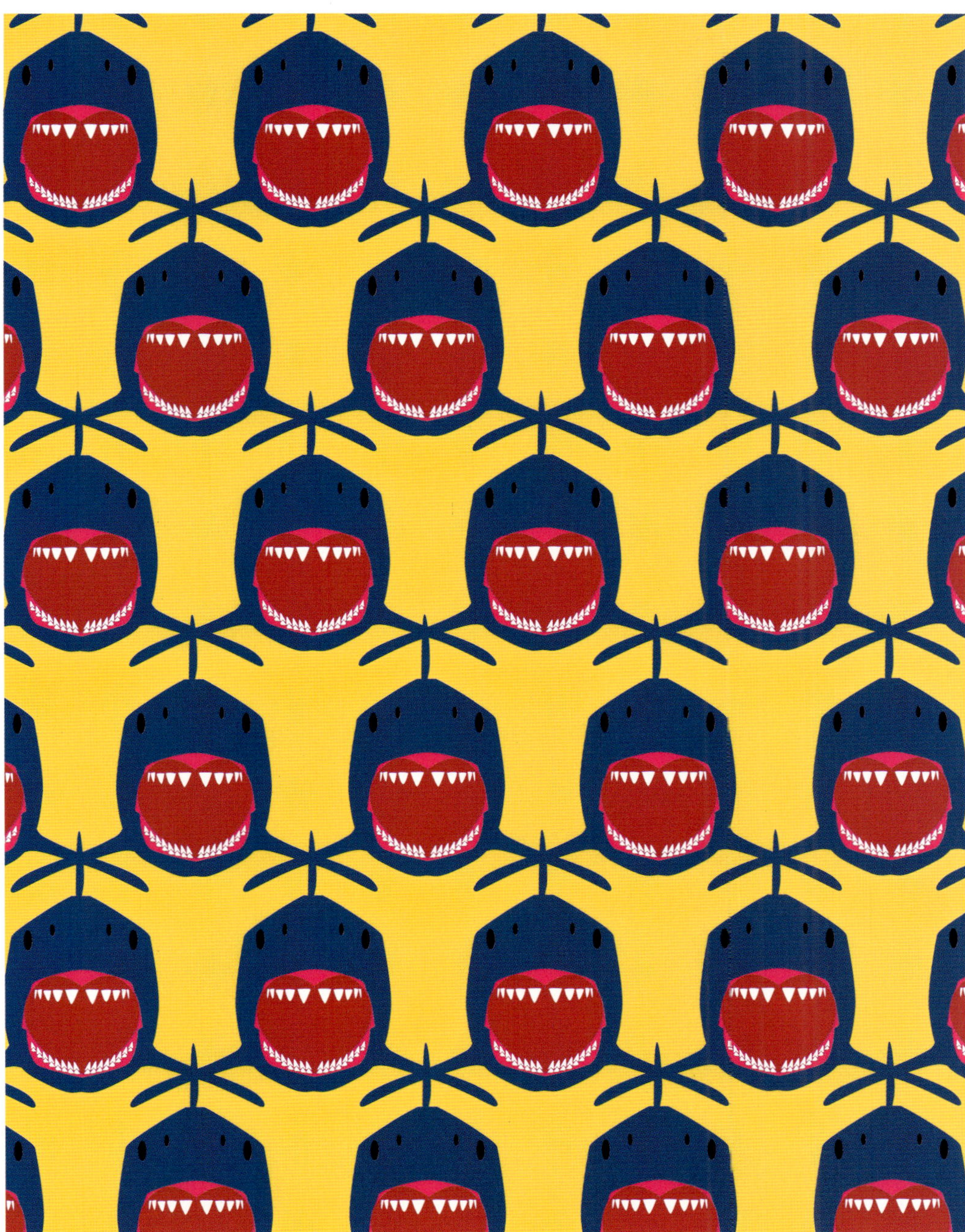

MA_T62

TEMPLATES

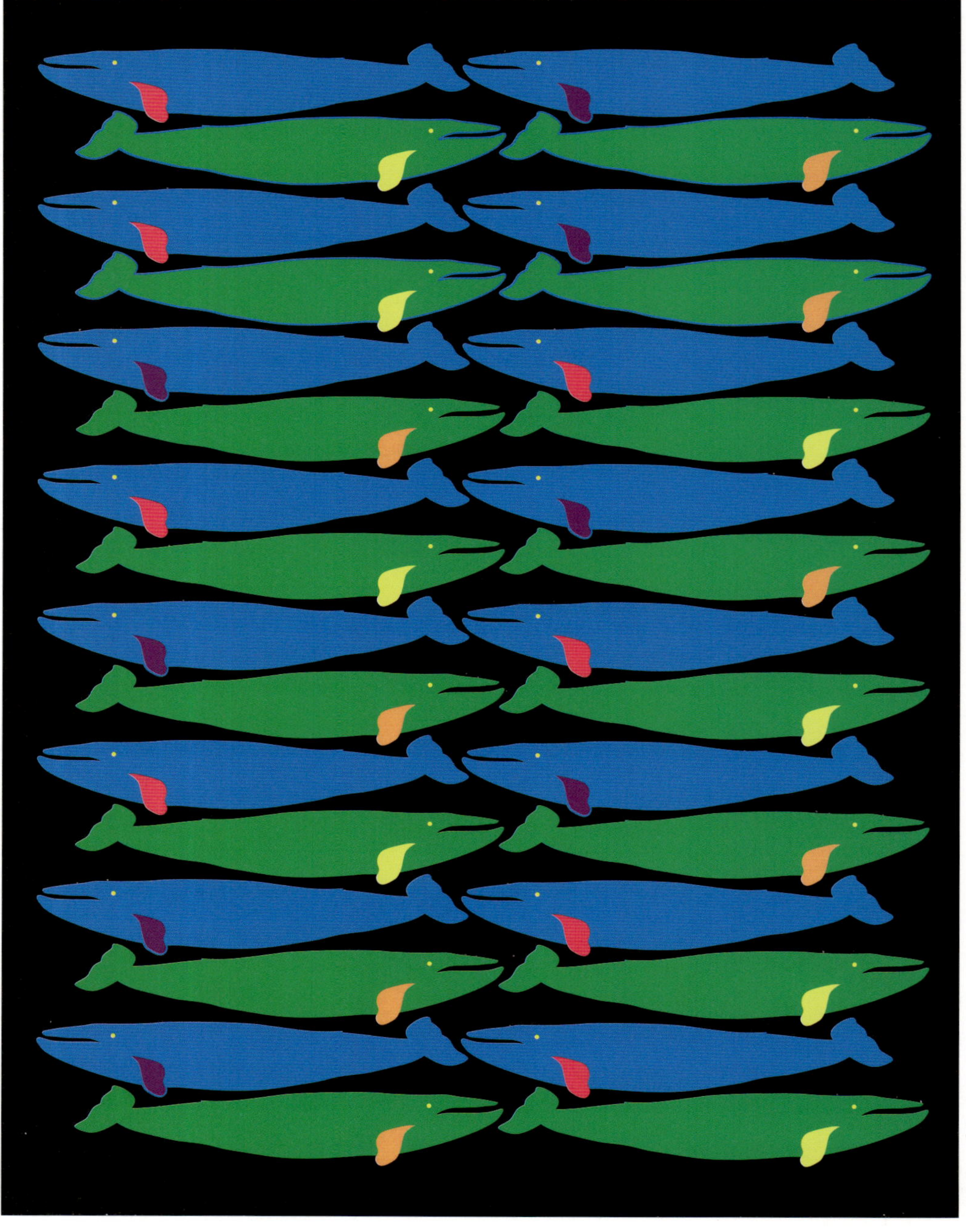

MA_T63

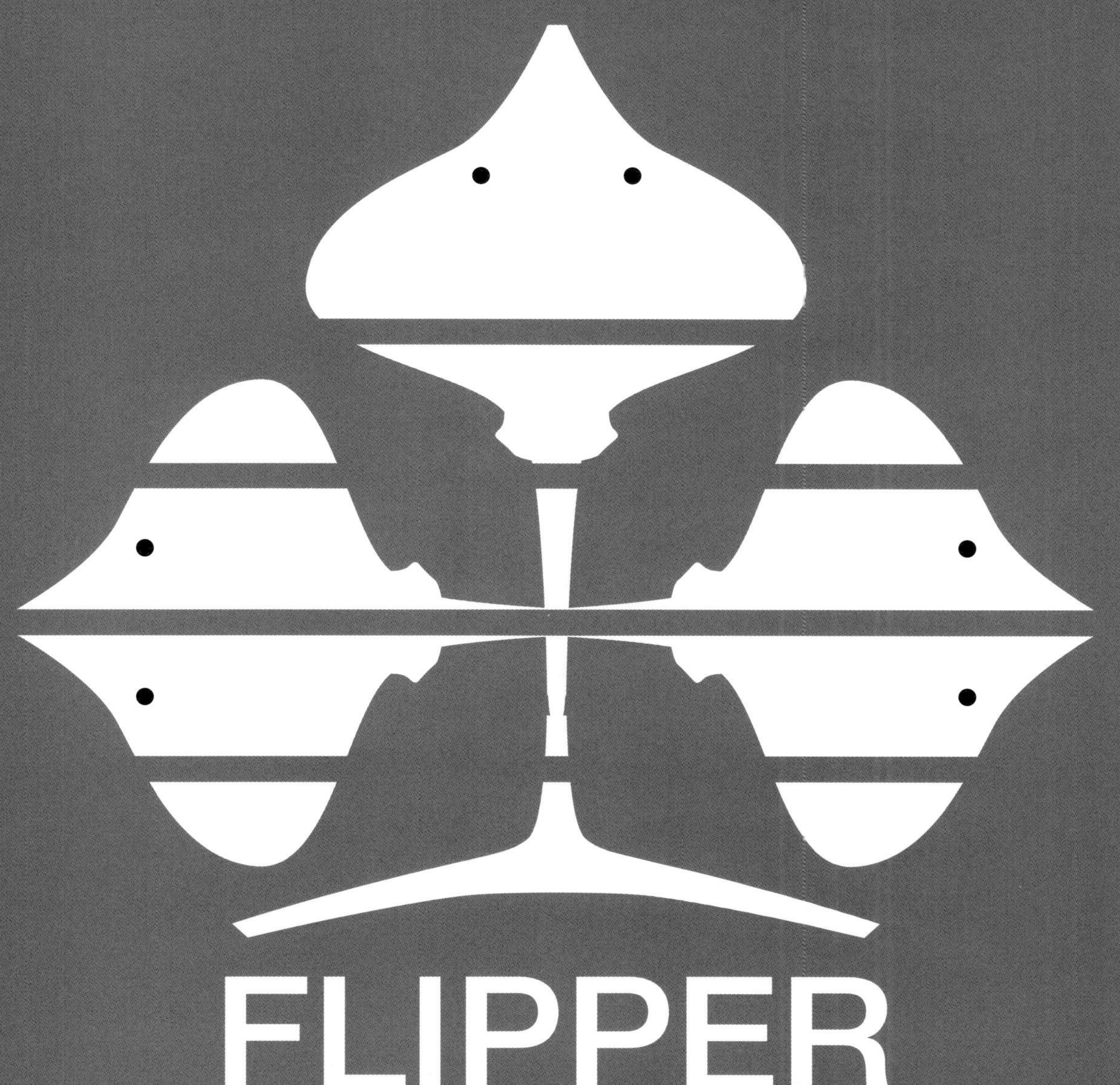

MA_T64

TEMPLATES

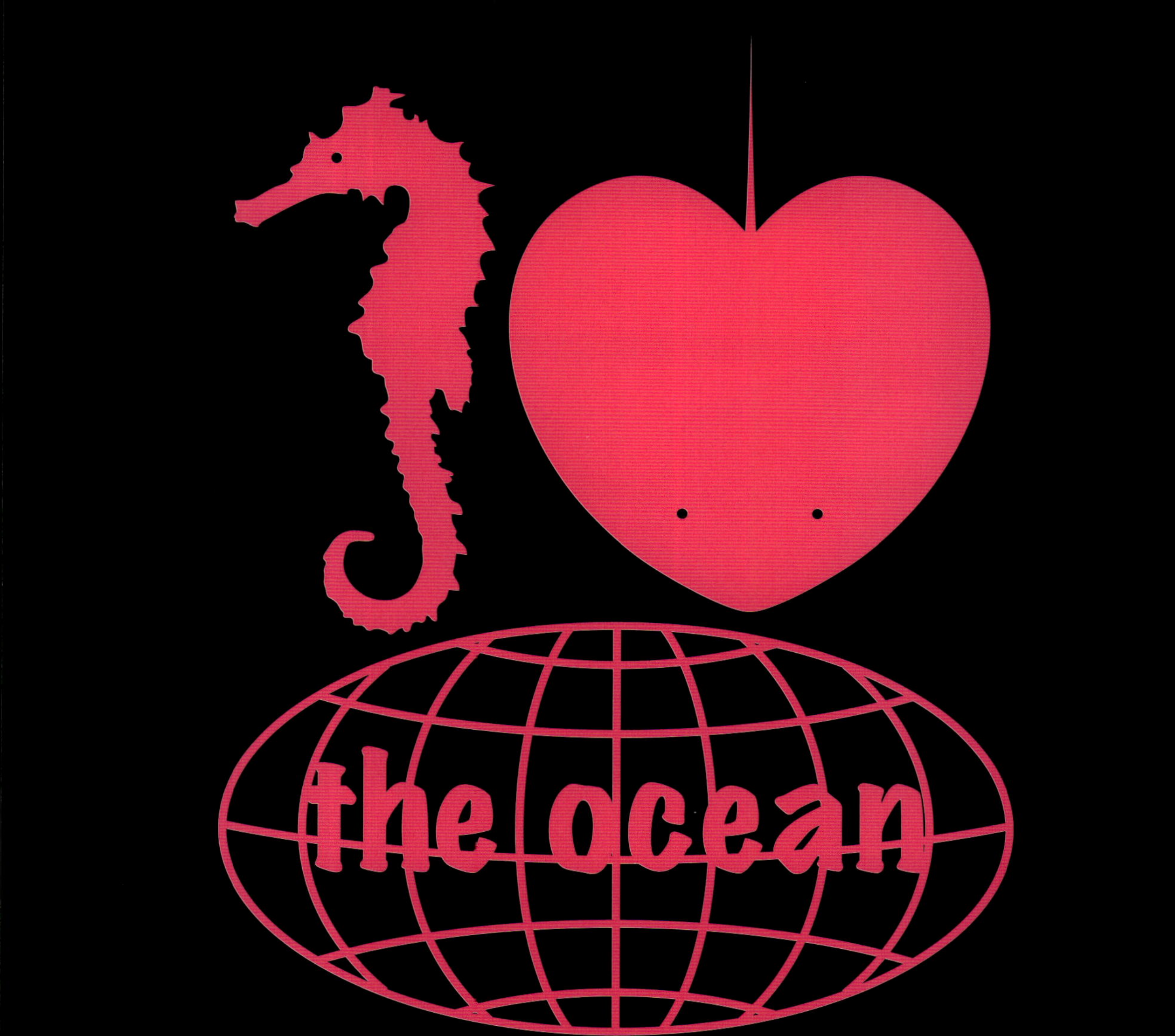

MA_T65

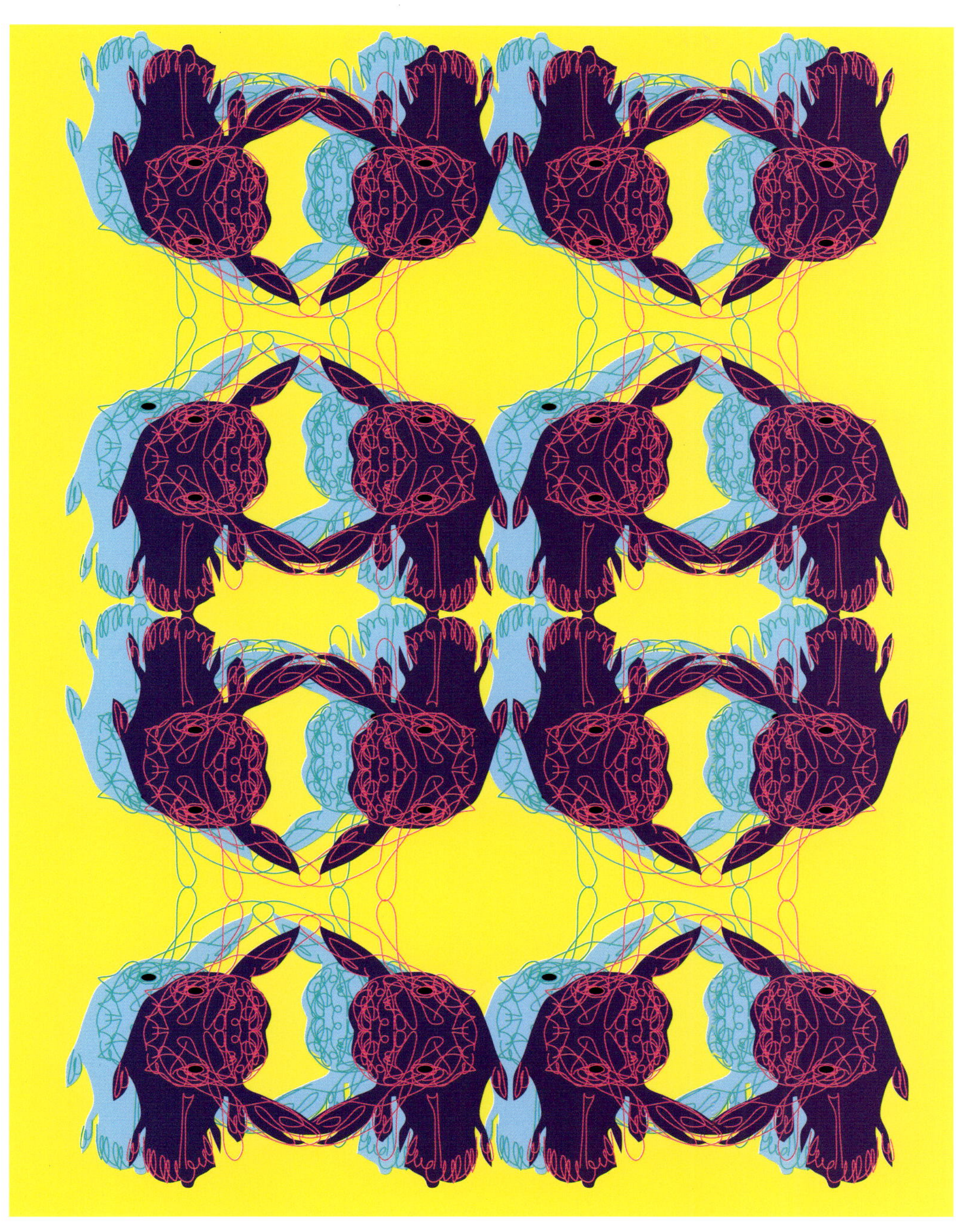

MA_T66

TEMPLATES

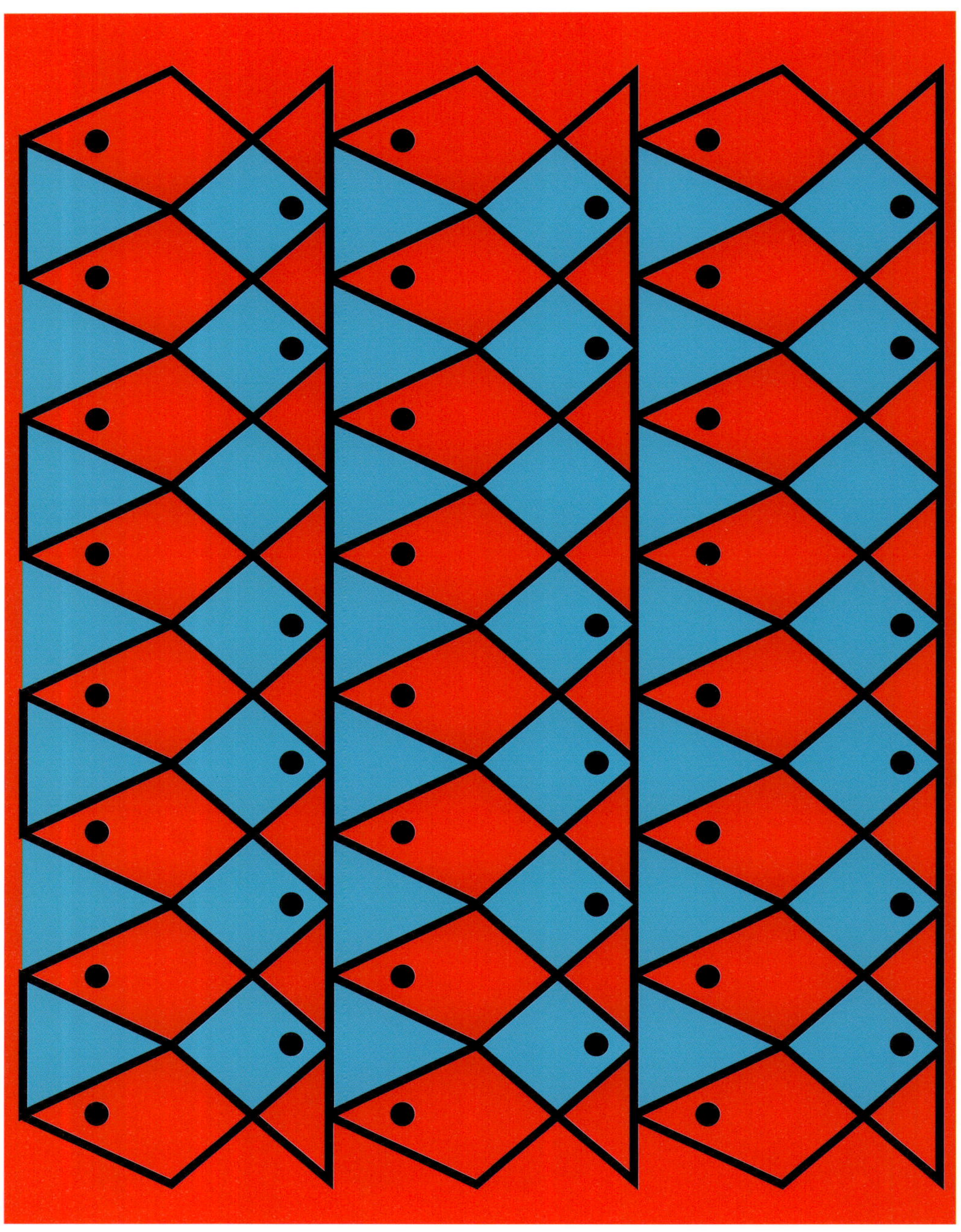

MA_T67

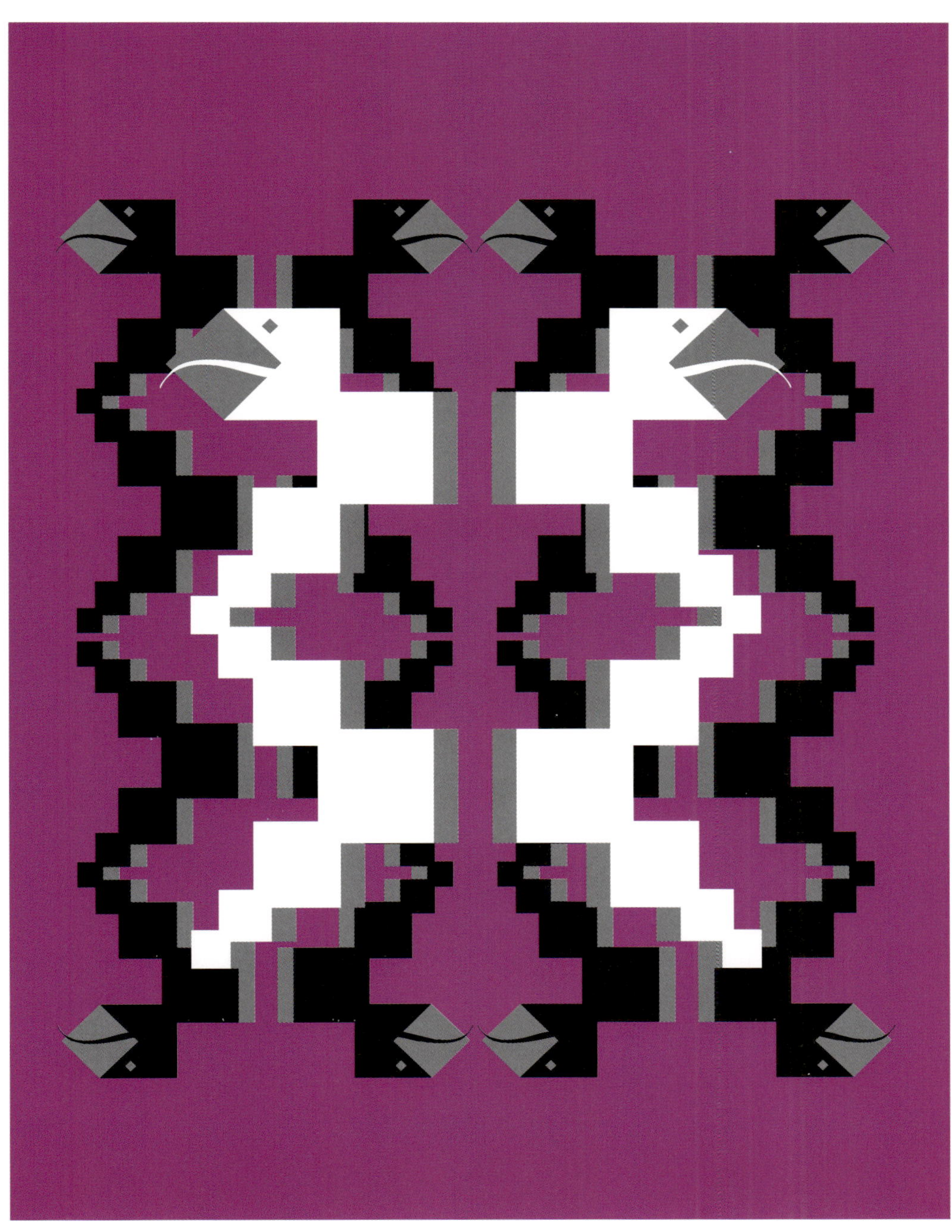

MA_T68

TEMPLATES

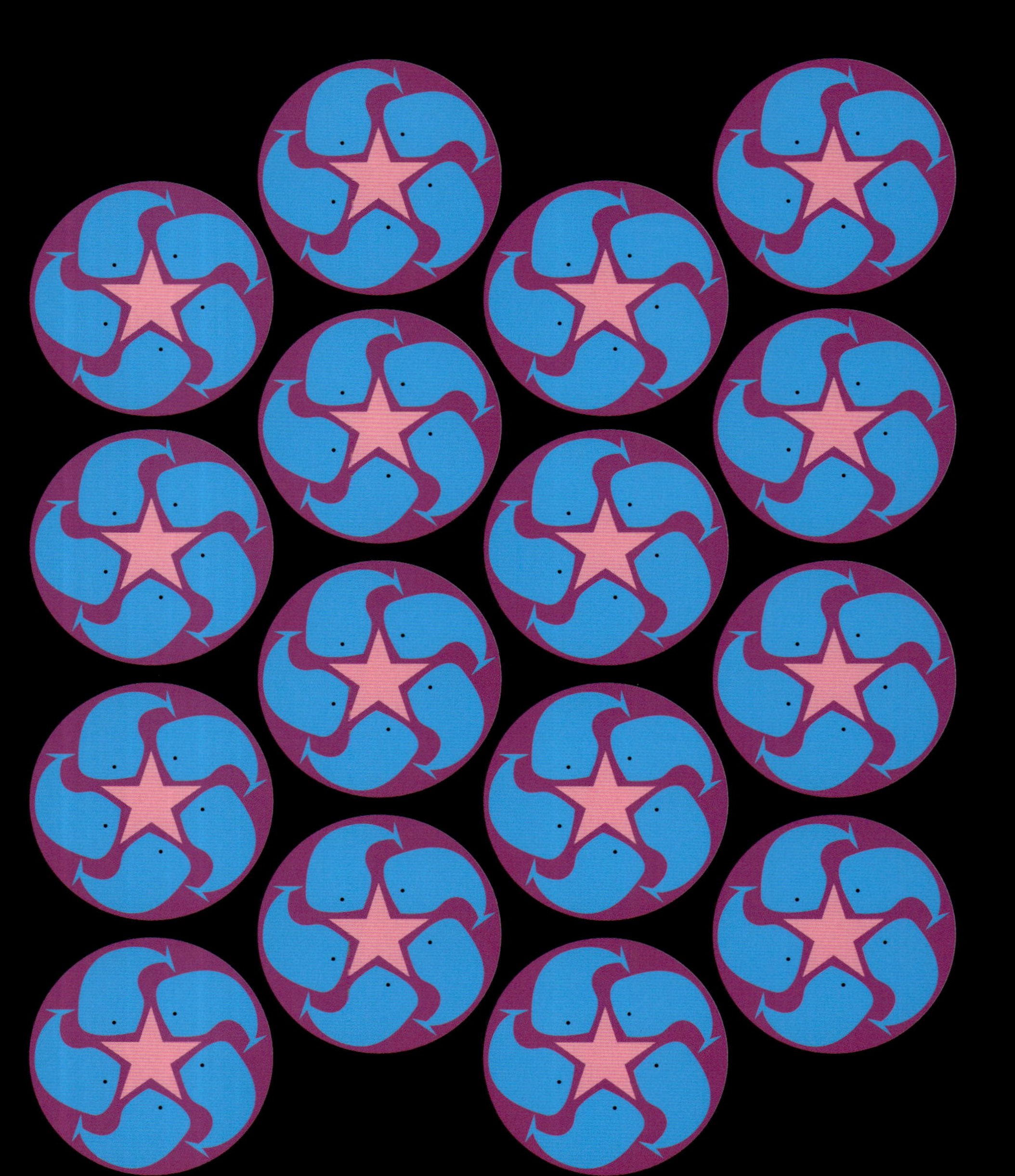

MA_T69

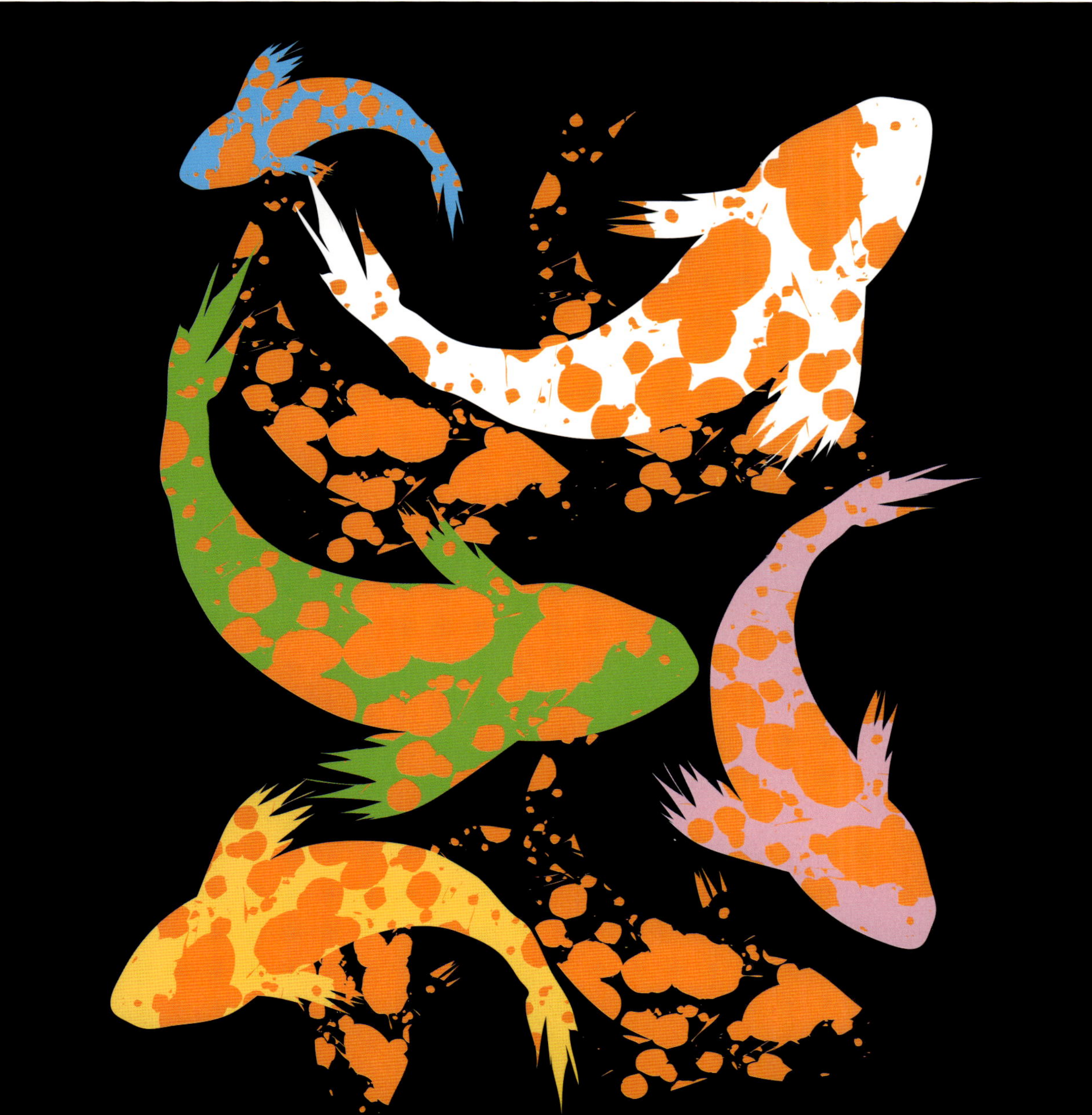

MA_T70

TEMPLATES

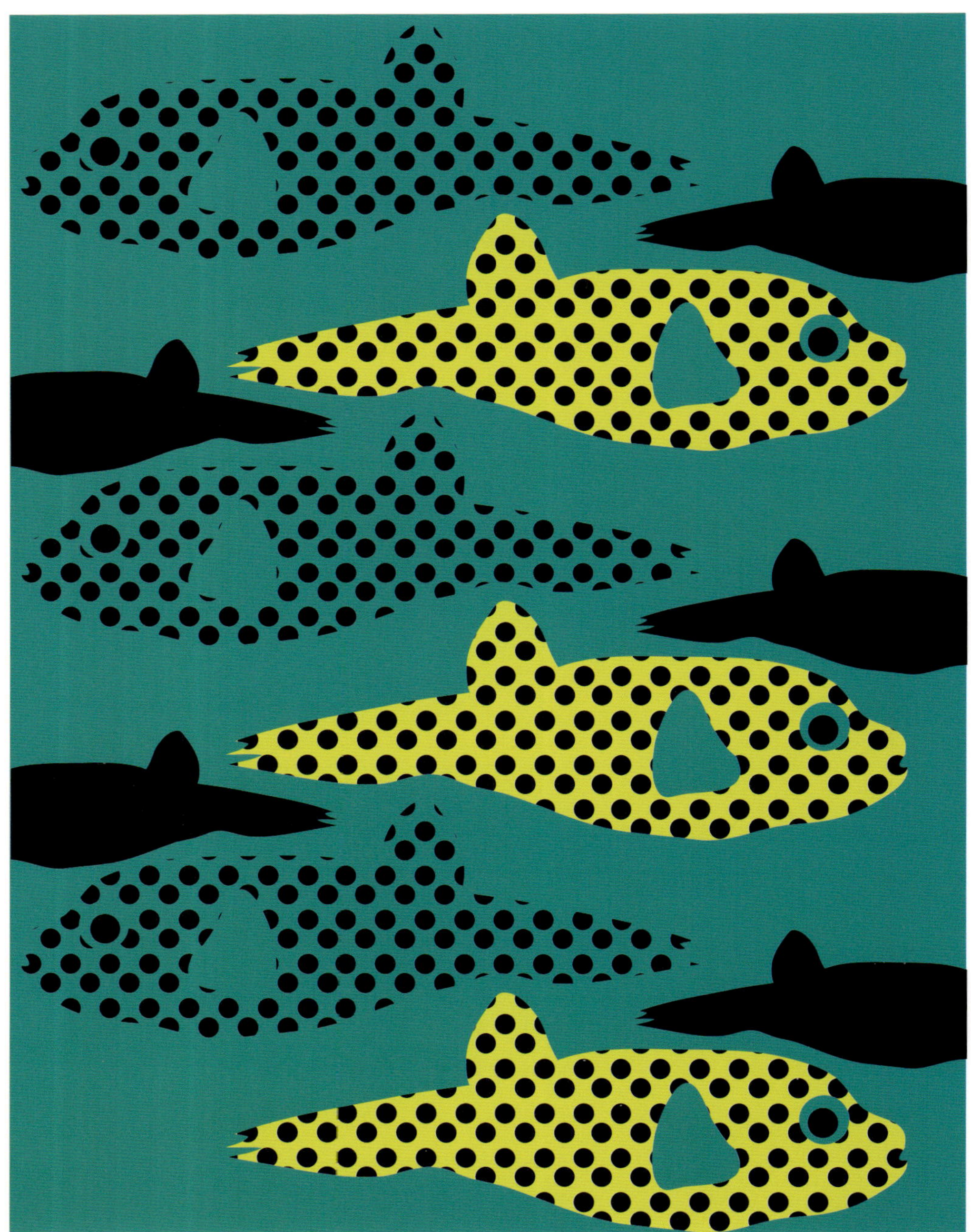

MA_T71

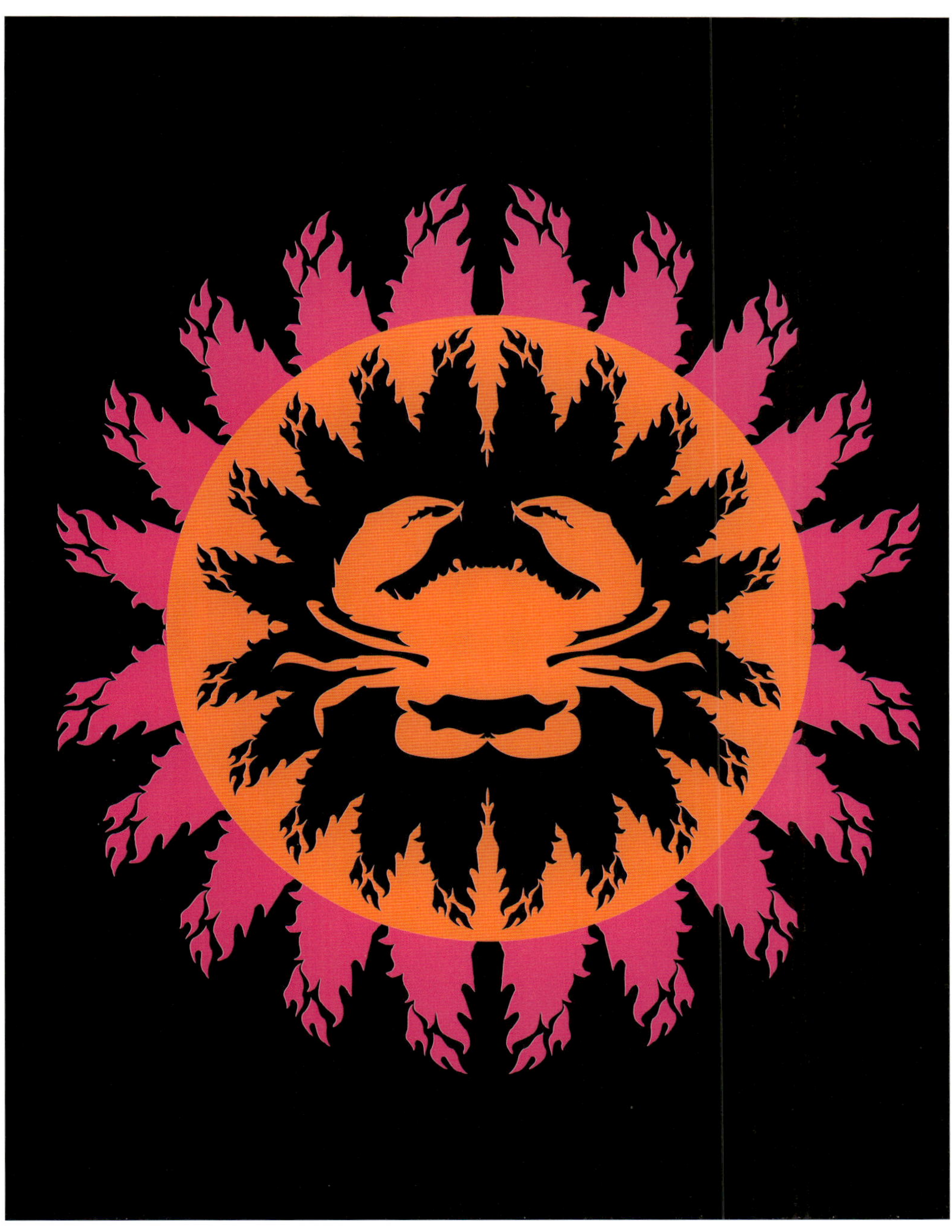

MA_T72

TEMPLATES

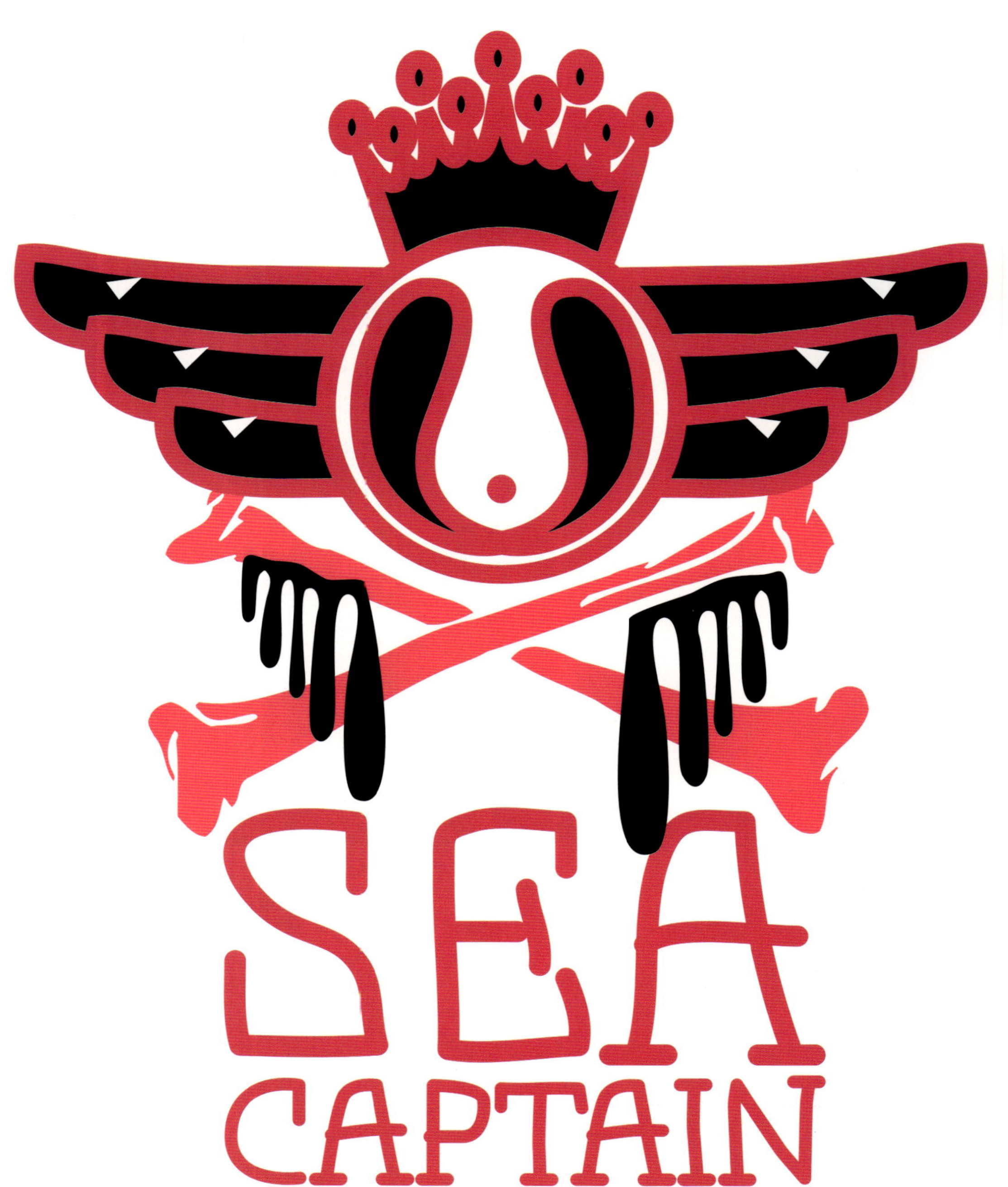

MA_T73

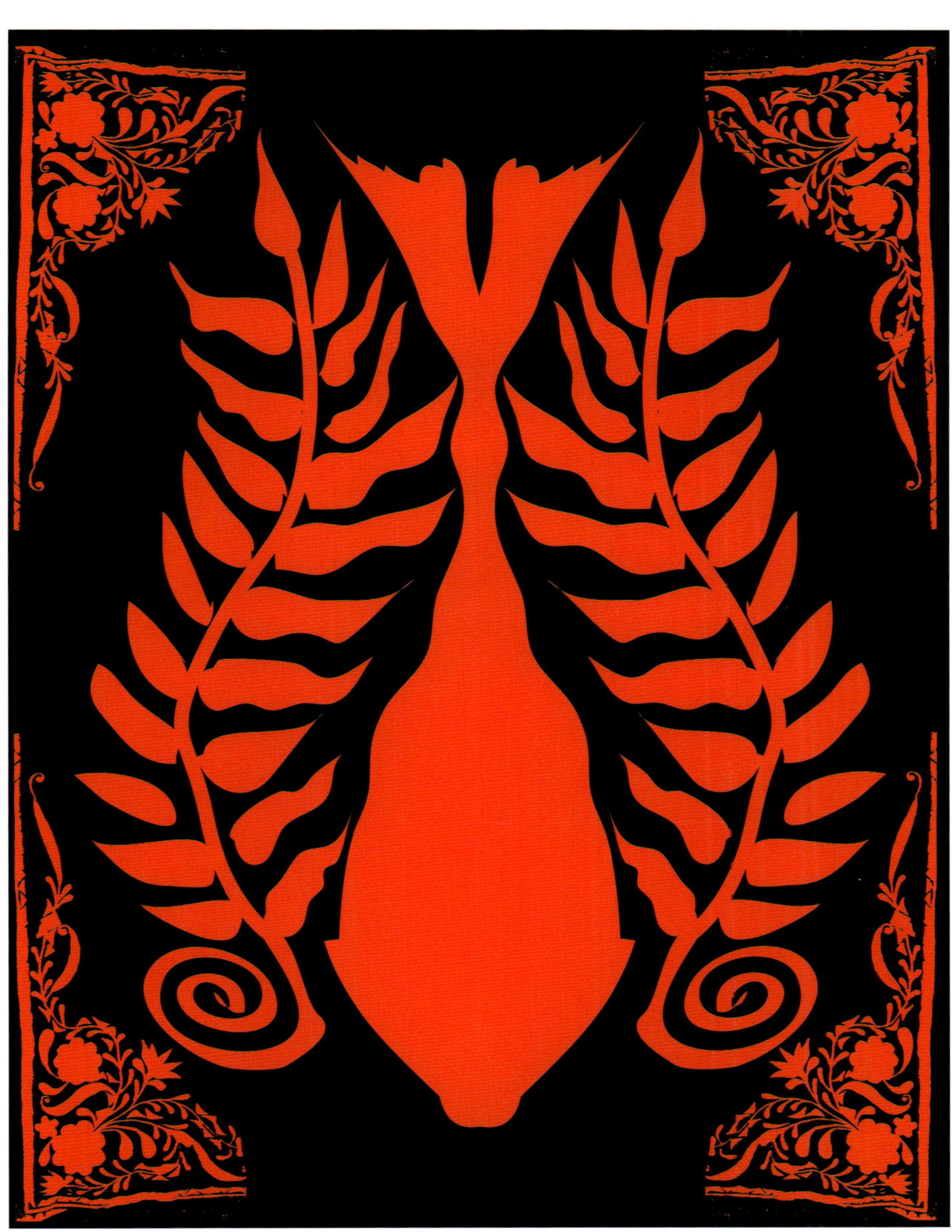

MA_T74

TEMPLATES

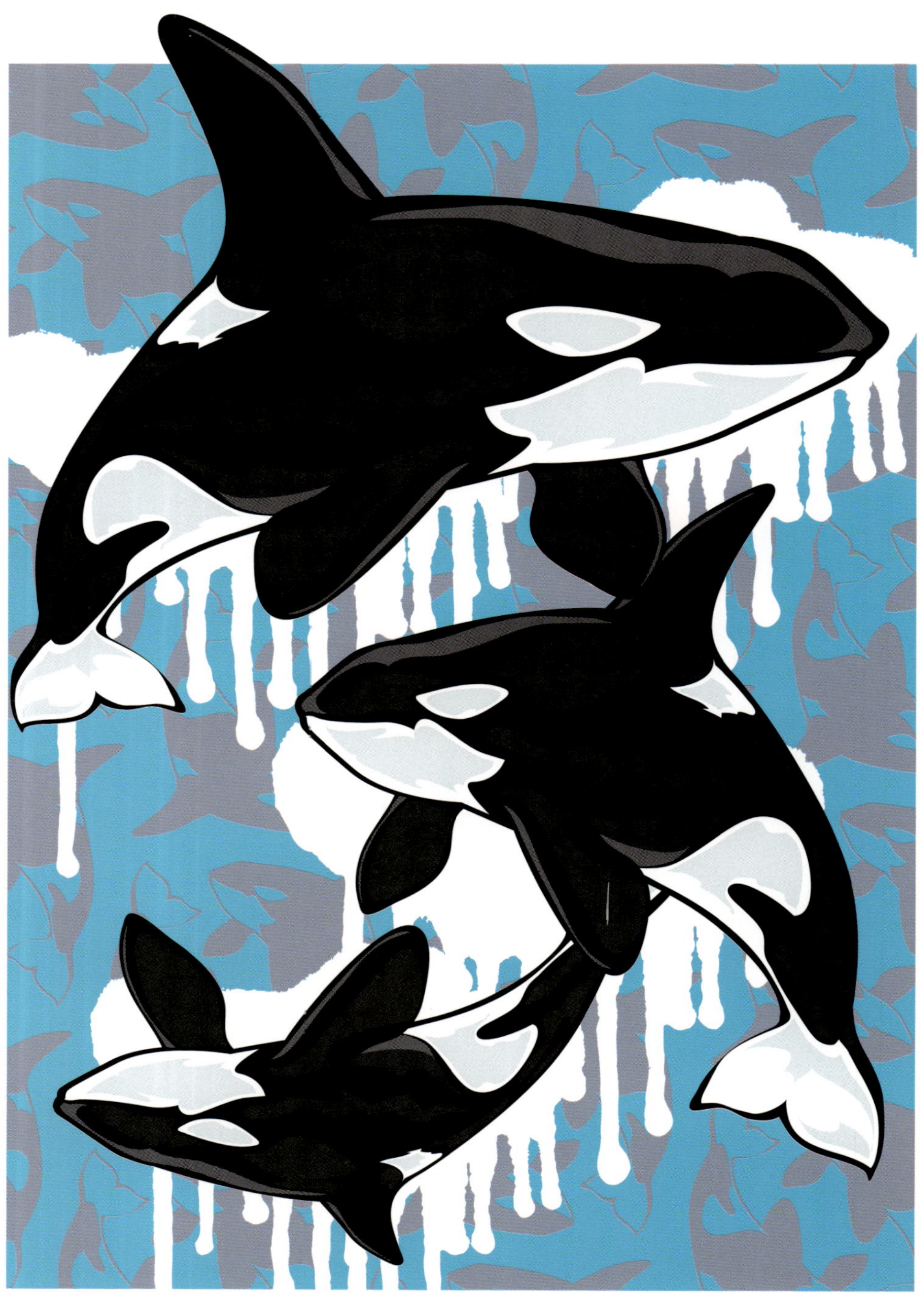

MA_T75

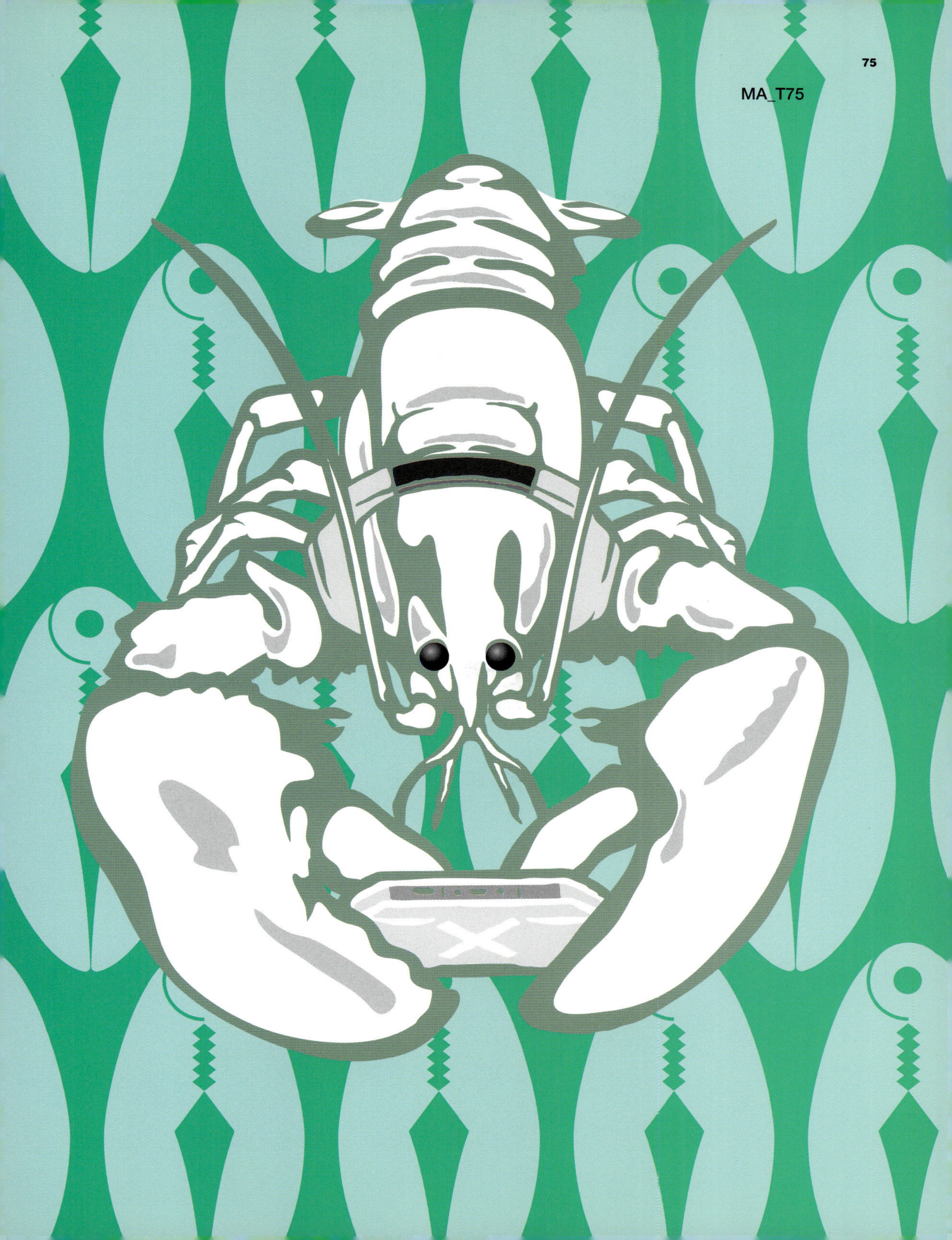

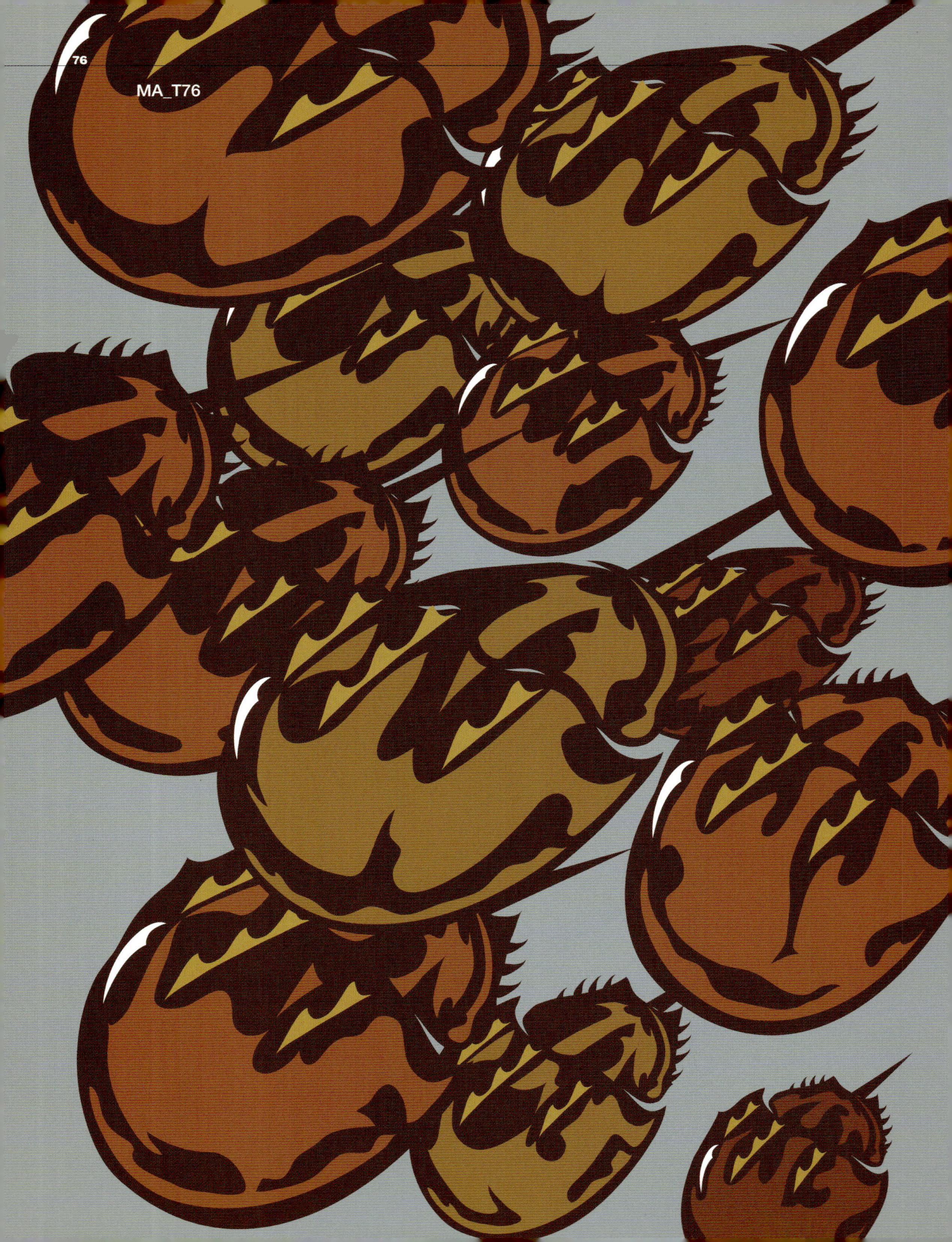
MA_T76

MA_T77

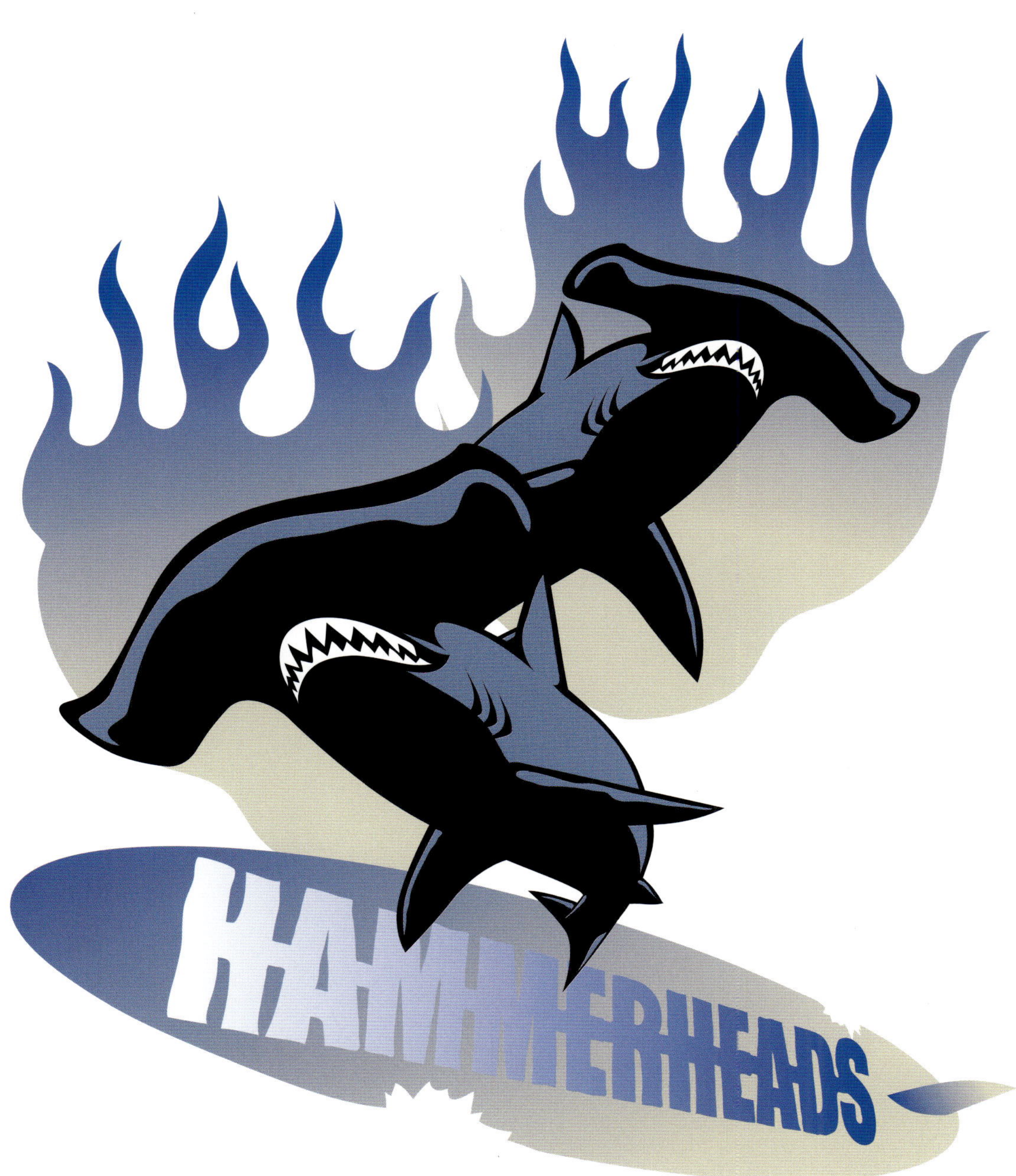

MA_T78

TEMPLATES

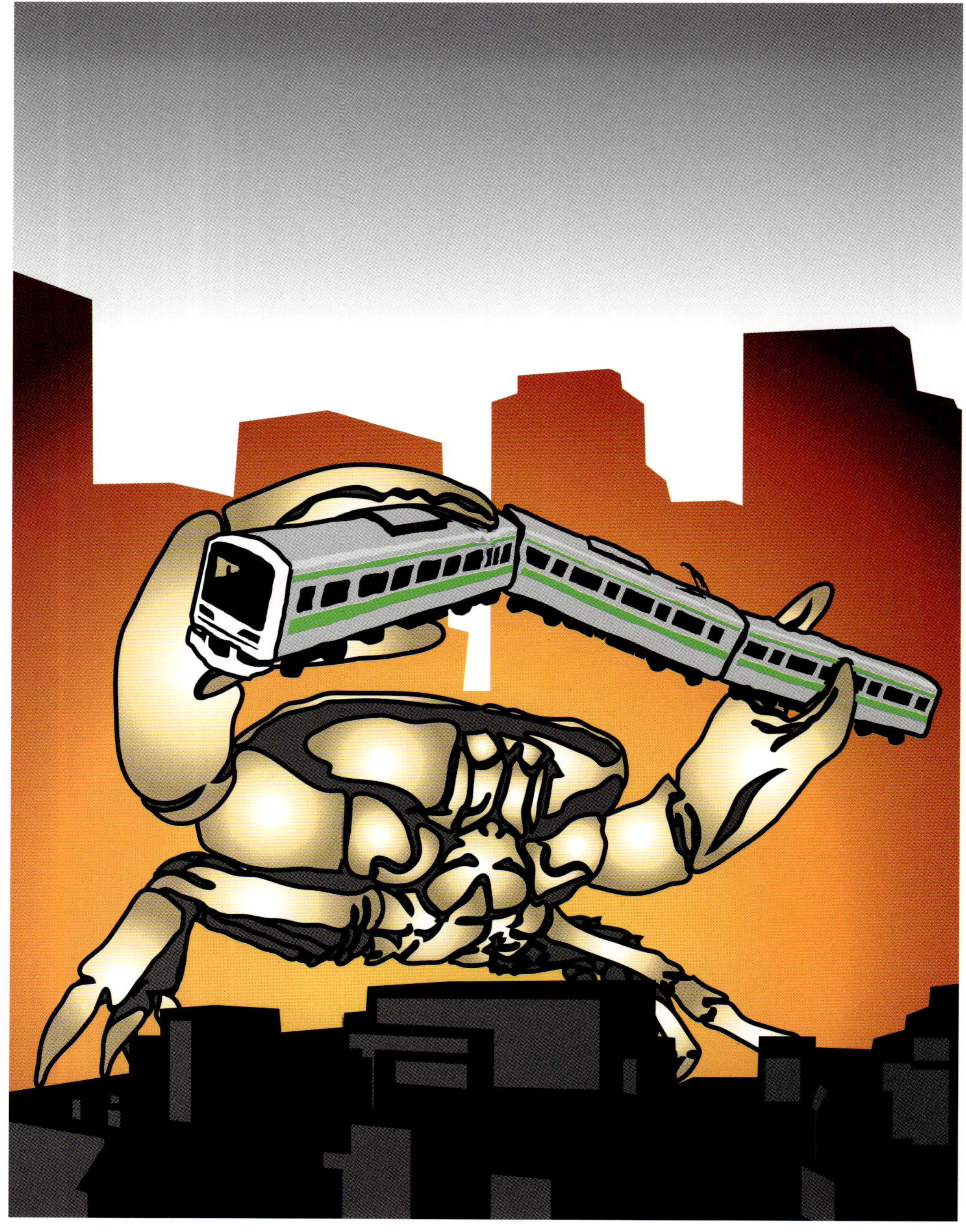

MA_T79

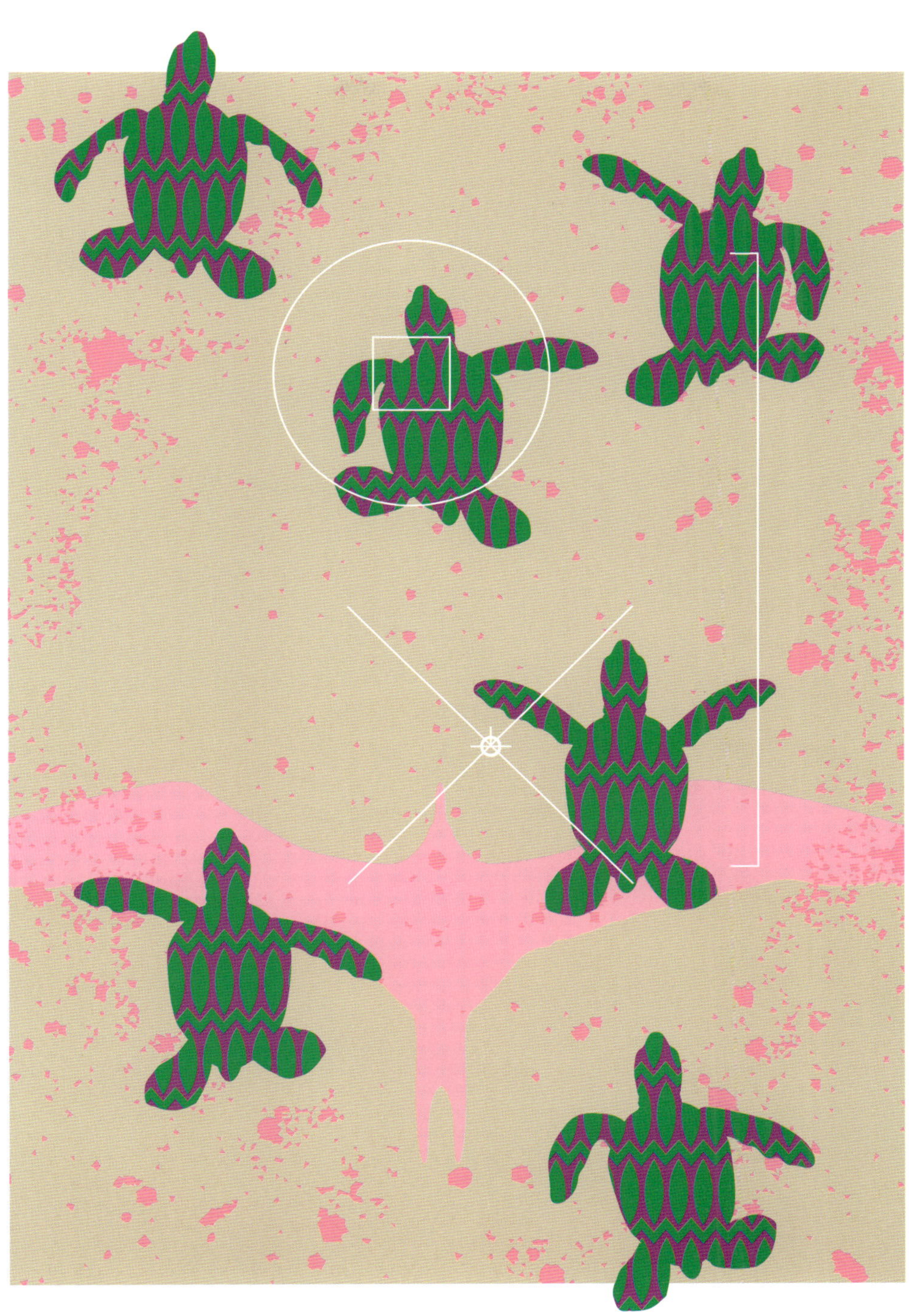

MA_T80

TEMPLATES

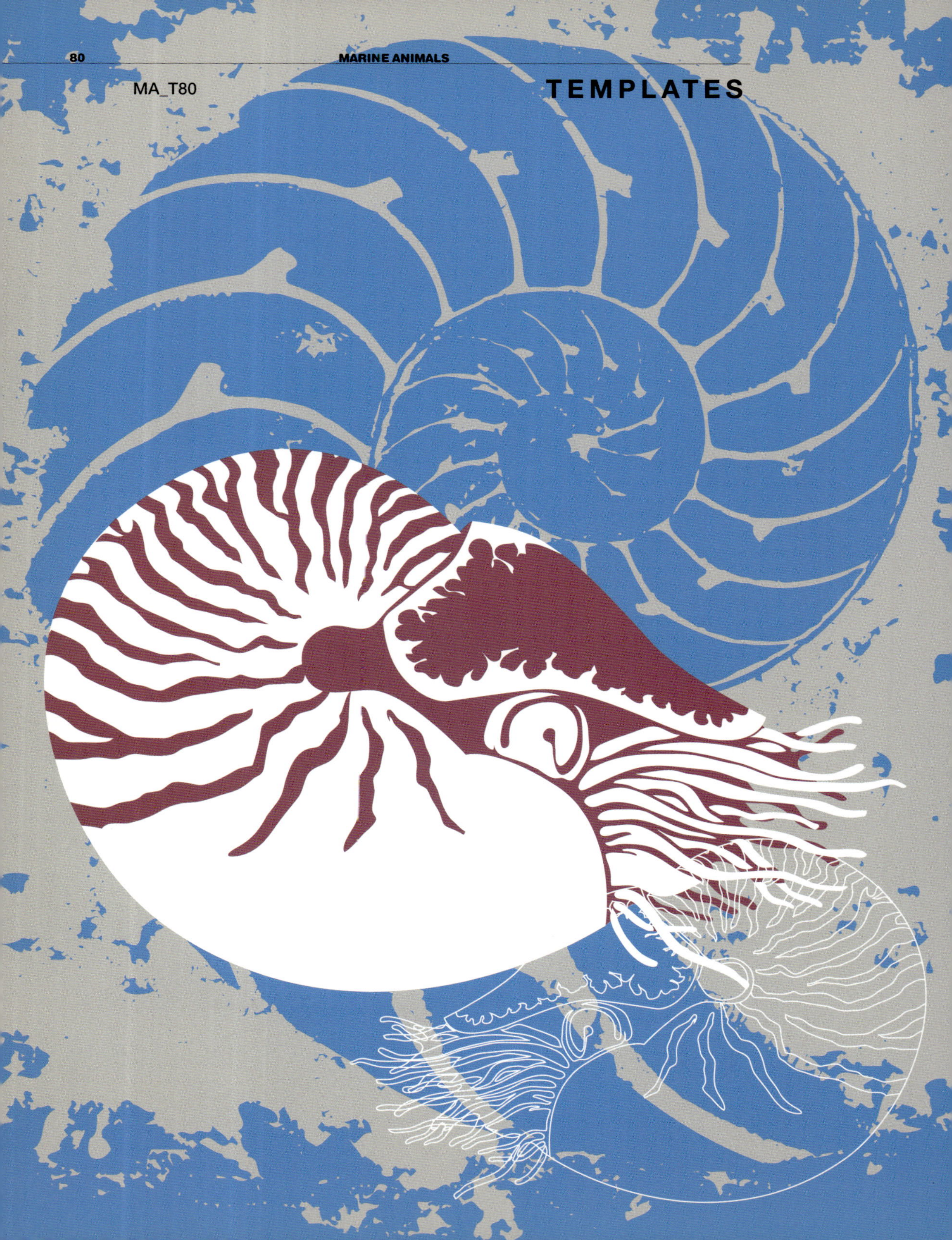

MA_T81

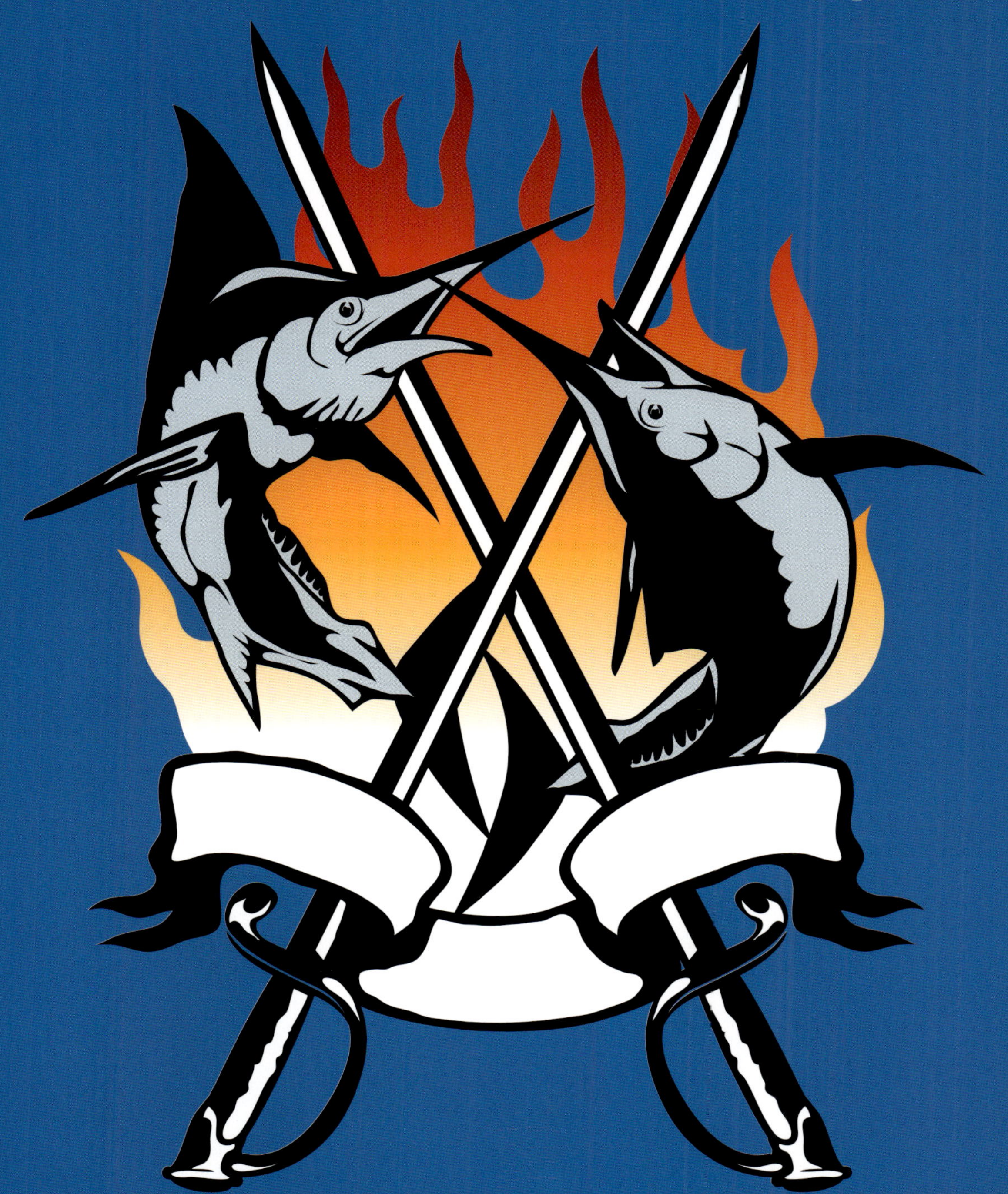

MA_T82

TEMPLATES

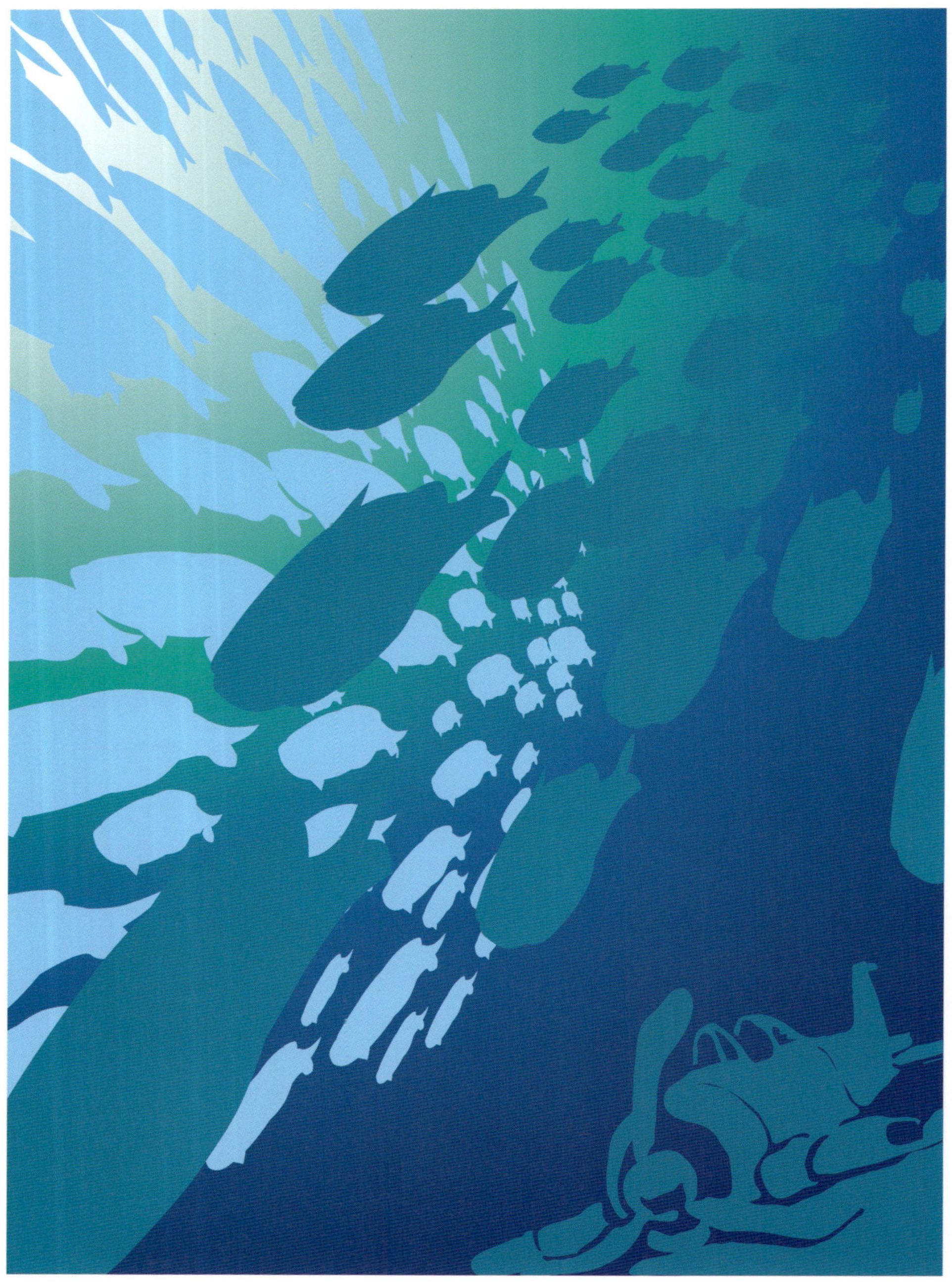

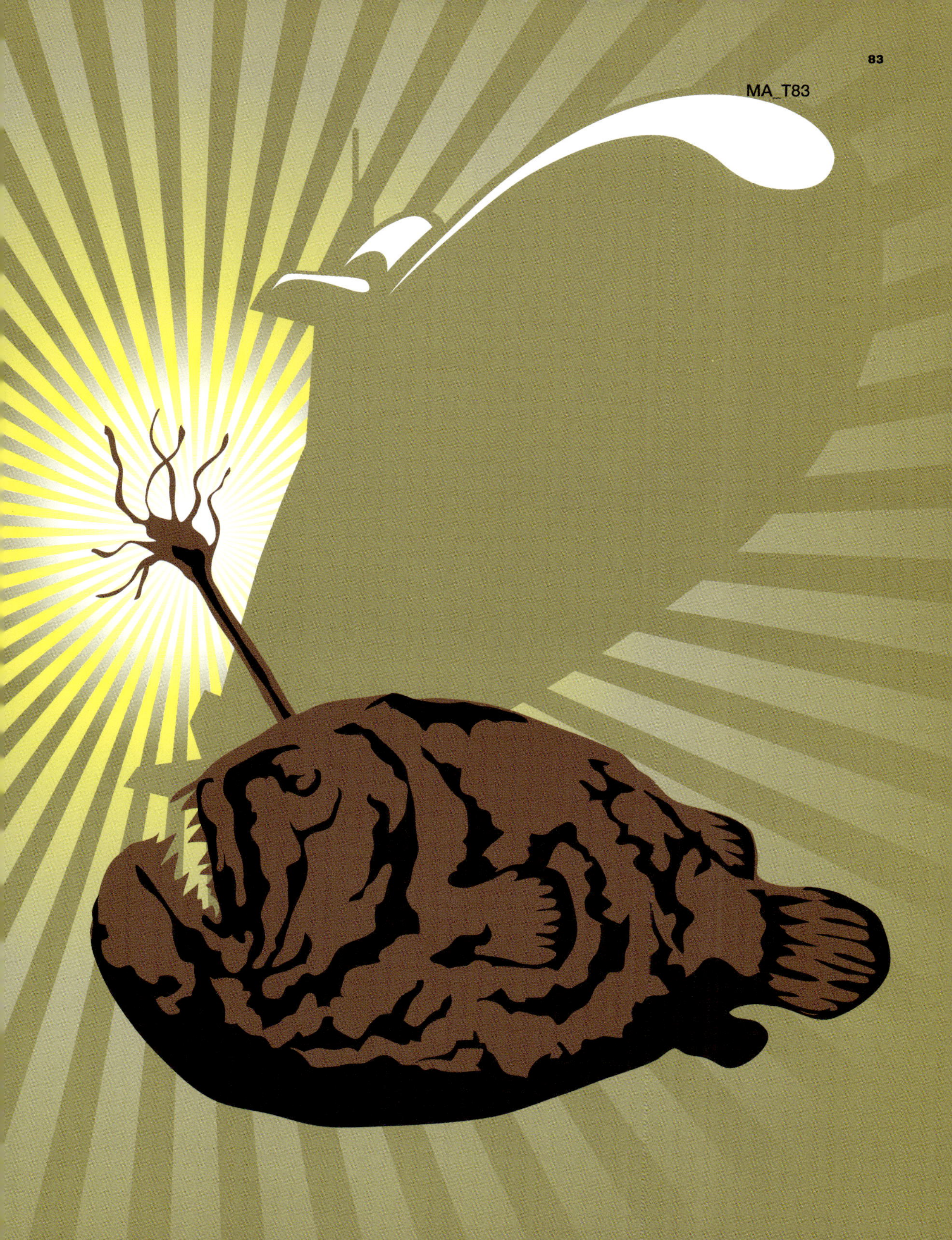
MA_T83

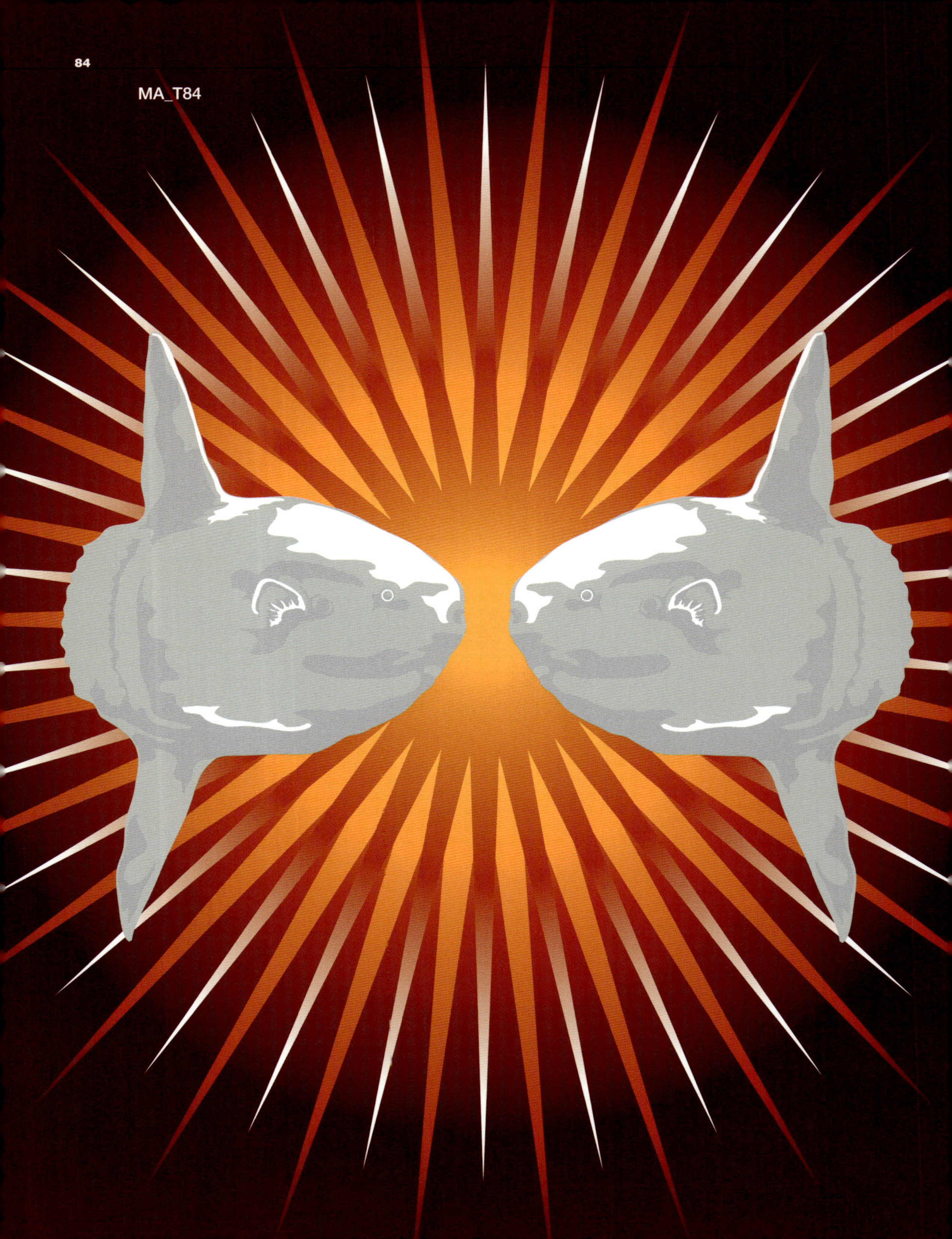
MA_T84

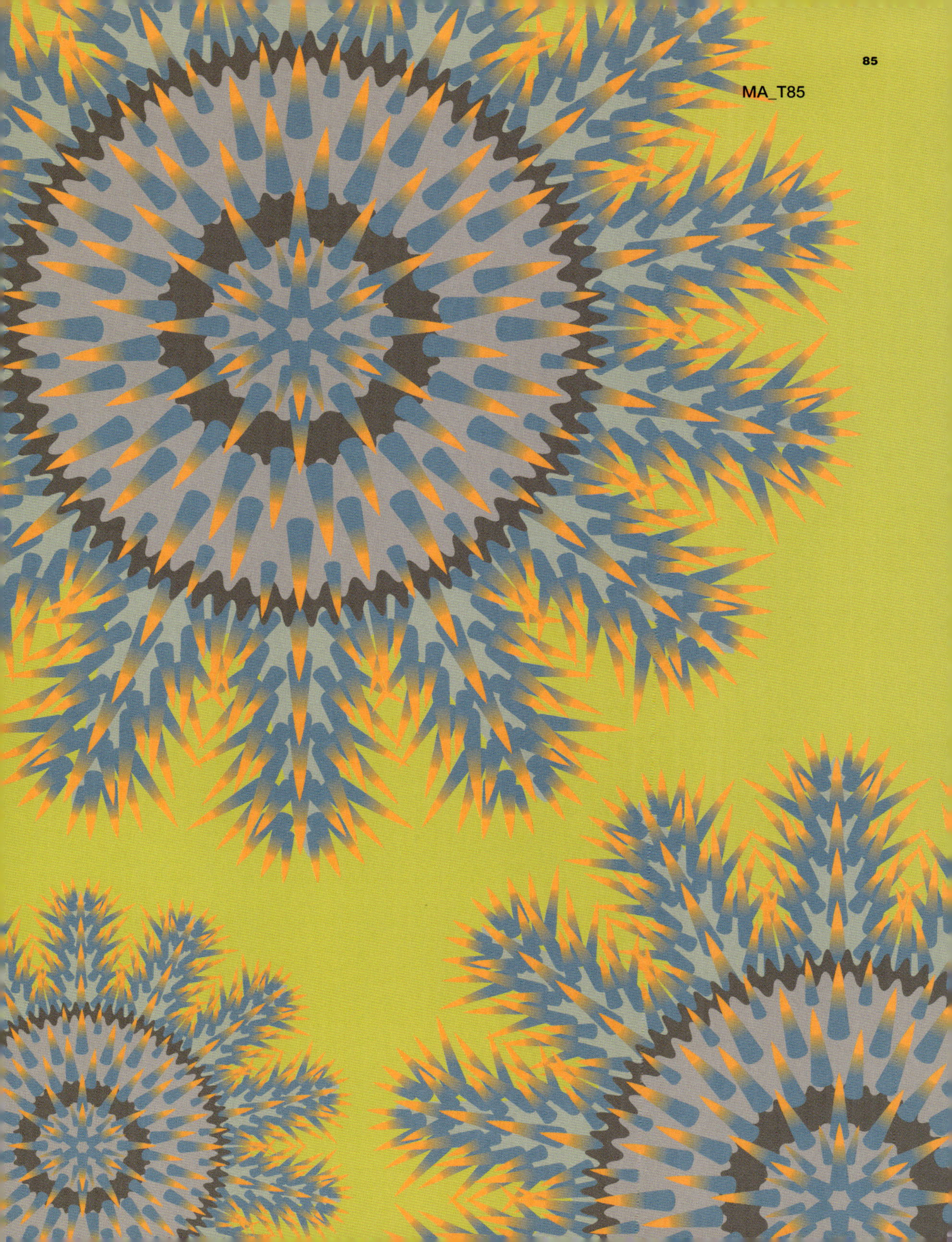
MA_T85

MA_T86

TEMPLATES

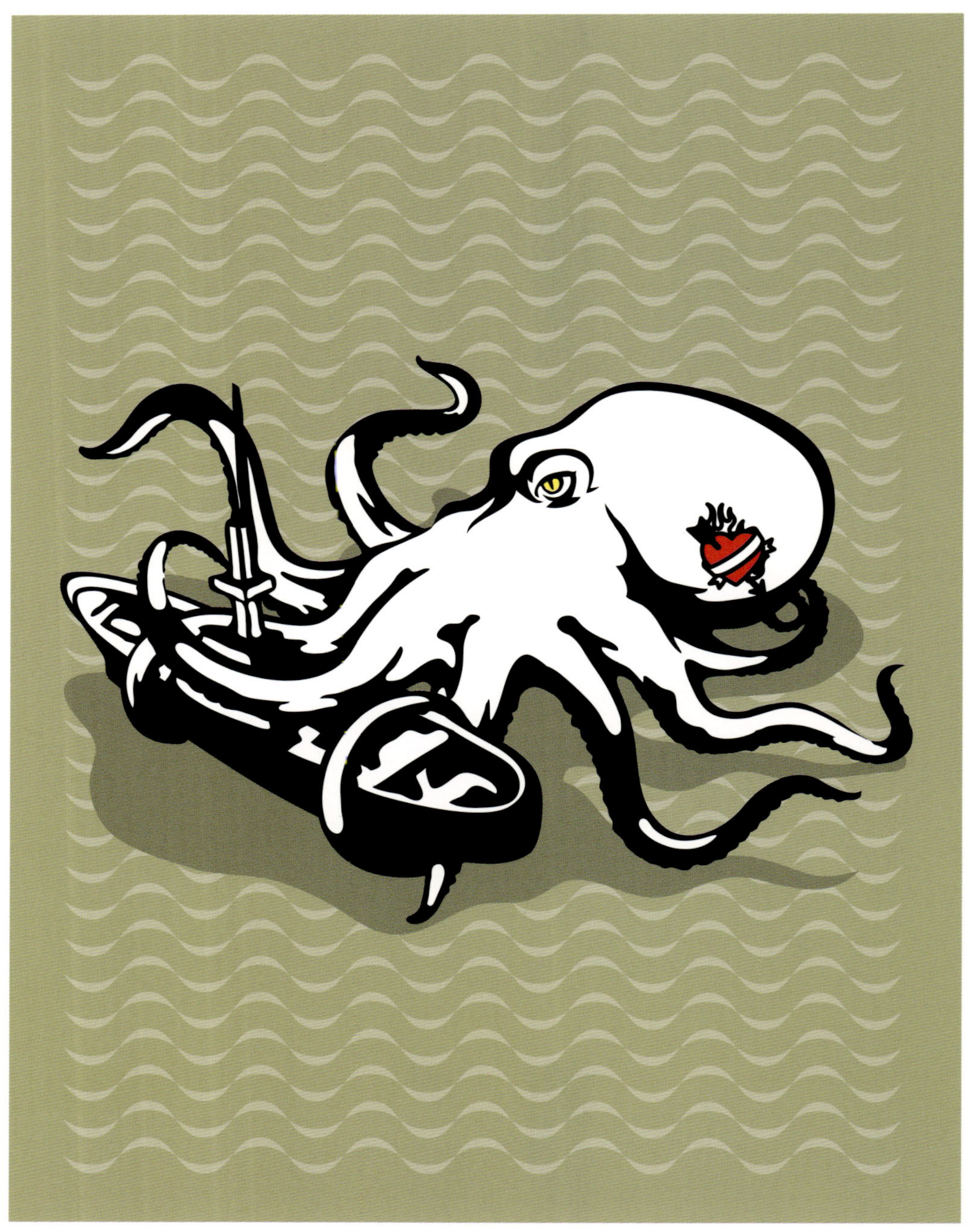

MA_T87

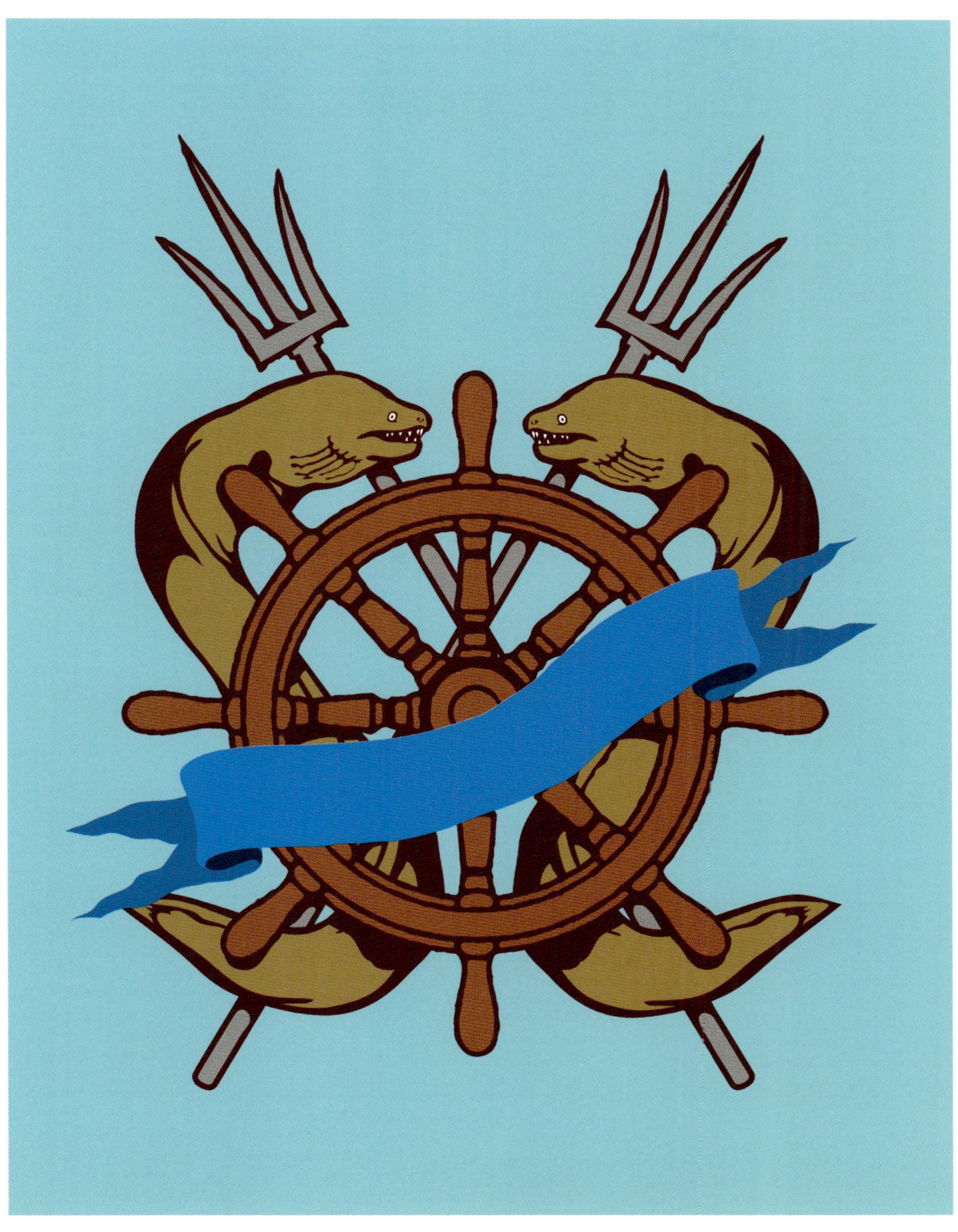

MA_T88

TEMPLATES

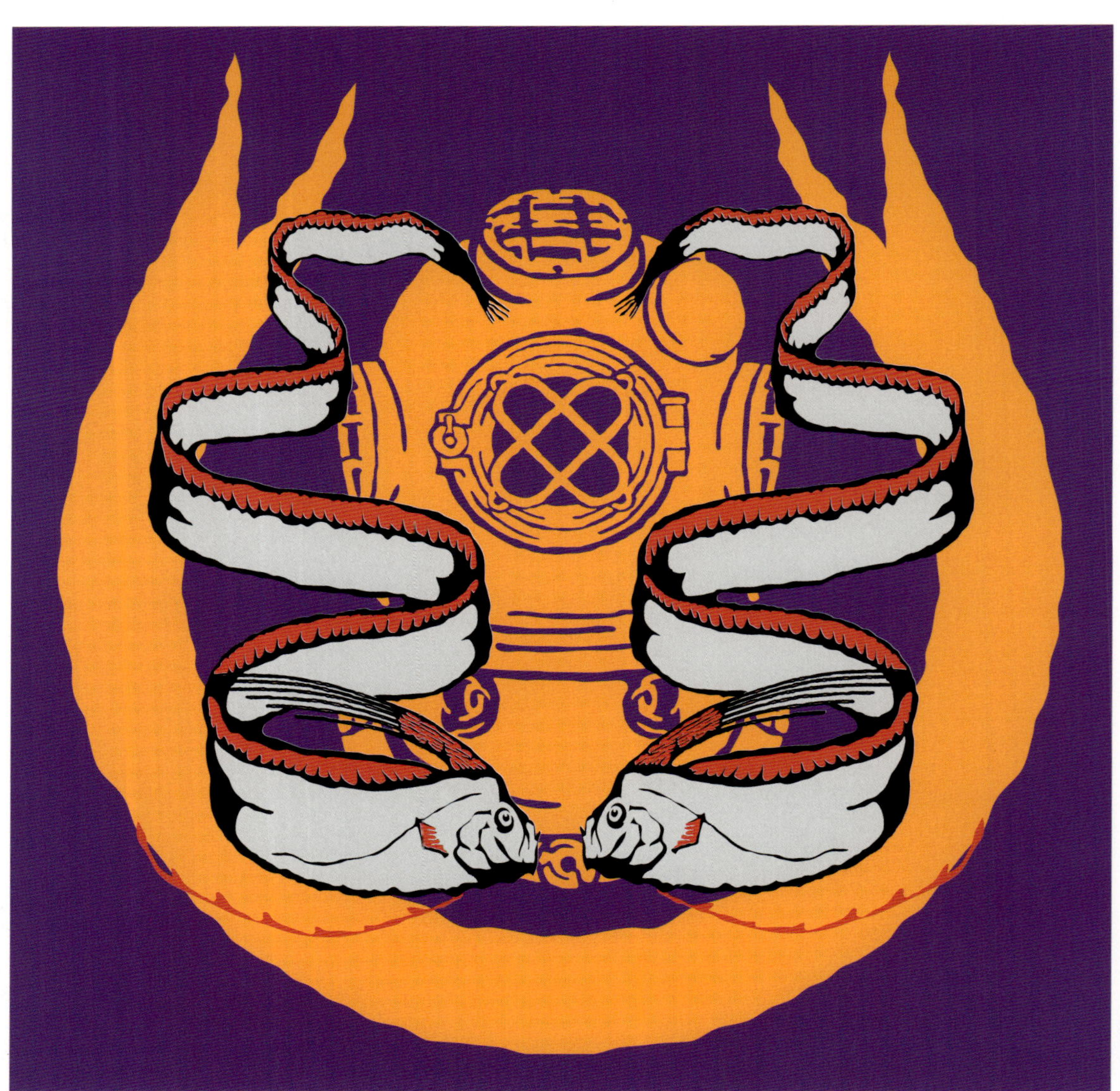

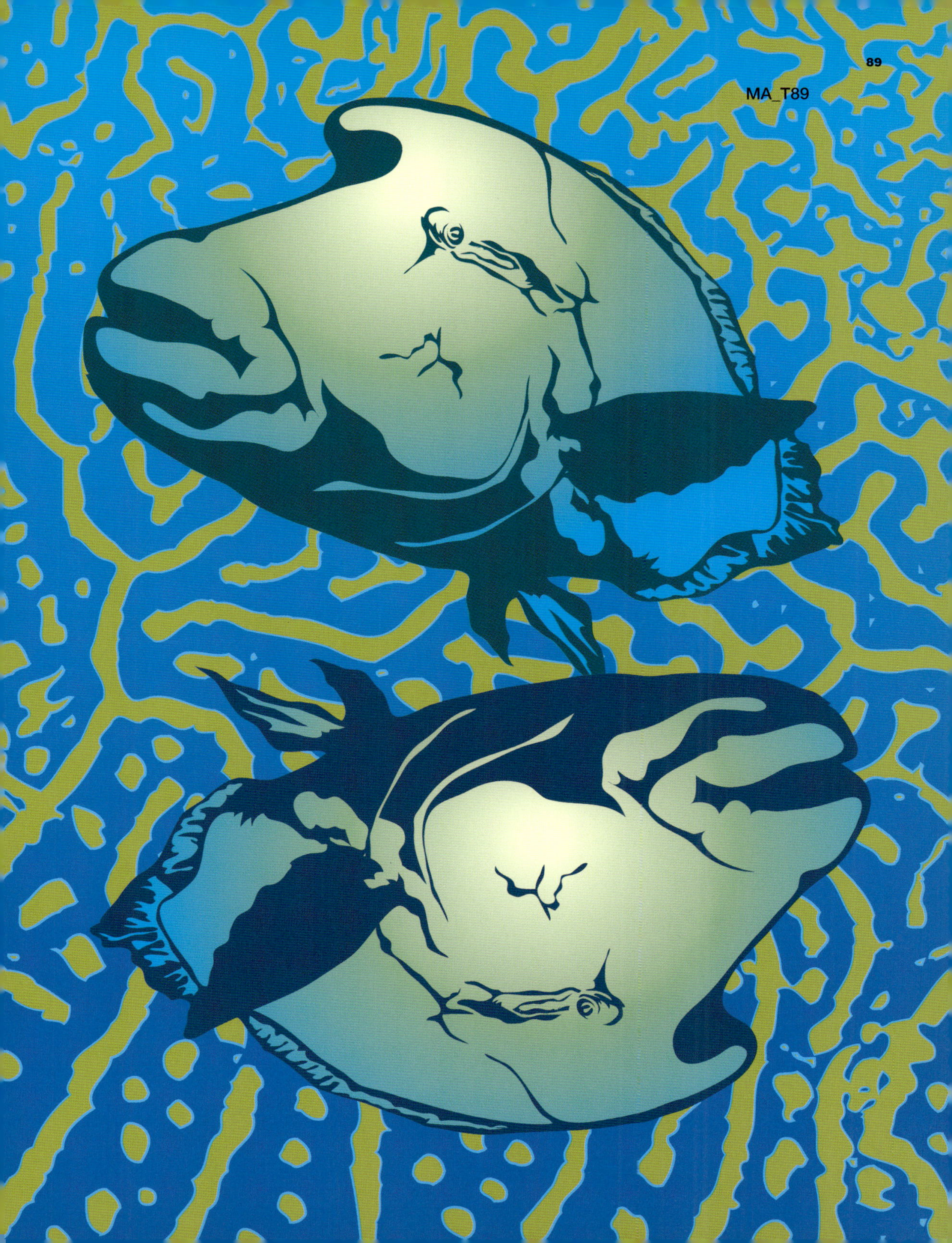
MA_T89

MA_T90

TEMPLATES

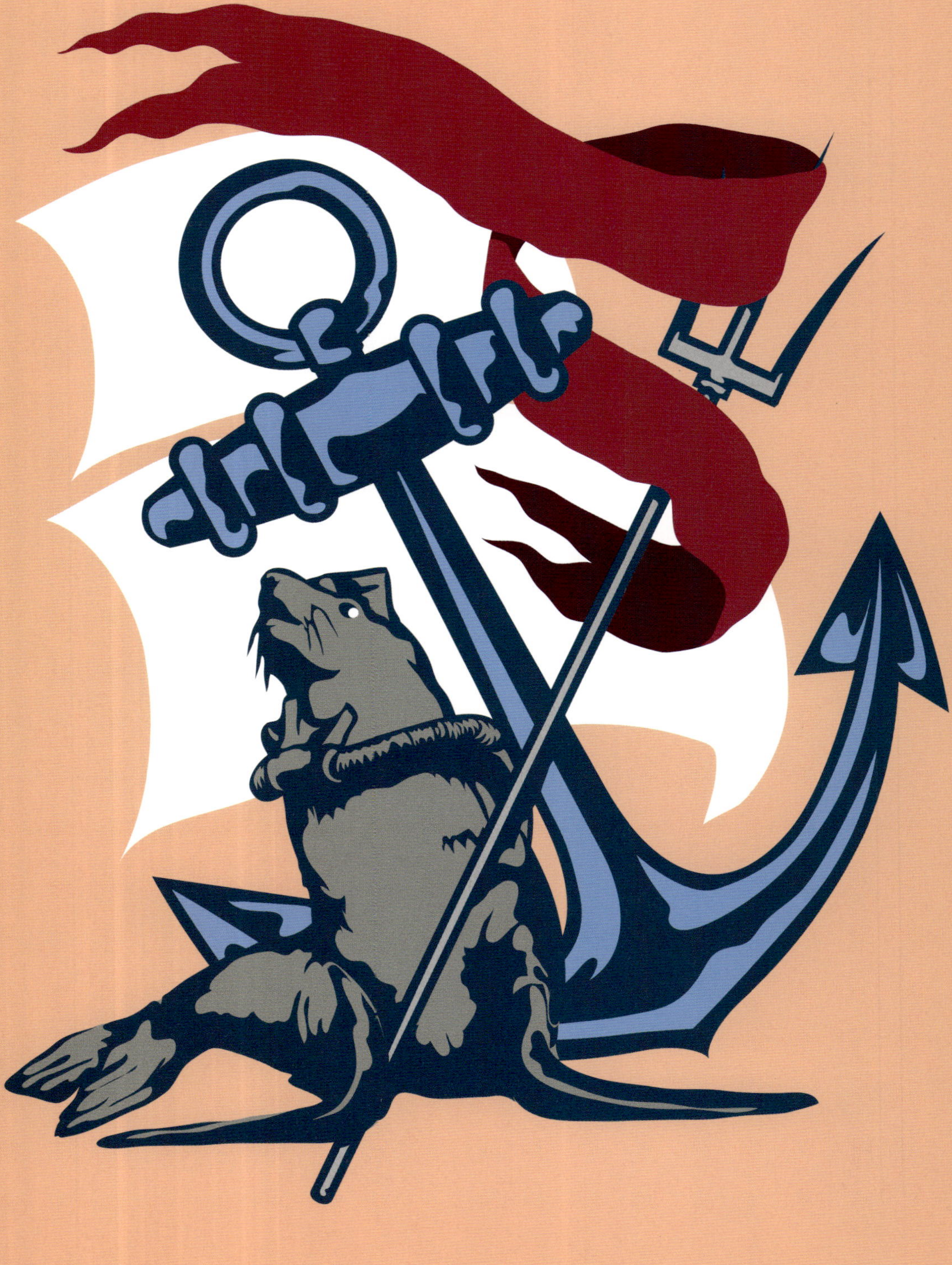

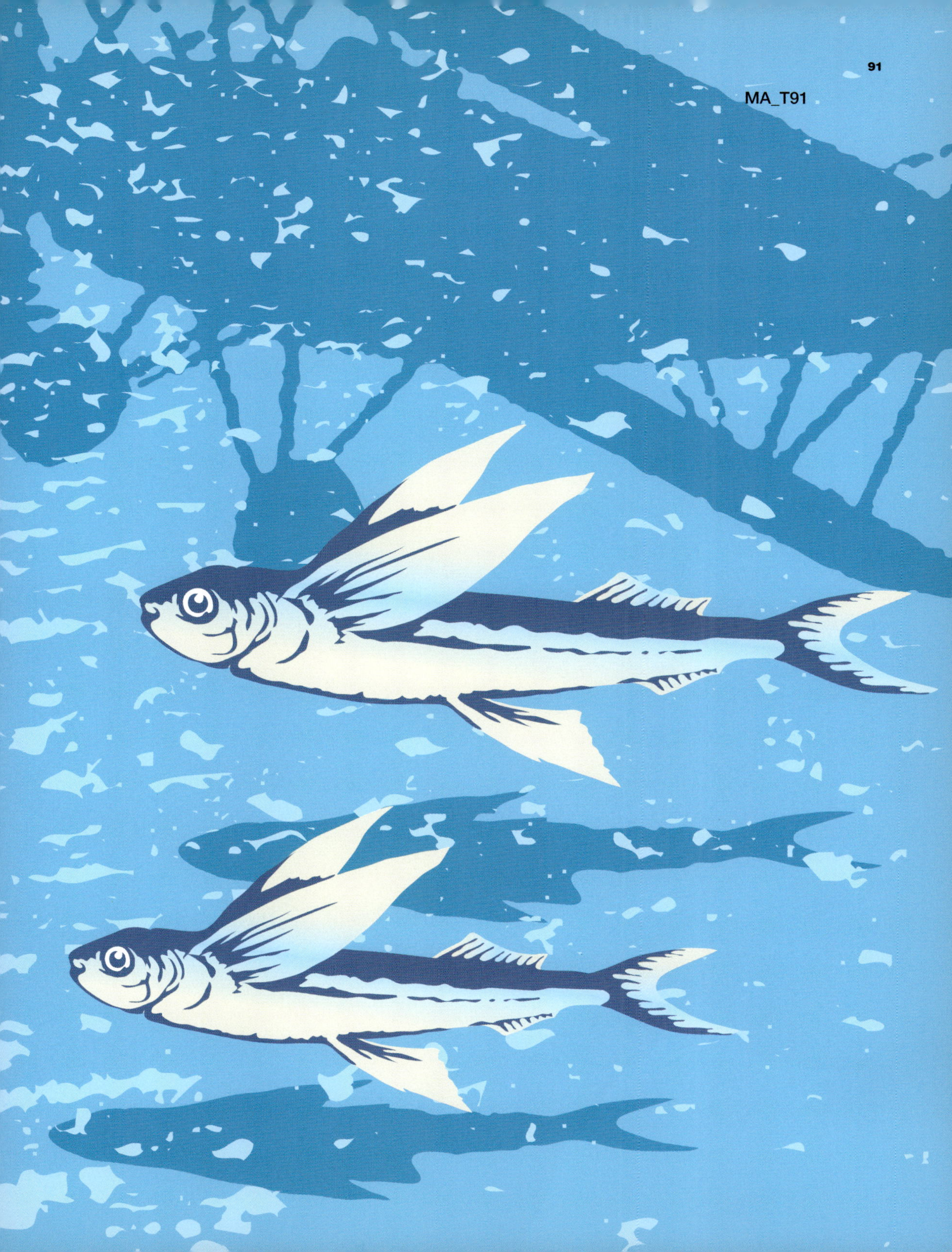
MA_T91

MA_T92

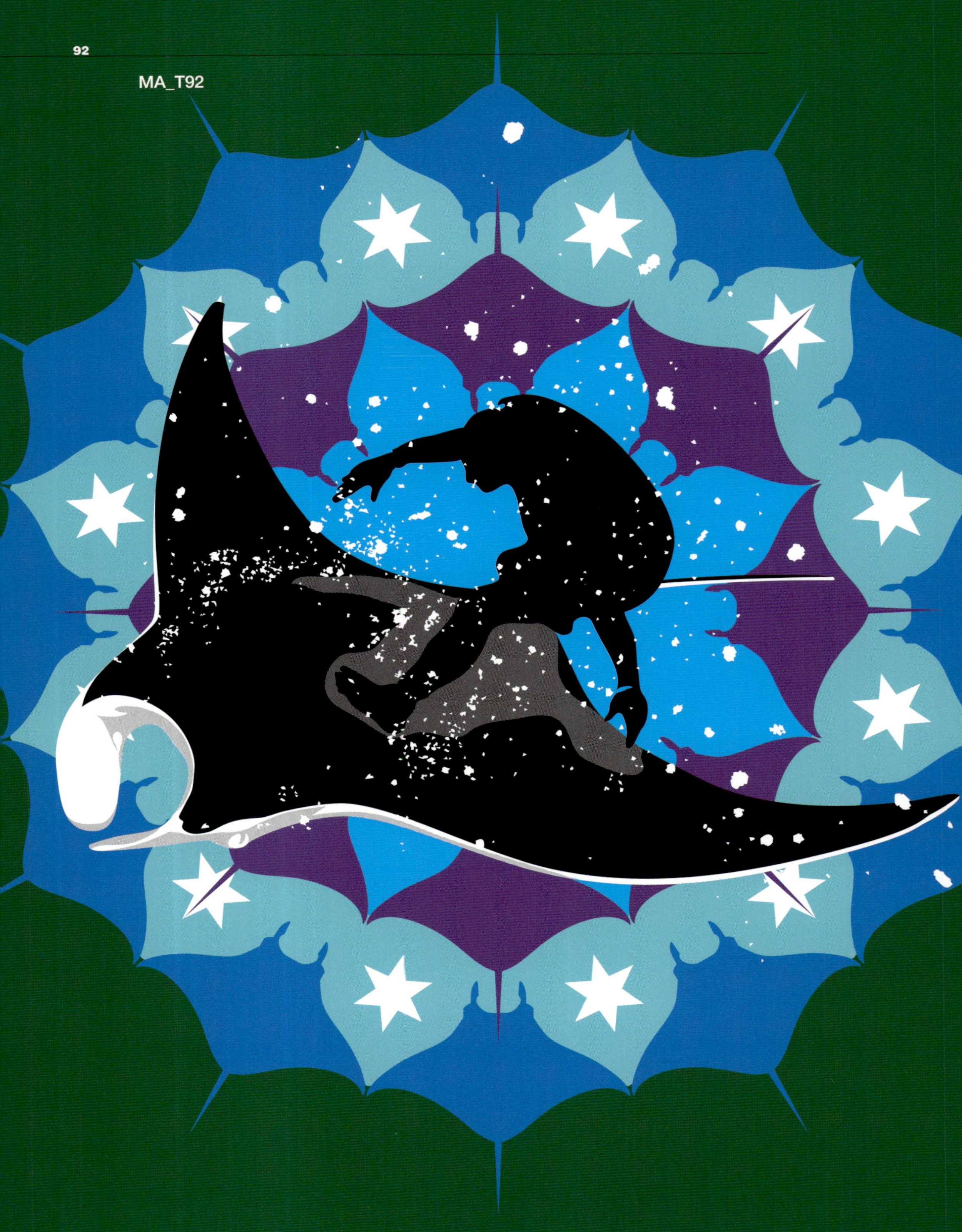

MA_T93

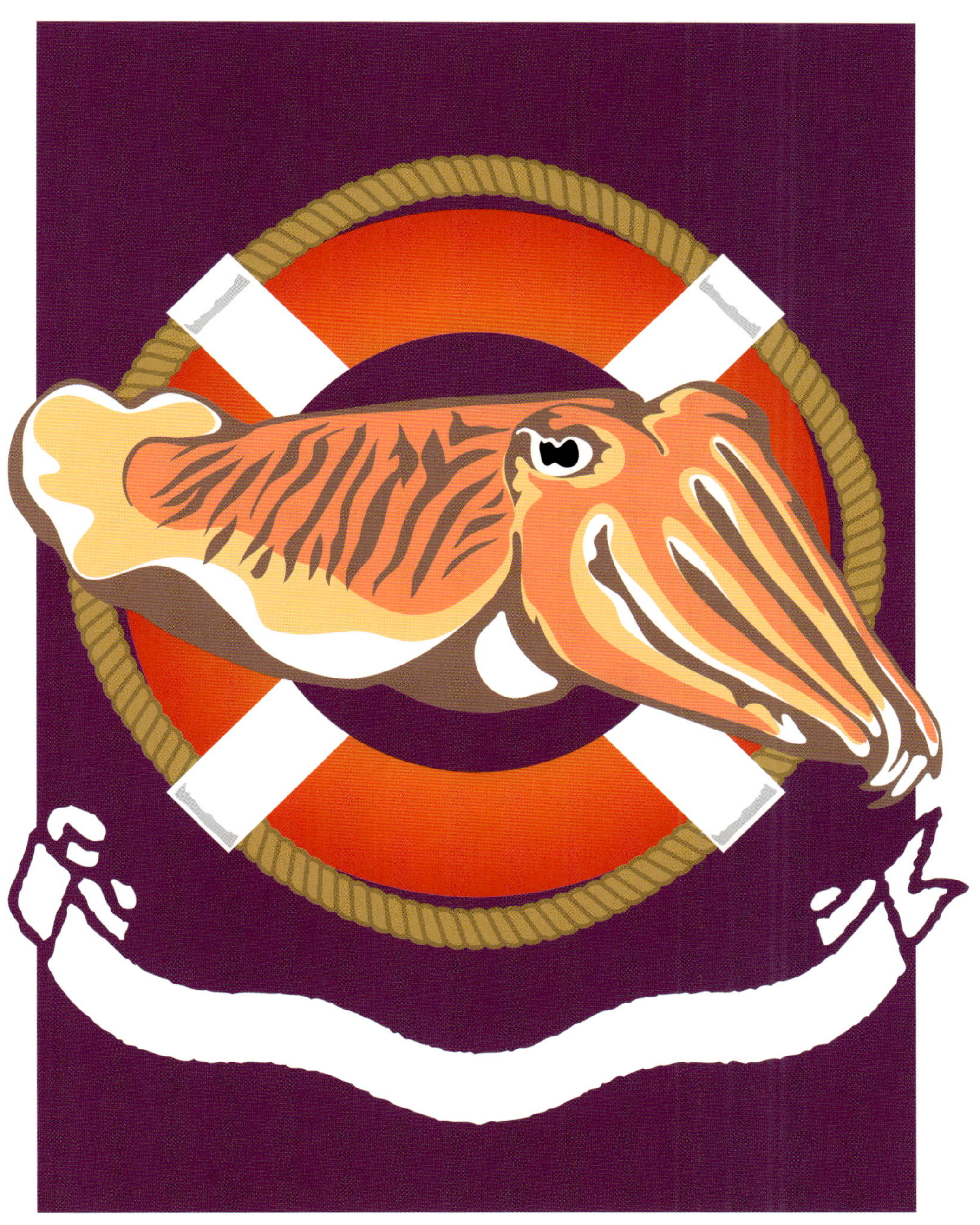

MA_T94

TEMPLATES

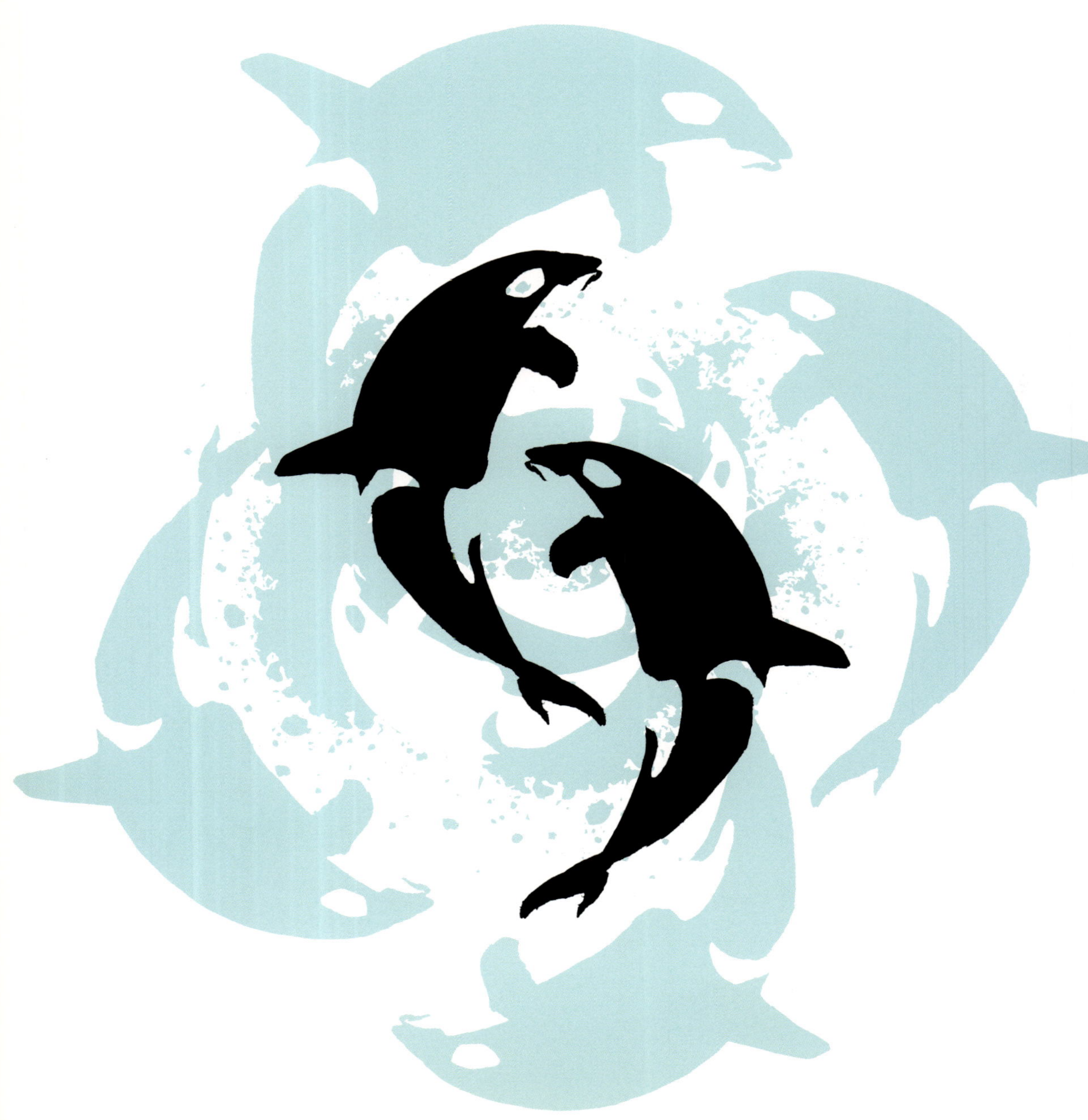

MA_T95

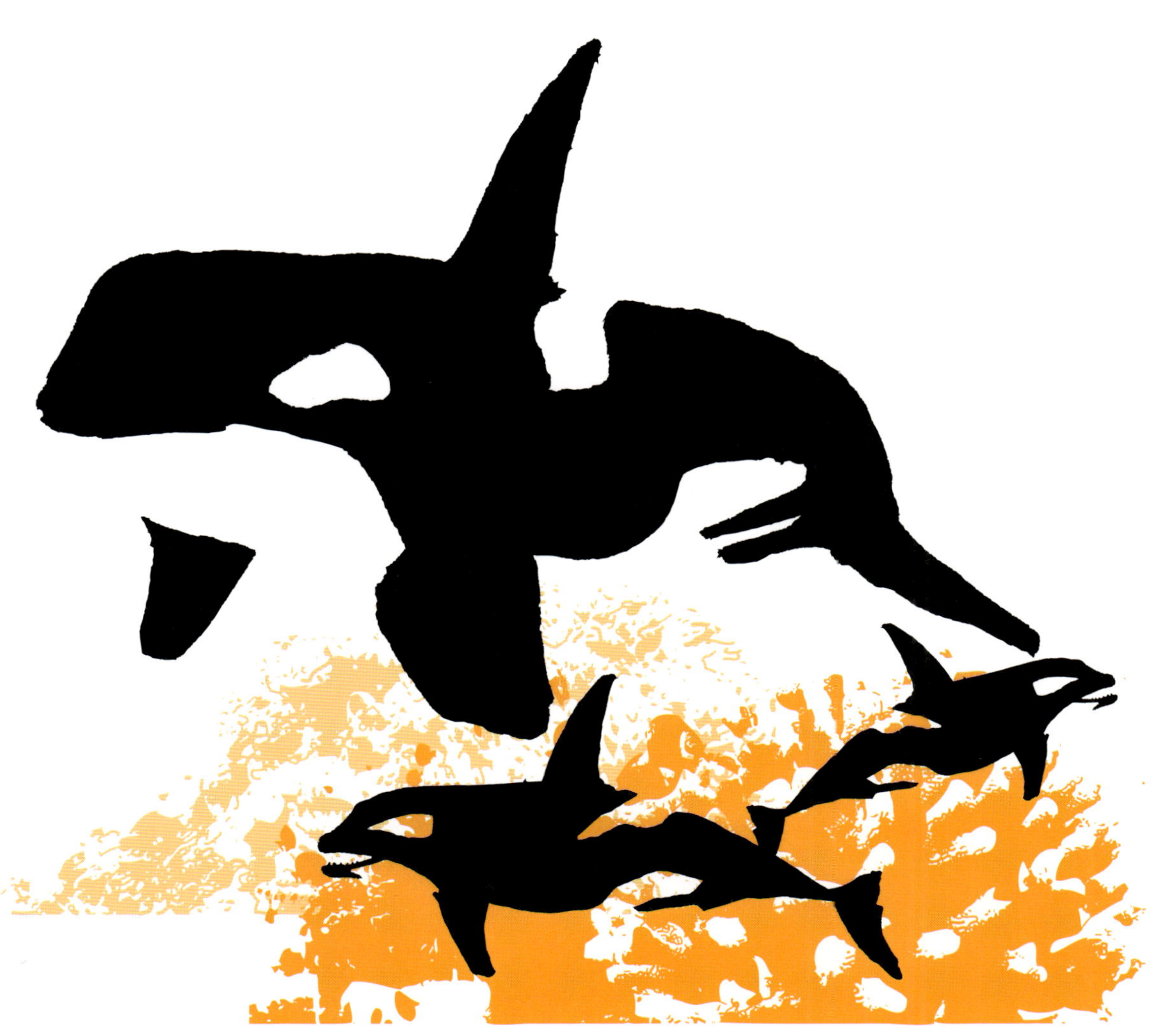

MA_T96

TEMPLATES

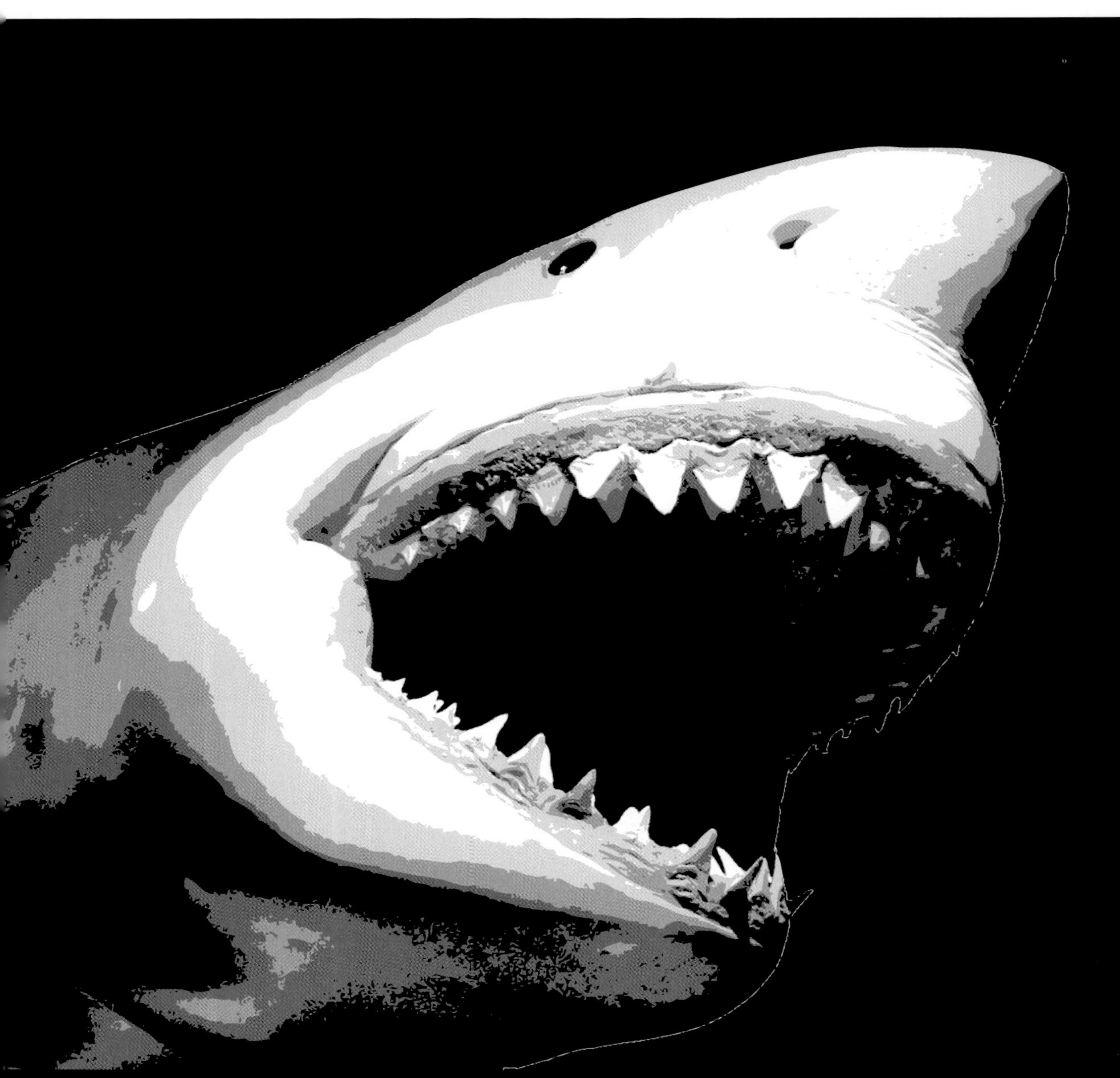

MA_T97

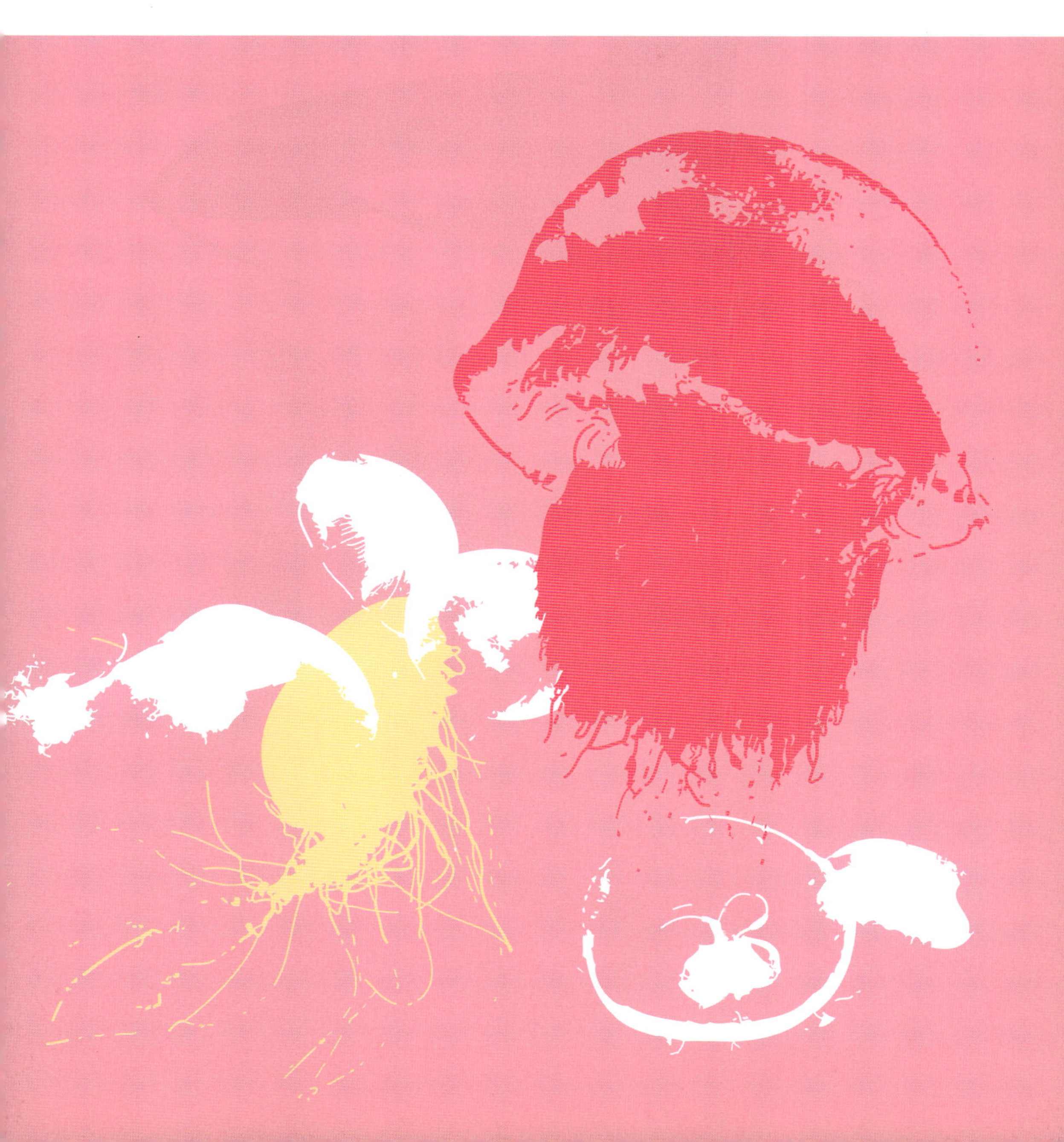

MA_T98

TEMPLATES

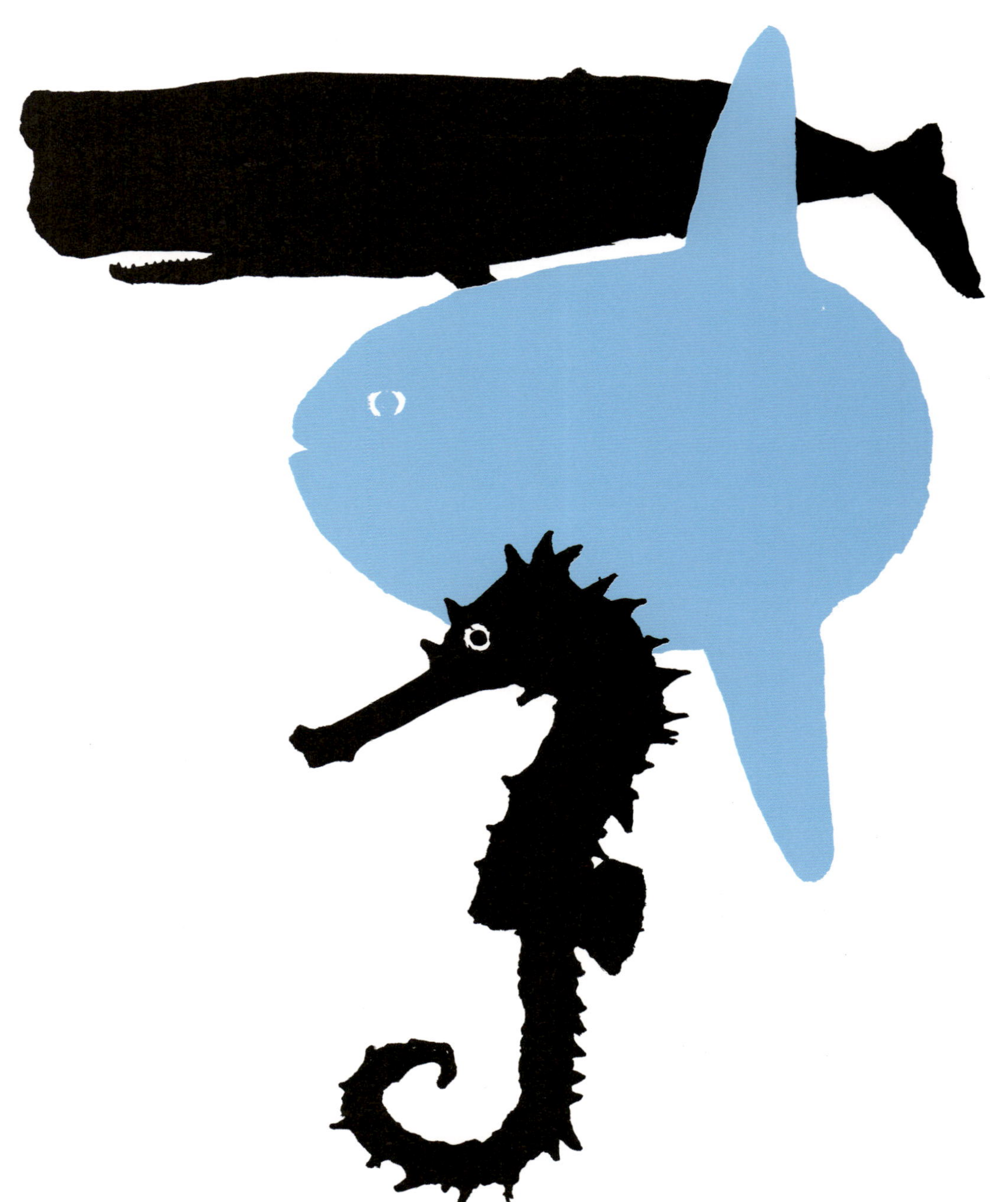

MA_T99

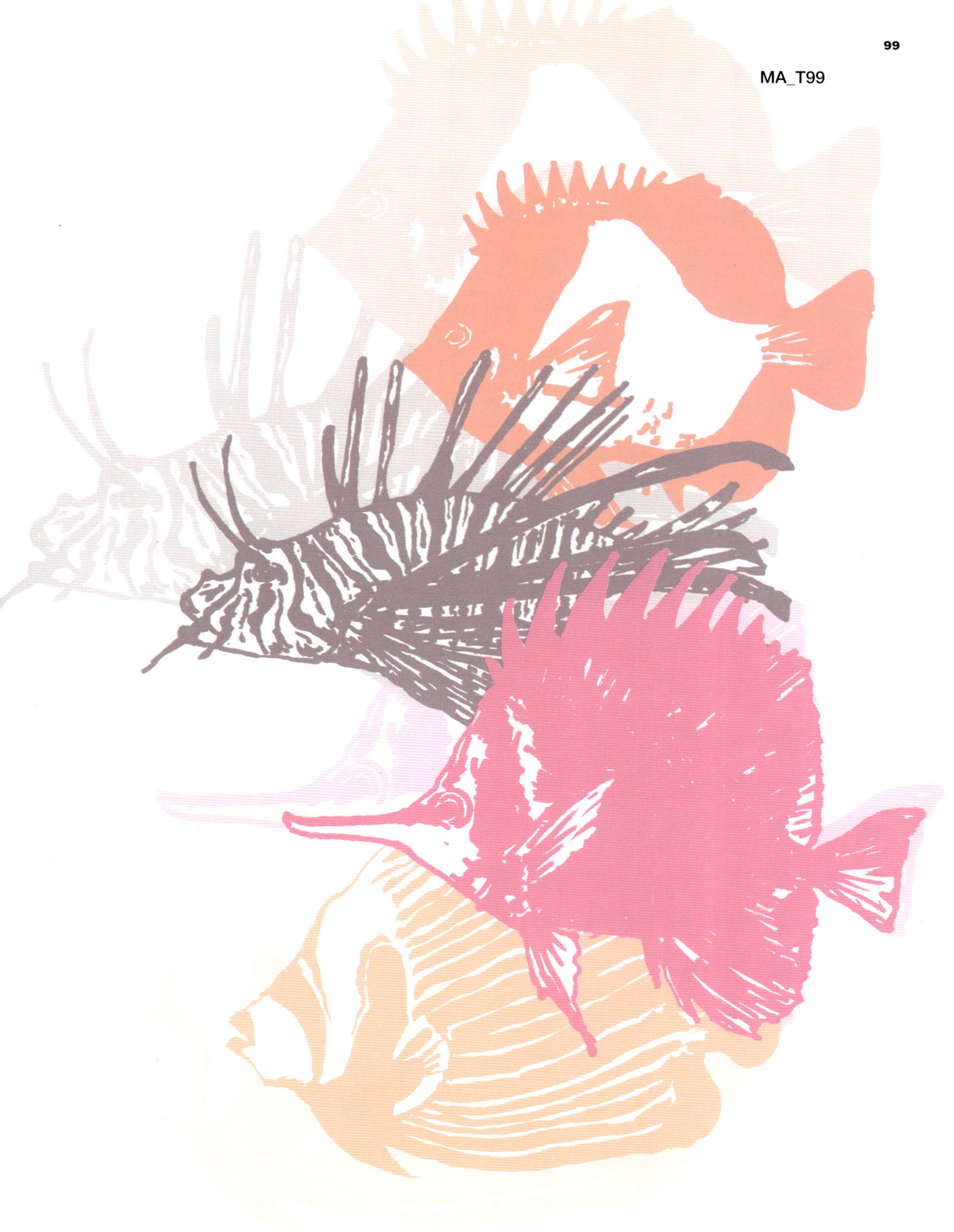

TEMPLATES

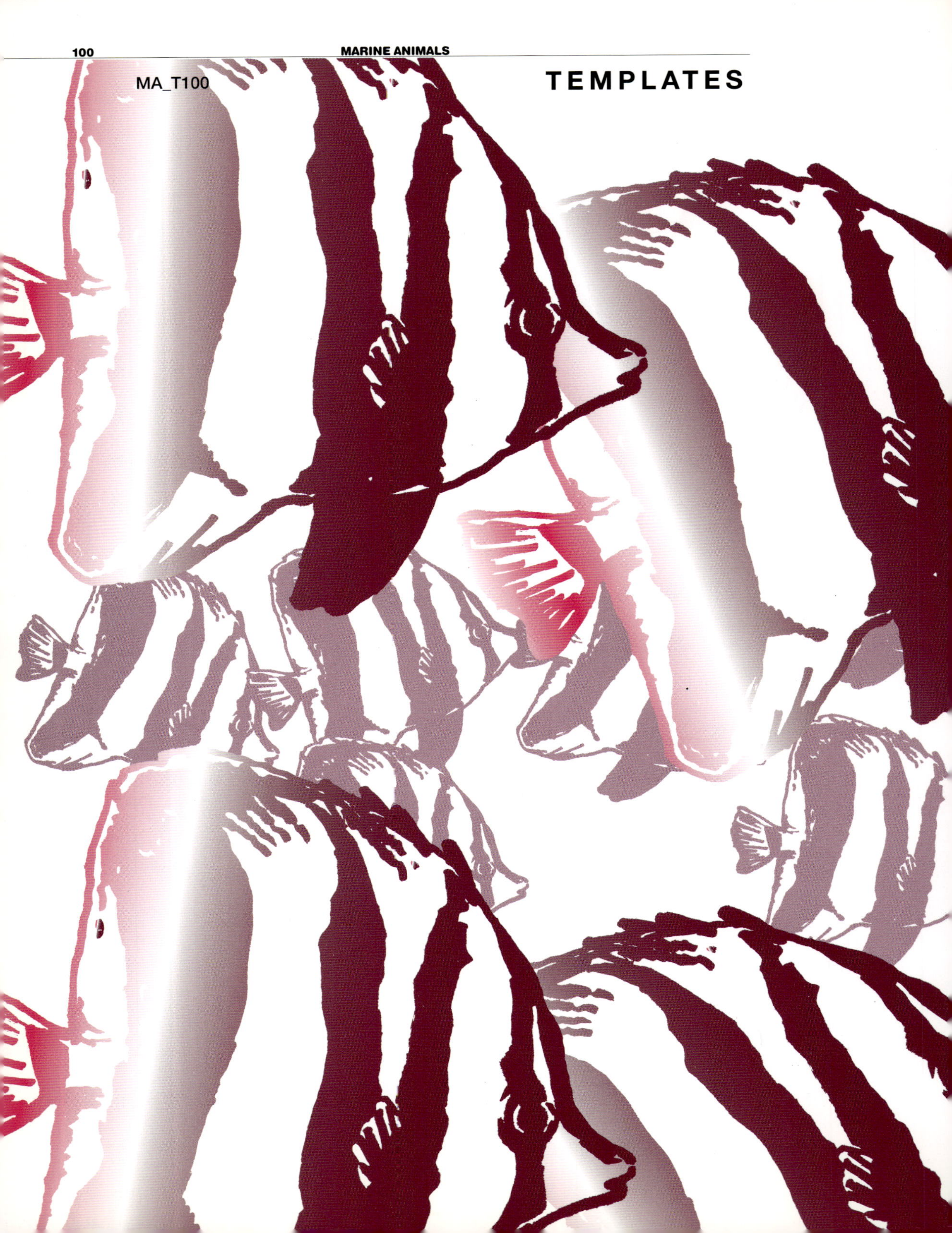

MA_T101

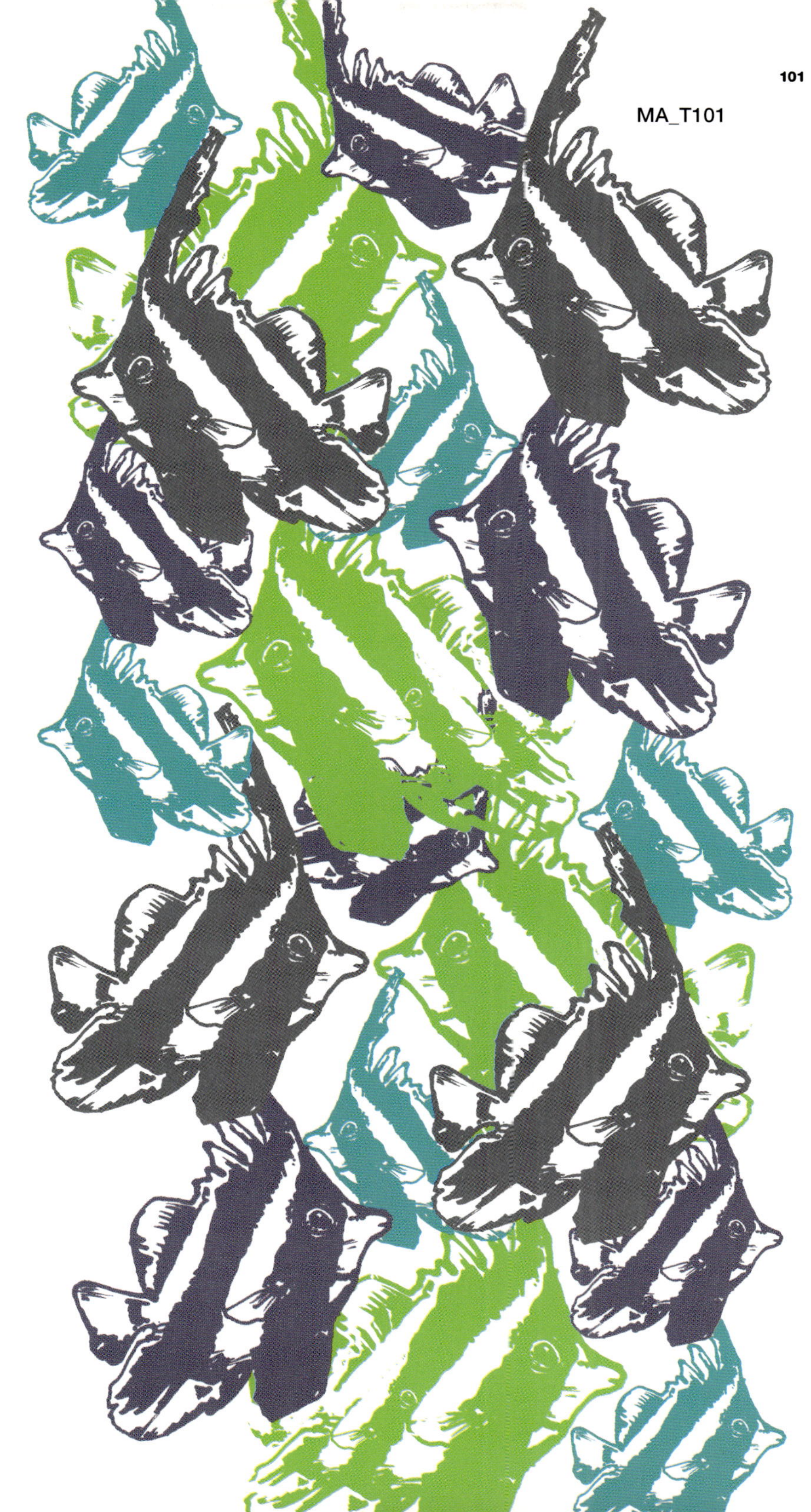

MA_T102

TEMPLATES

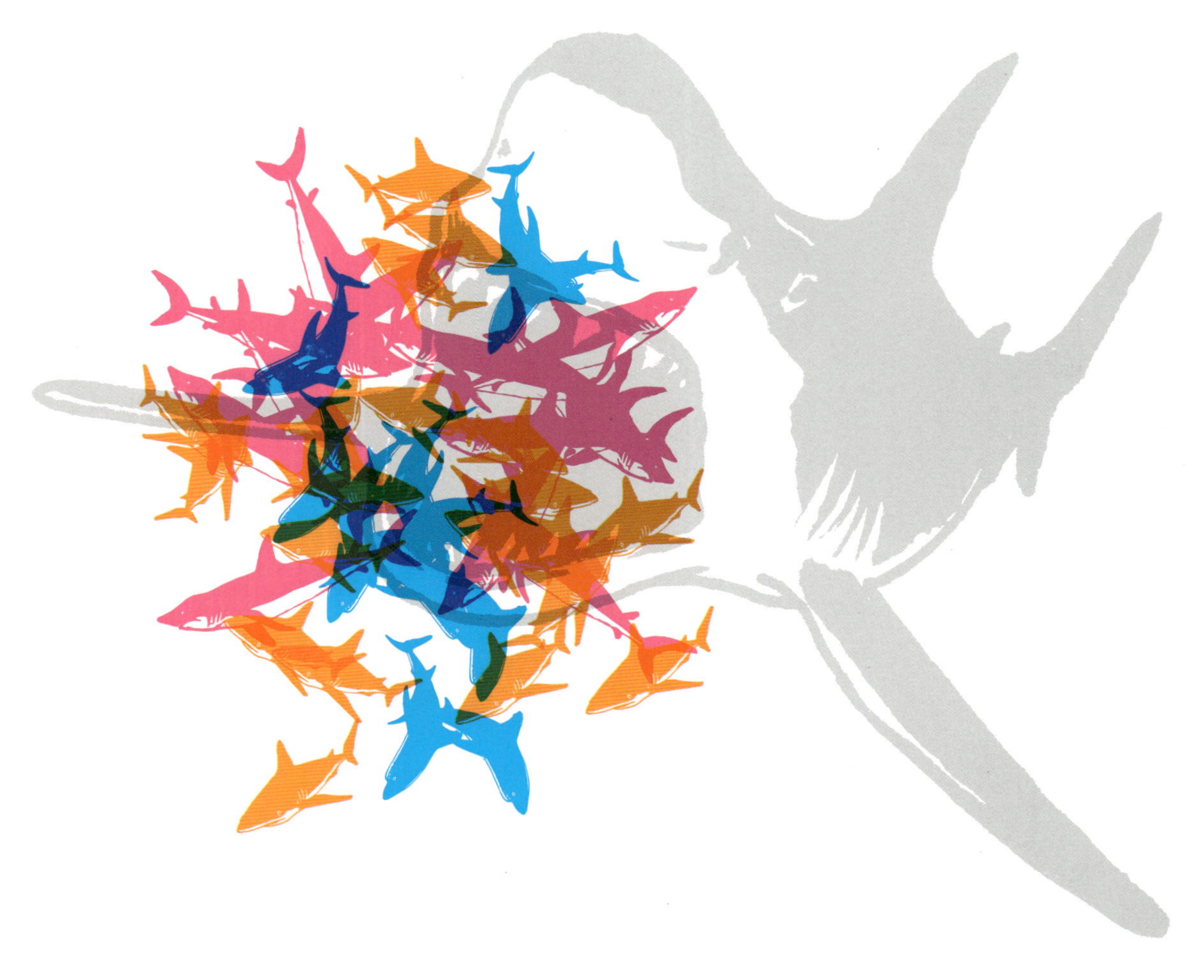

MA_T103

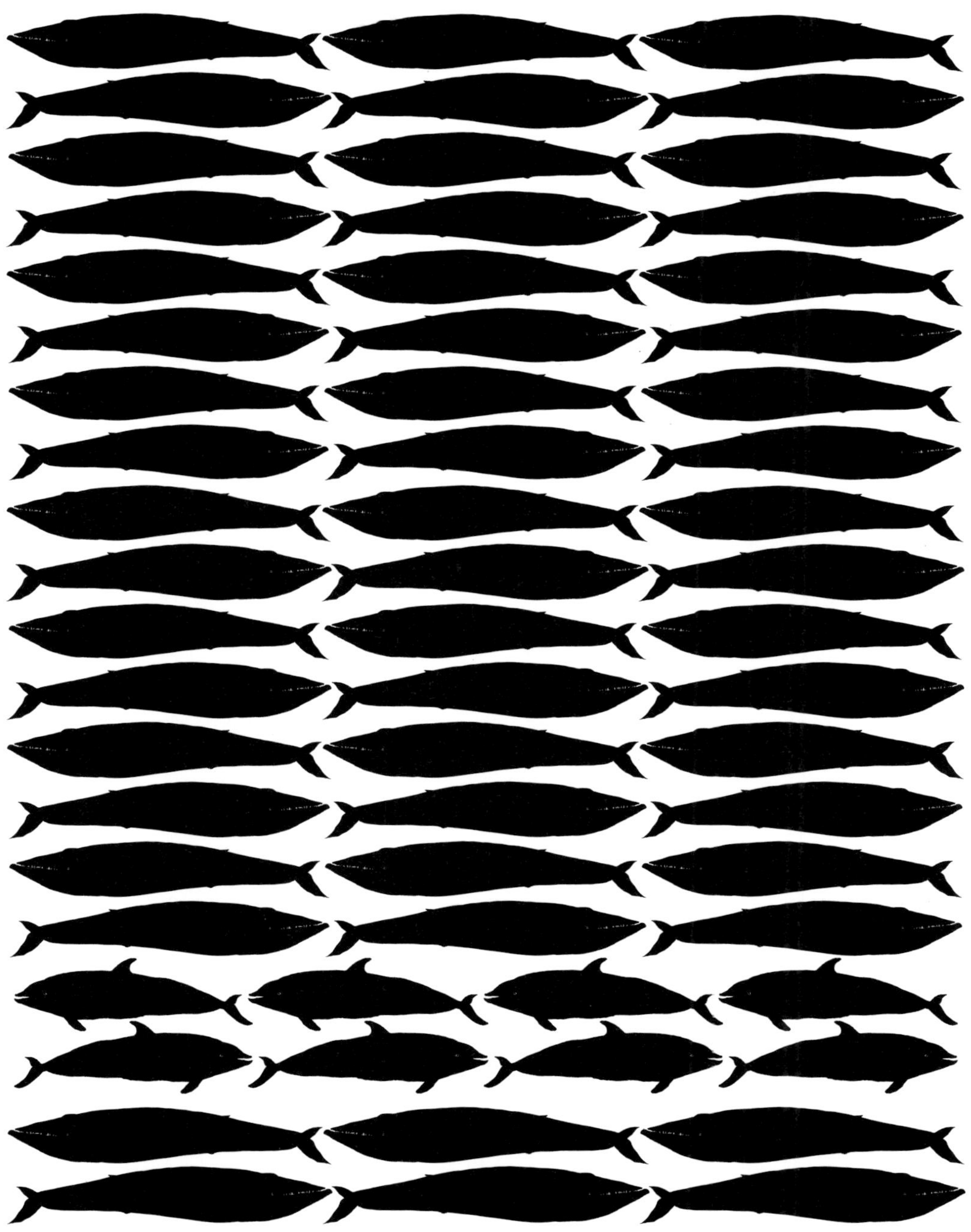

MA_T104

TEMPLATES

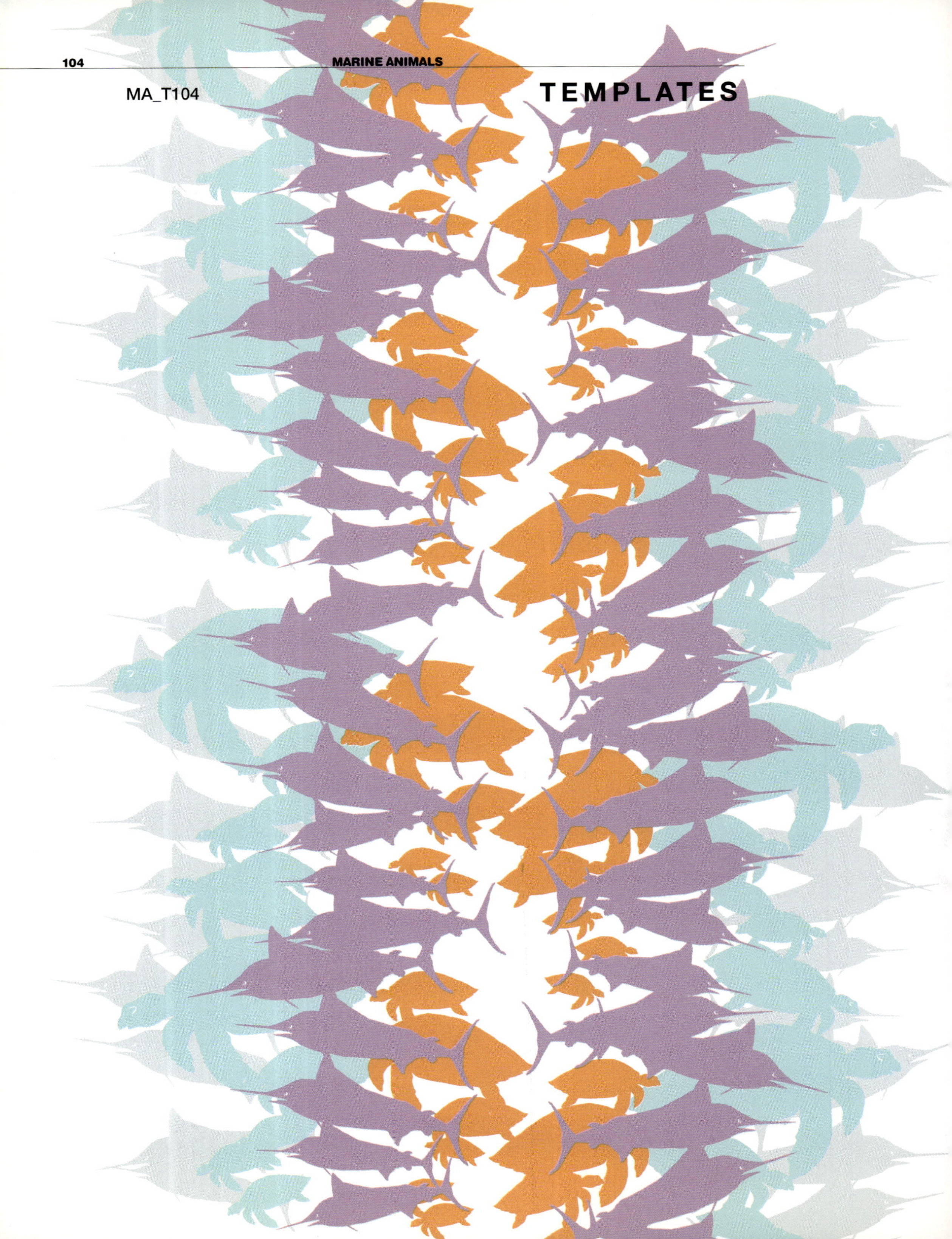

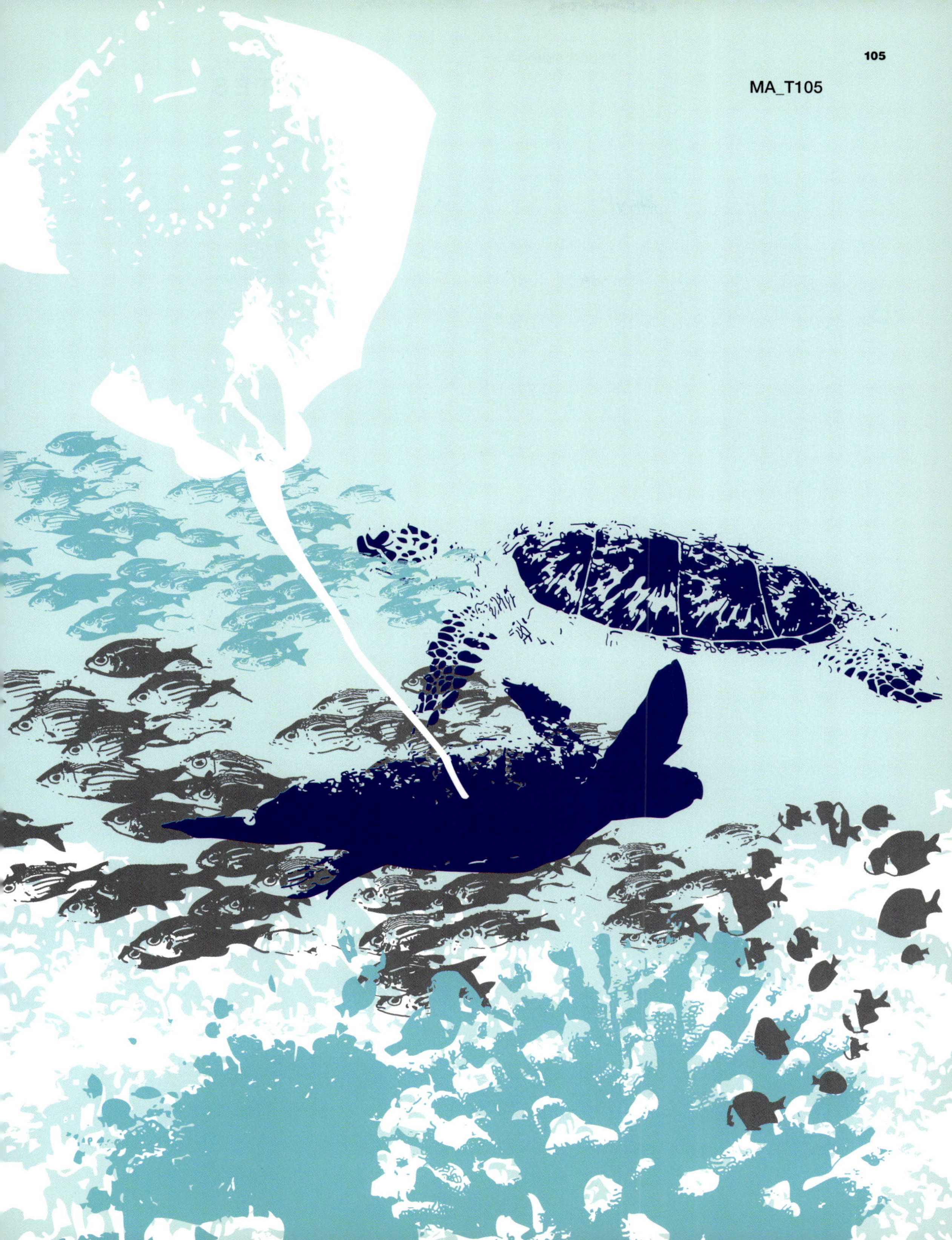
MA_T105

MA_T106

TEMPLATES

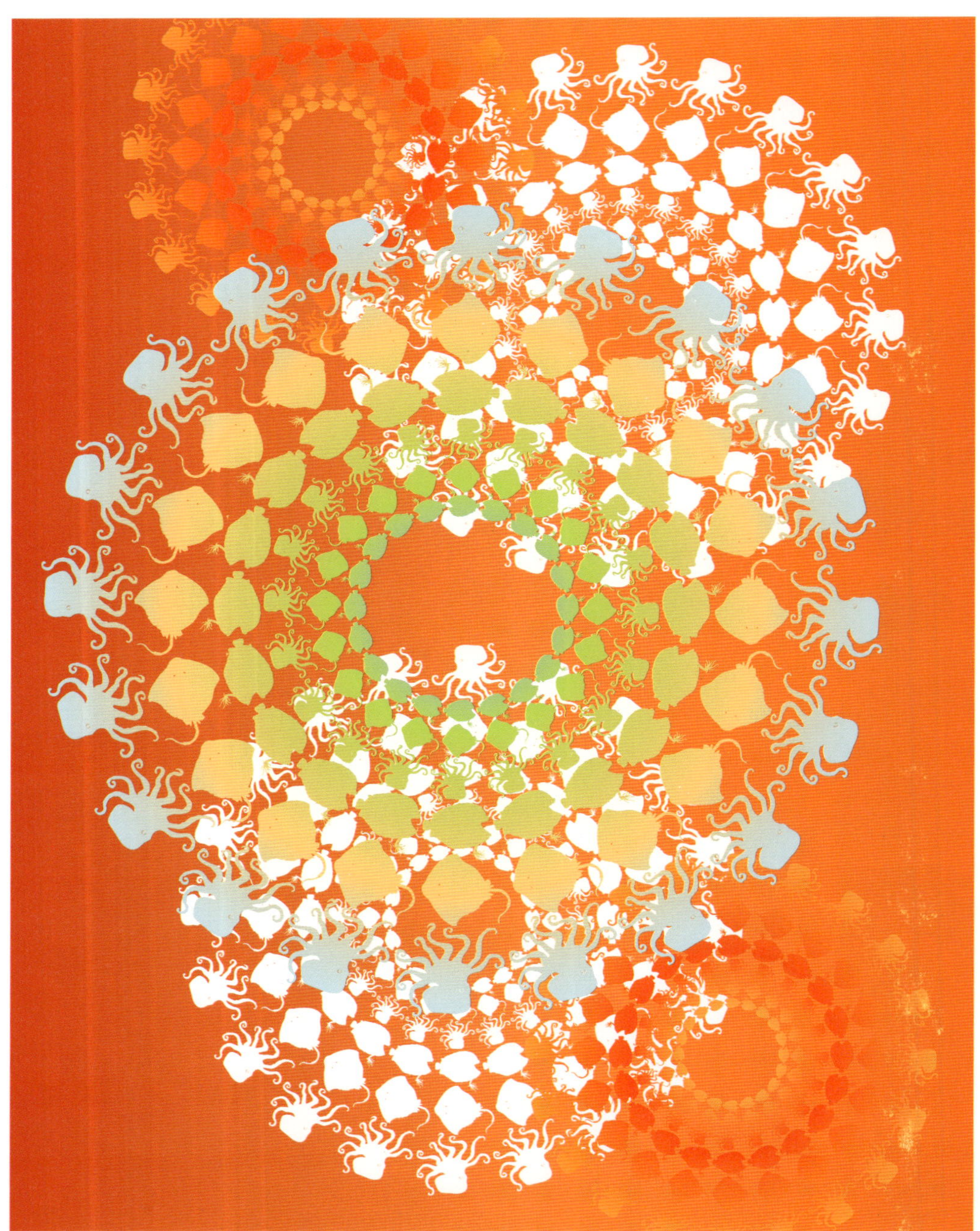

MA_T107

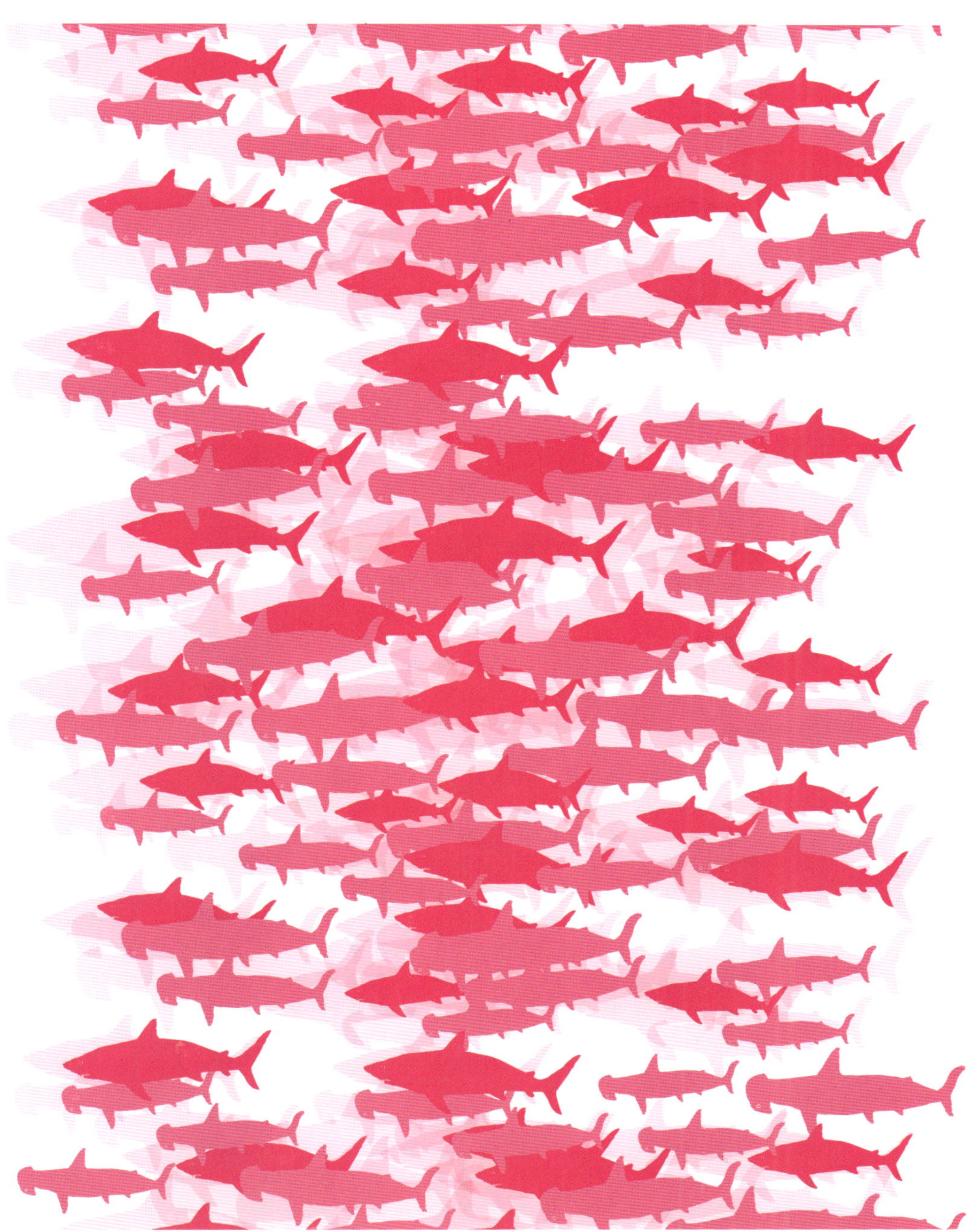

MA_T108

TEMPLATES

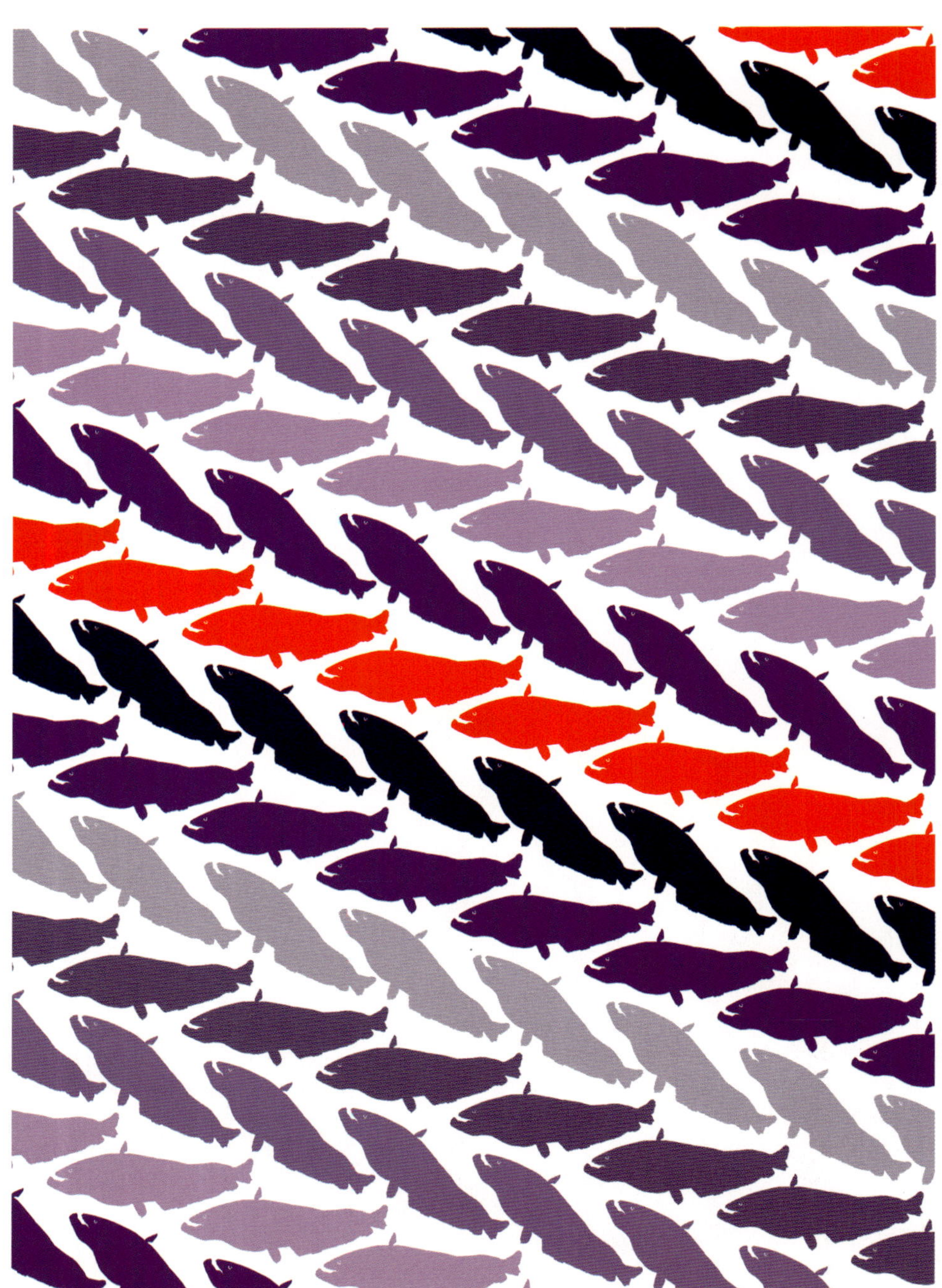

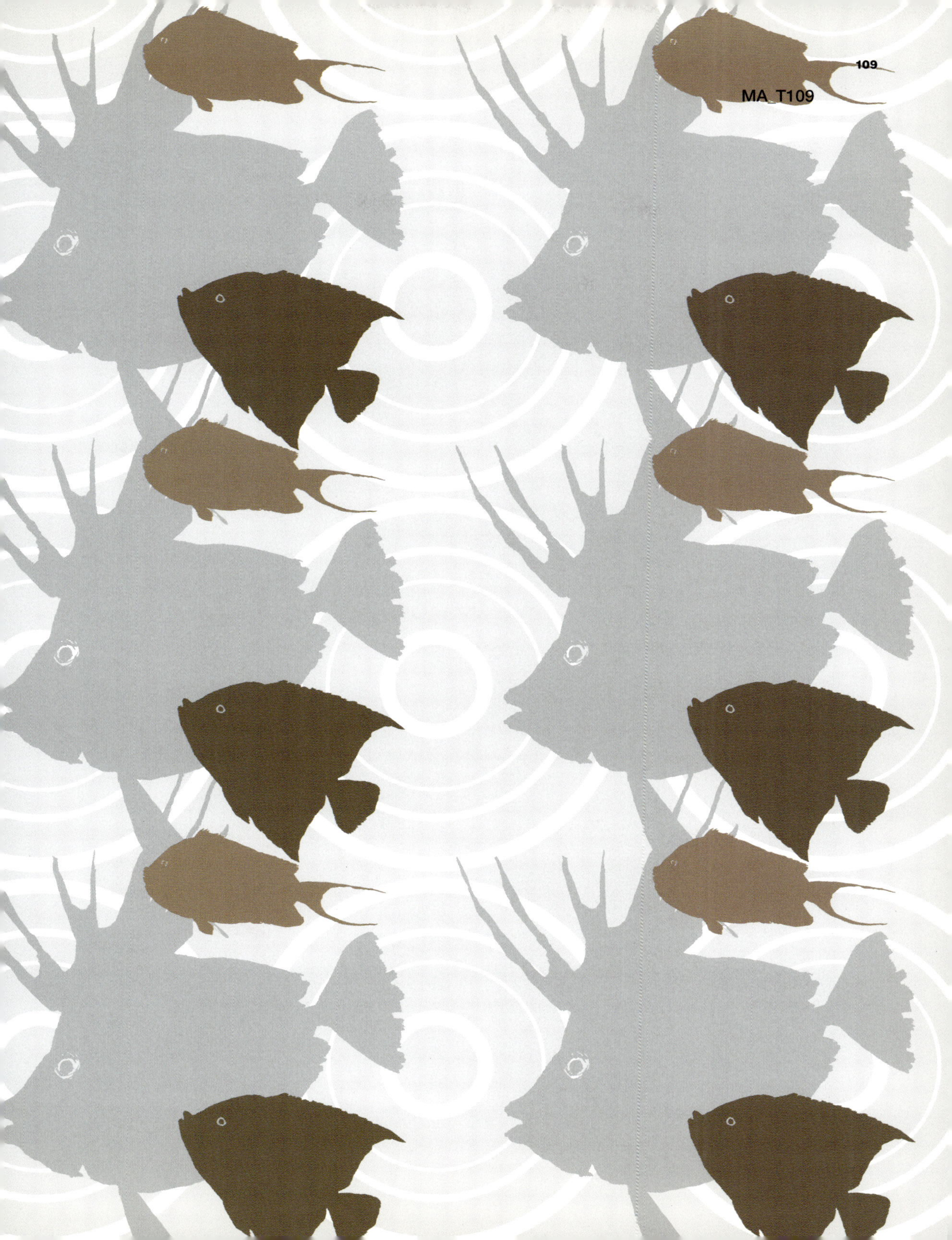
MA_T109

MA_T110

TEMPLATES

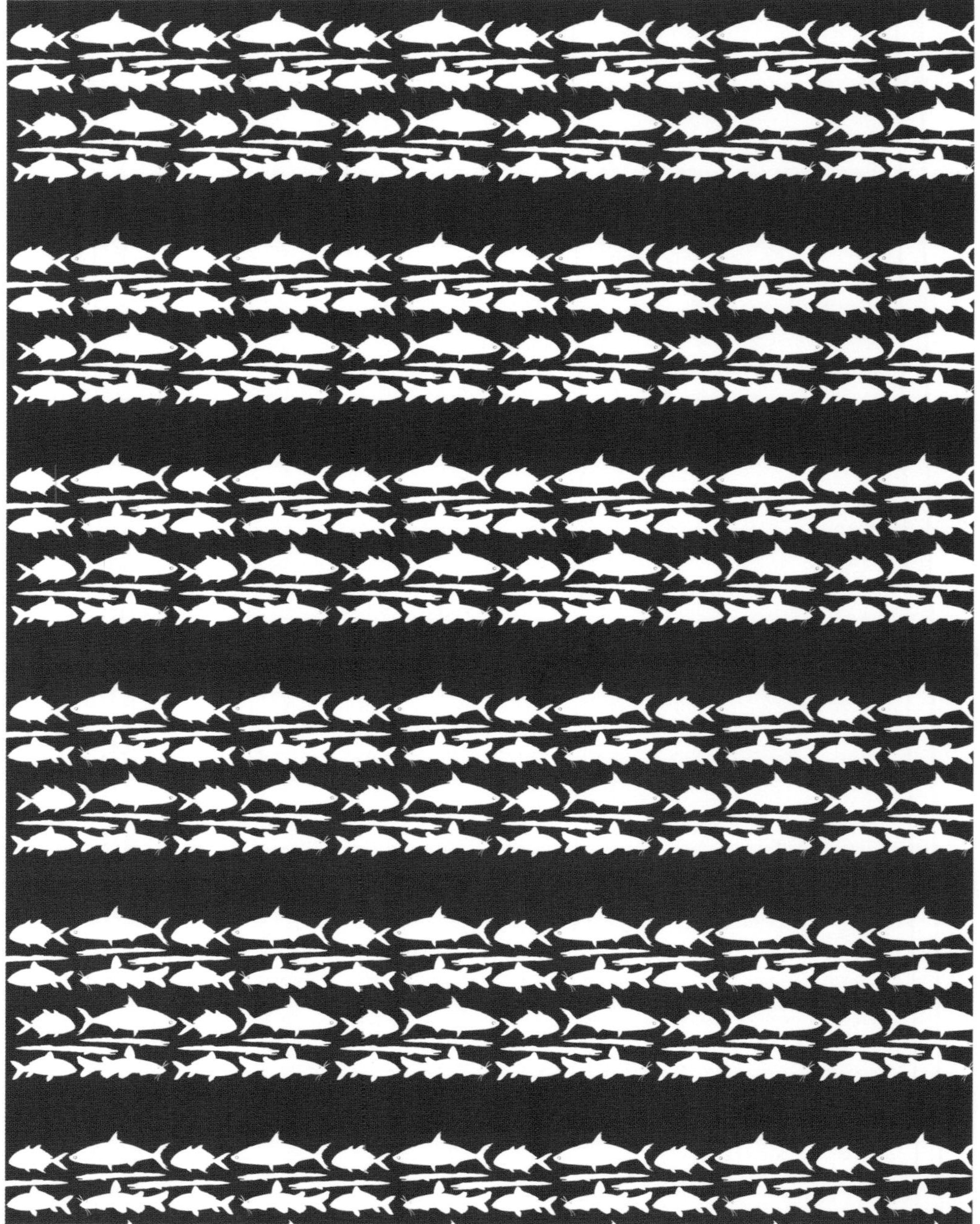

MA_T111

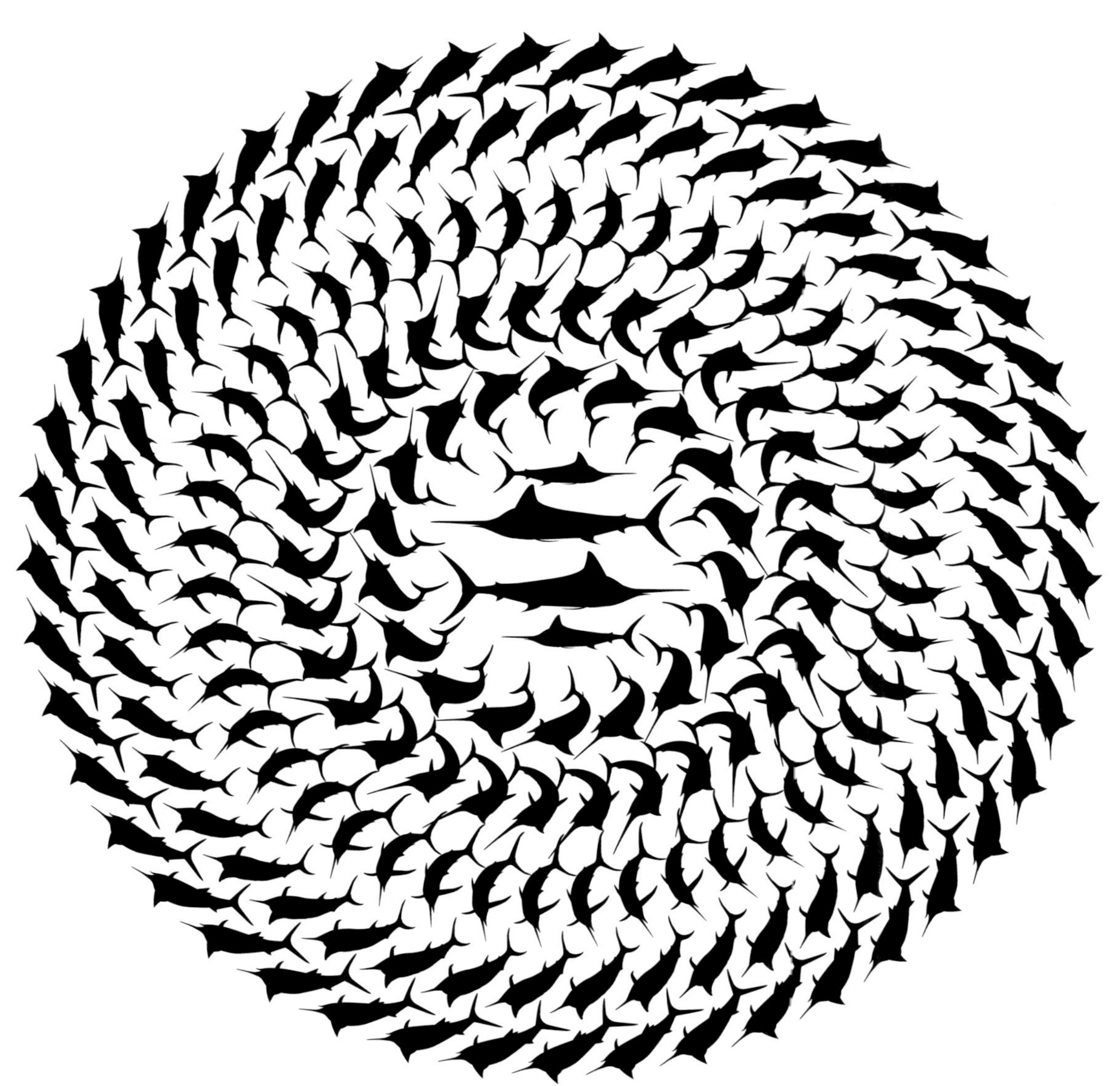

MA_T112

TEMPLATES

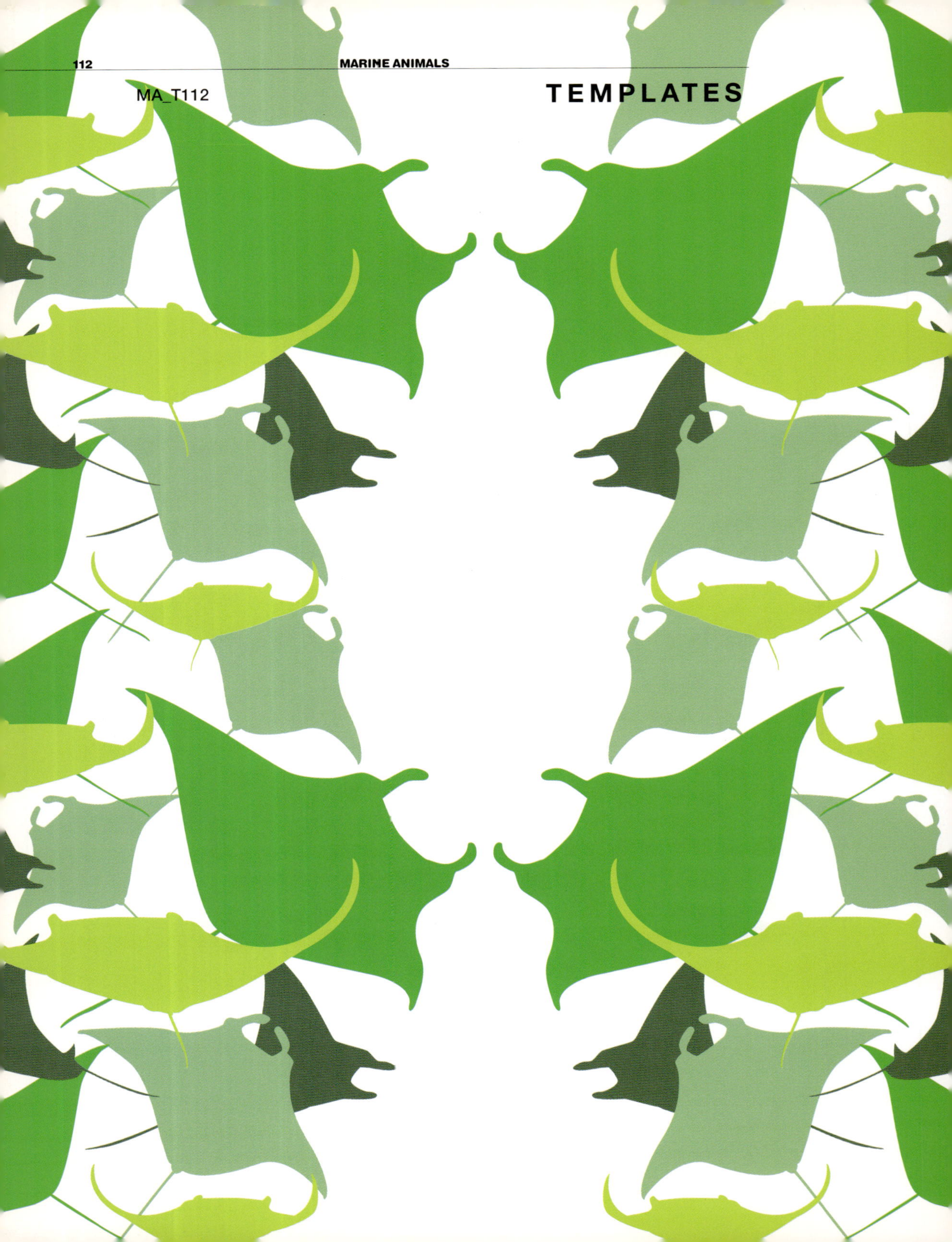

MA_T113

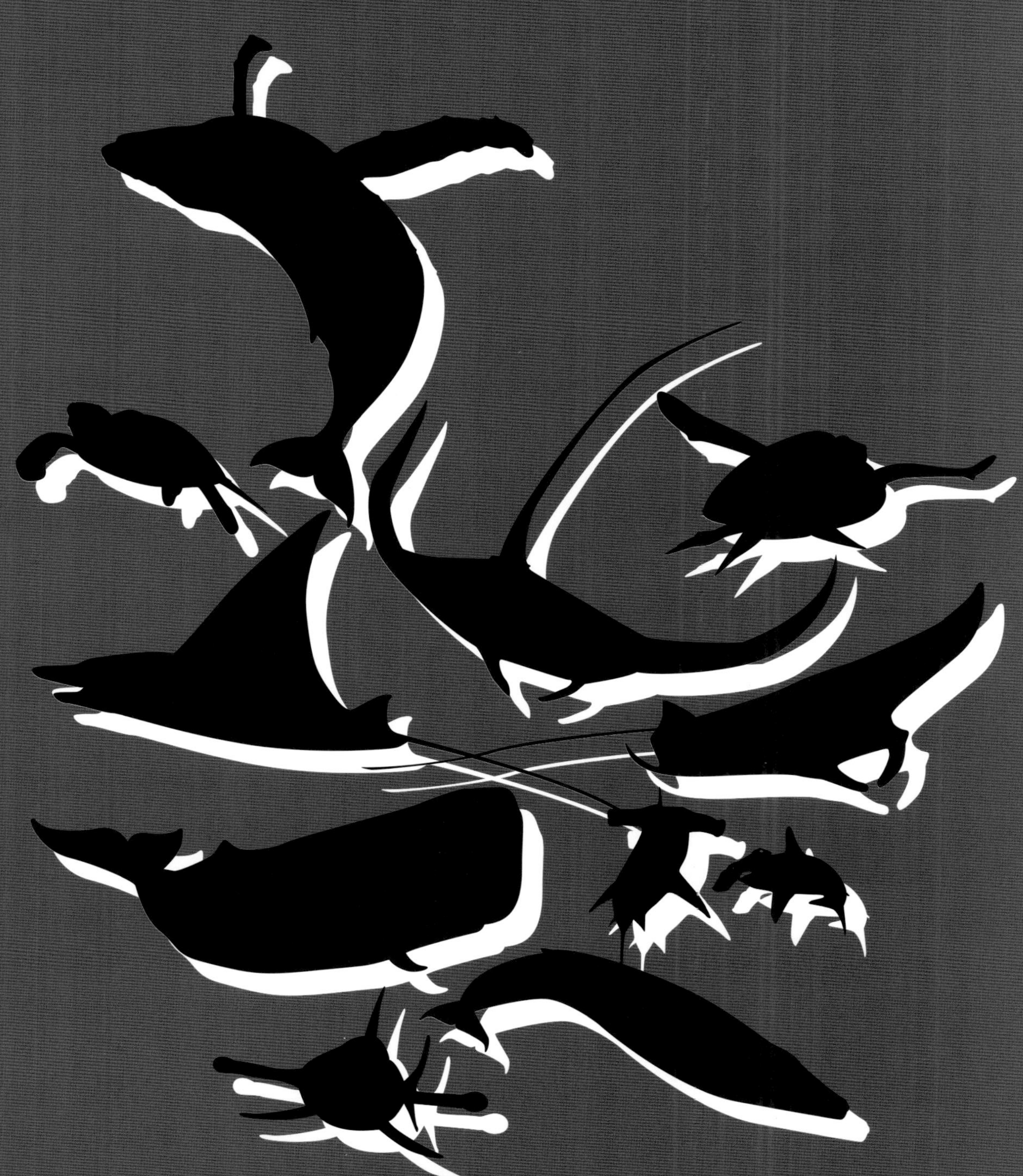

COMPONENTS

COMPONENTS

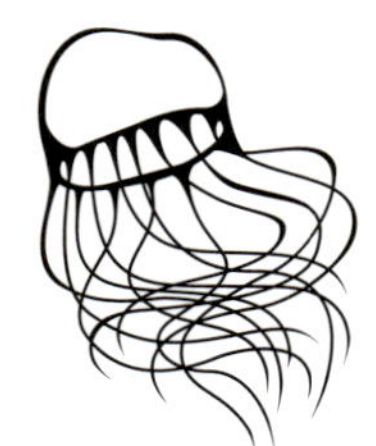

File name: MA_T22_01
Page 22

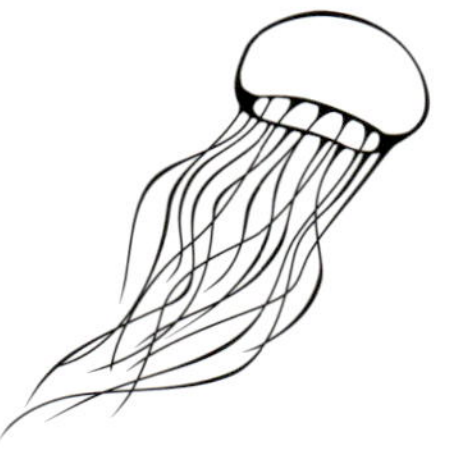

File name: MA_T22_02
Page 22

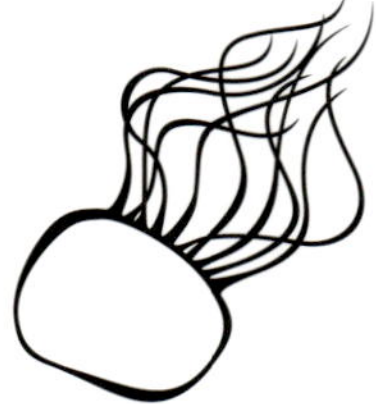

File name: MA_T22_03
Page 22

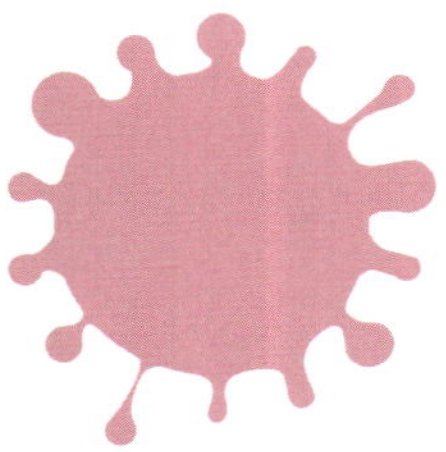

File name: MA_T22_04
Page 22

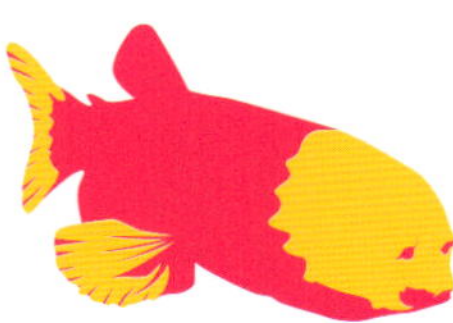

File name: MA_T23_01
Page 23

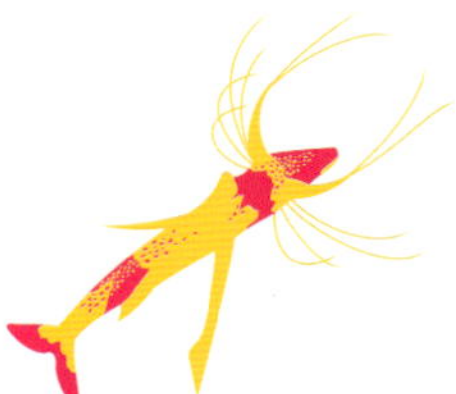

File name: MA_T23_02
Page 23

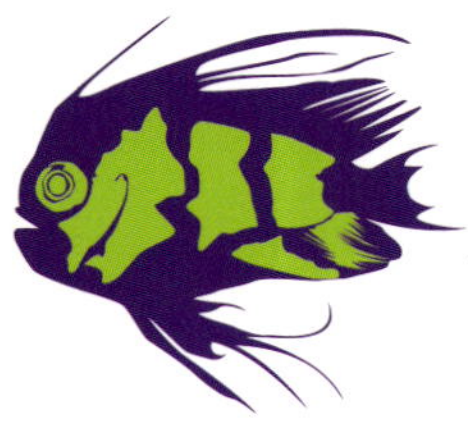

File name: MA_T23_03
Page 23

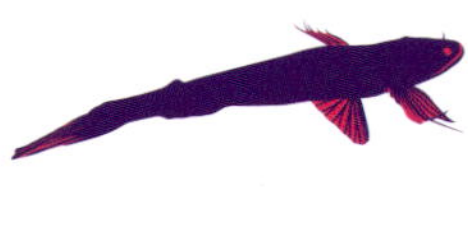

File name: MA_T23_04
Page 23

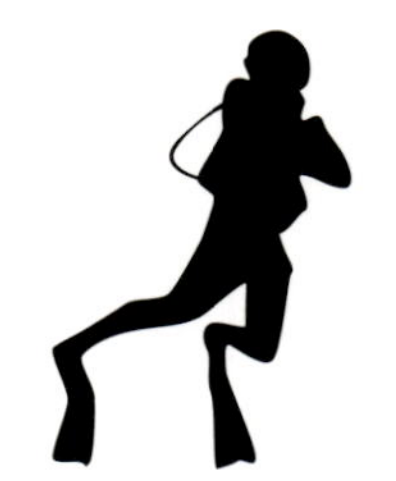

File name: MA_T23_05
Page 23

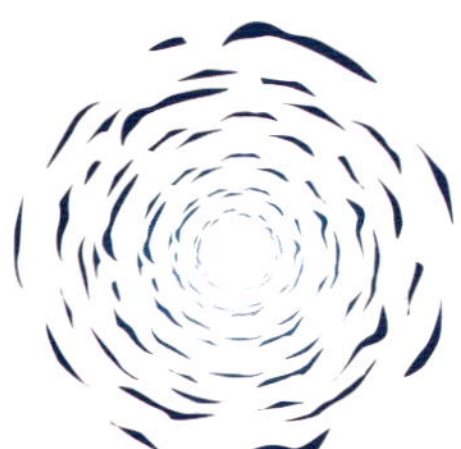

File name: MA_T23_06
Page 23

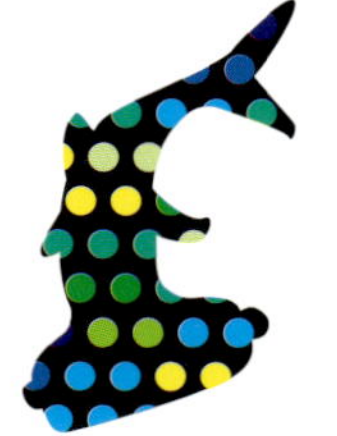

File name: MA_T24_01
Page 24

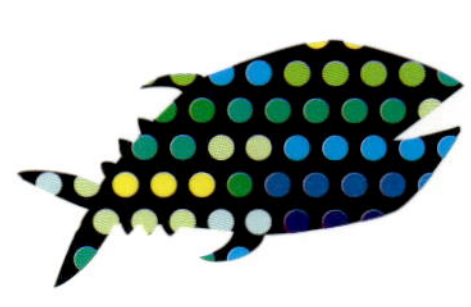

File name: MA_T24_02
Page 24

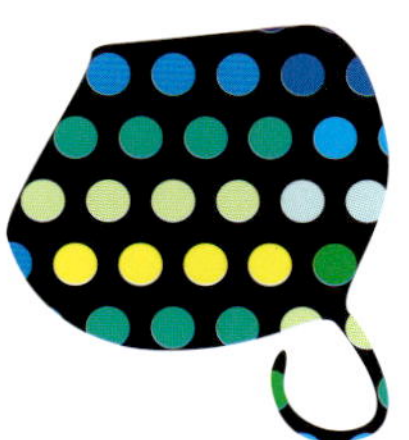

File name: MA_T24_03
Page 24

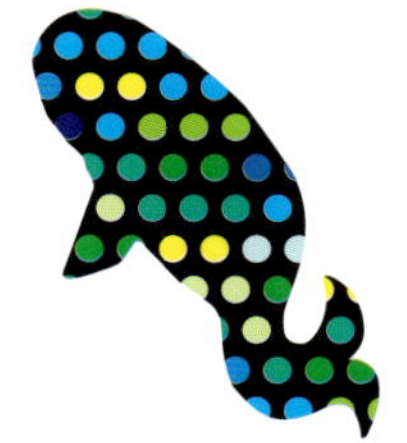

File name: MA_T24_04
Page 24

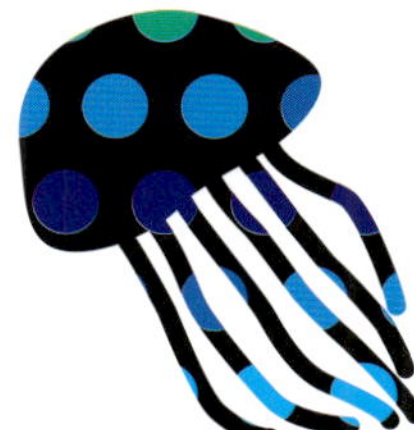

File name: MA_T24_05
Page 24

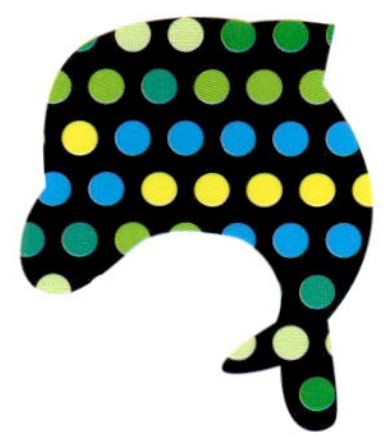

File name: MA_T24_06
Page 24

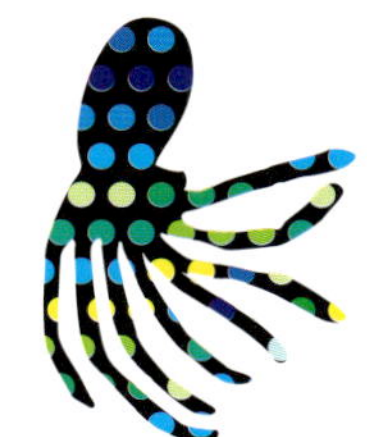

File name: MA_T24_07
Page 24

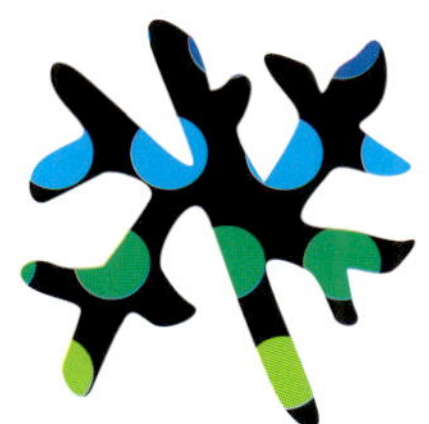

File name: MA_T24_08
Page 24

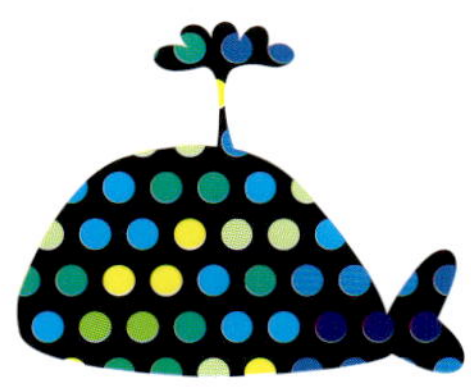

File name: MA_T24_09
Page 24

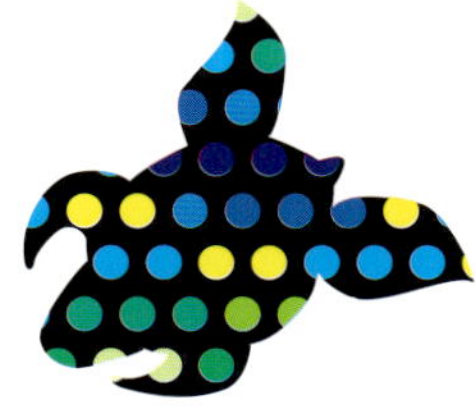

File name: MA_T24_10
Page 24

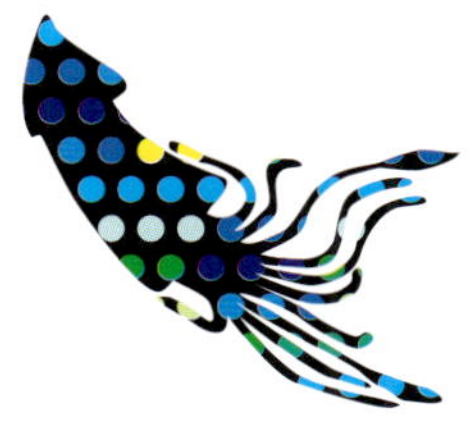

File name: MA_T24_11
Page 24

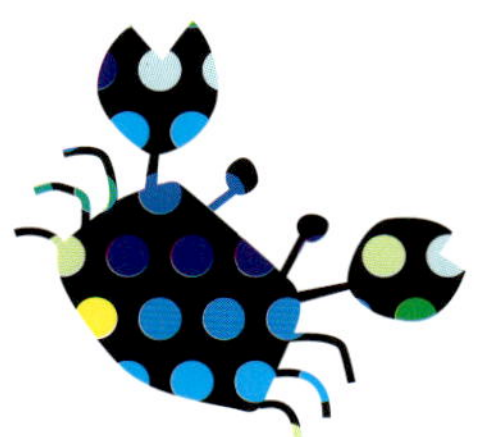

File name: MA_T24_12
Page 24

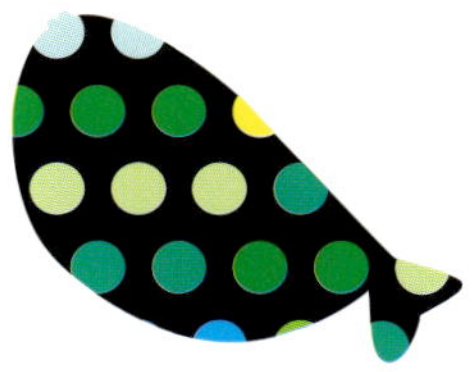

File name: MA_T24_13
Page 24

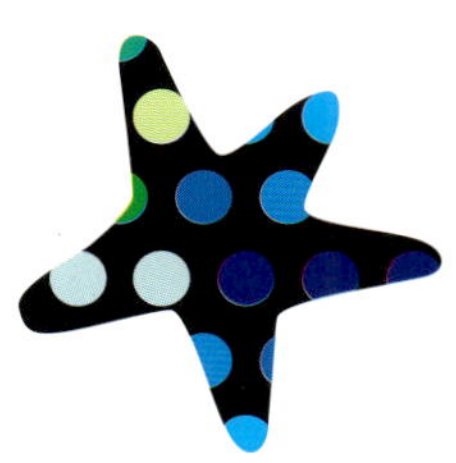

File name: MA_T24_14
Page 24

COMPONENTS

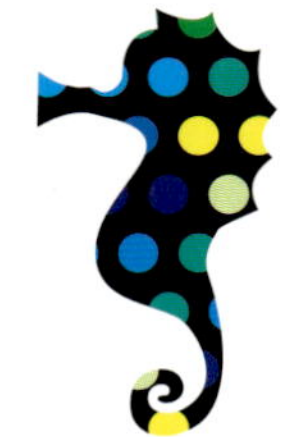

File name: MA_T24_15
Page 24

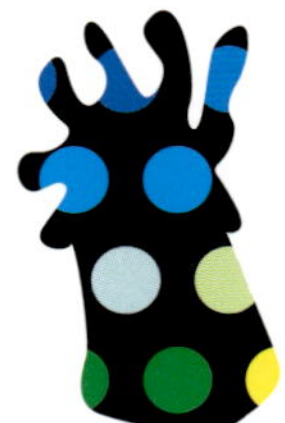

File name: MA_T24_16
Page 24

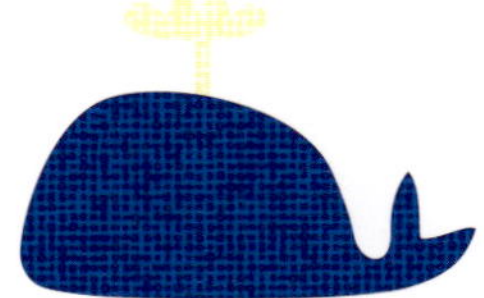

File name: MA_T25_01
Page 25

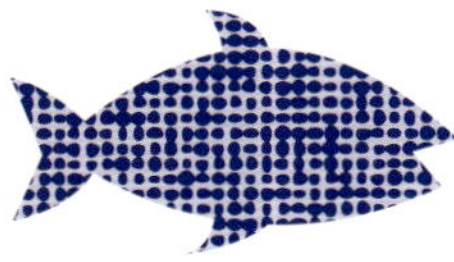

File name: MA_T25_02
Page 25

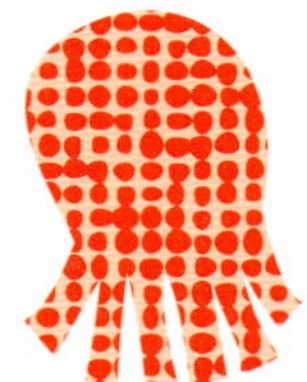

File name: MA_T25_03
Page 25

File name: MA_T25_04
Page 25

File name: MA_T25_05
Page 25

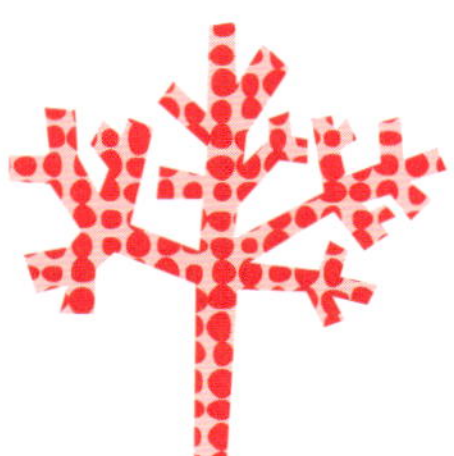

File name: MA_T25_06
Page 25

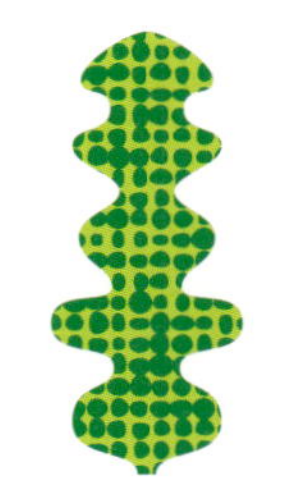

File name: MA_T25_07
Page 25

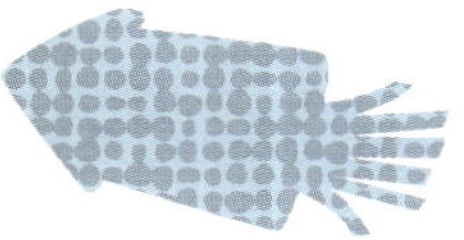

File name: MA_T25_08
Page 25

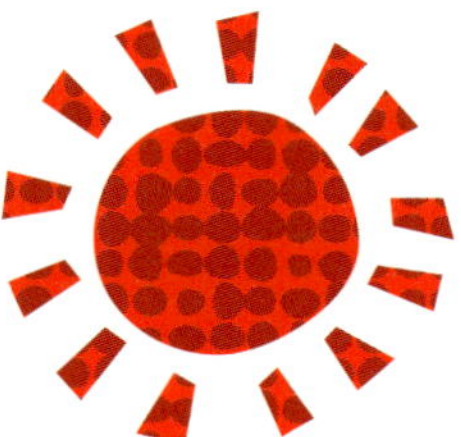

File name: MA_T25_09
Page 25

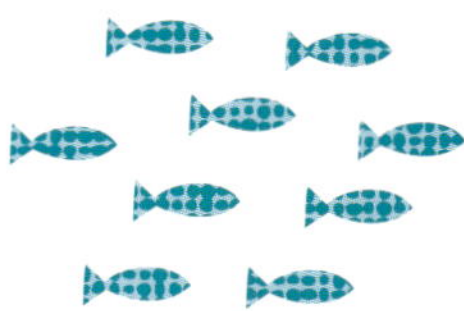

File name: MA_T25_10
Page 25

File name: MA_T25_11
Page 25

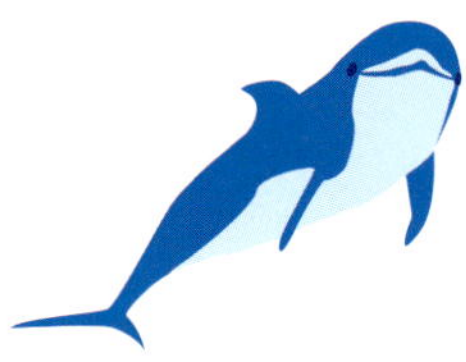

File name: MA_T26_01
Page 26

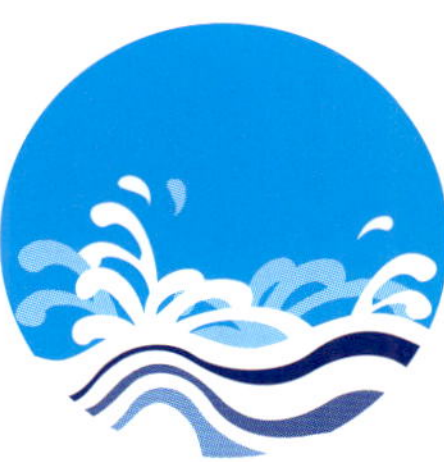

File name: MA_T26_02
Page 26

File name: MA_T26_03
Page 26

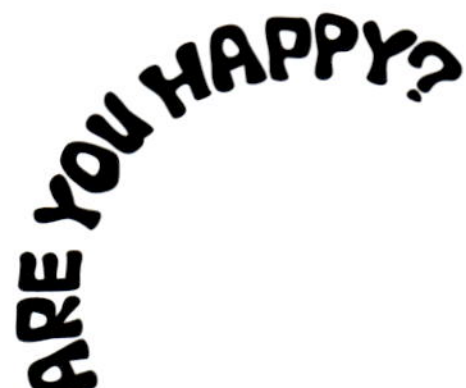

File name: MA_T26_04
Page 26

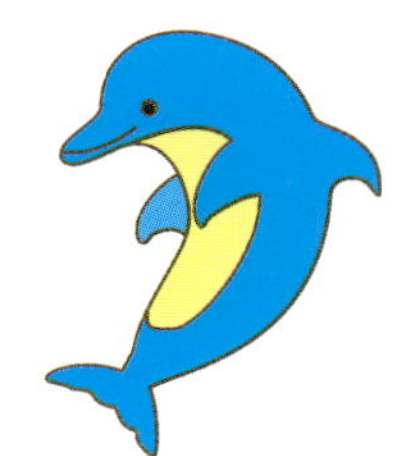

File name: MA_T27_01
Page 27

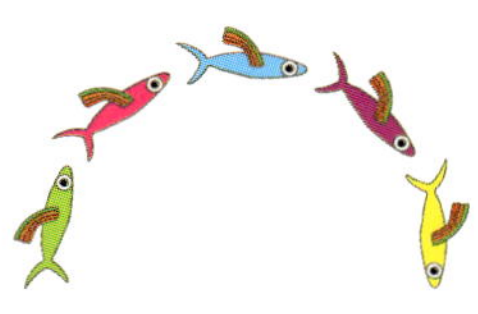

File name: MA_T27_02
Page 27

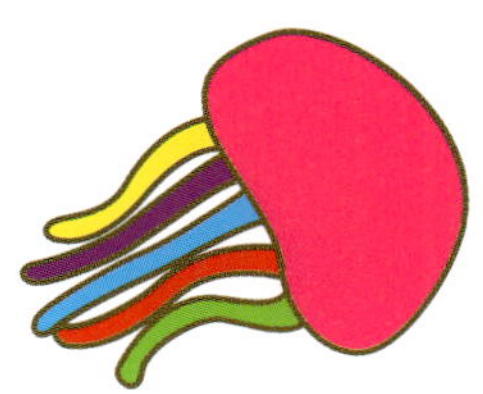

File name: MA_T27_03
Page 27

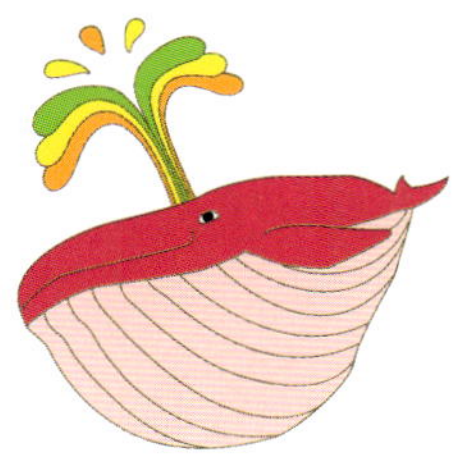

File name: MA_T27_04
Page 27

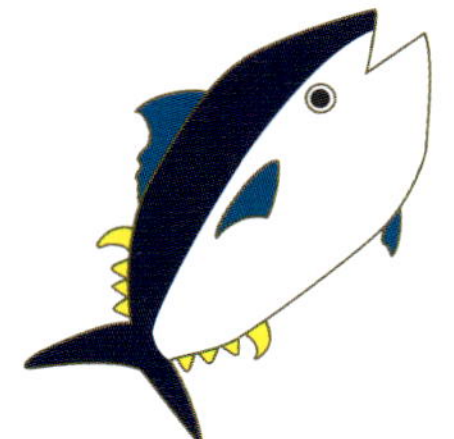

File name: MA_T27_05
Page 27

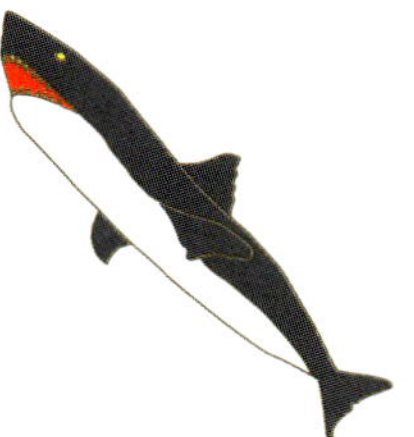
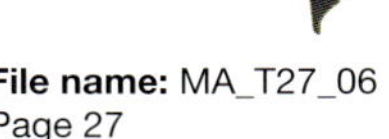

File name: MA_T27_06
Page 27

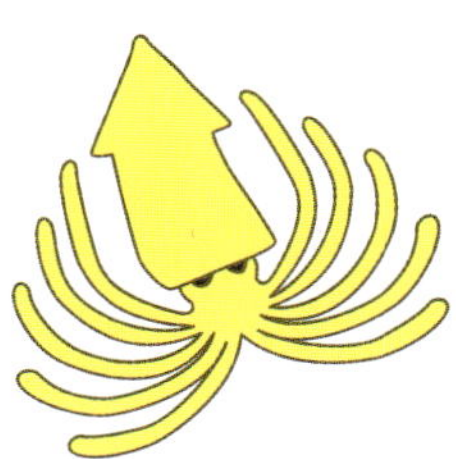

File name: MA_T27_07
Page 27

COMPONENTS

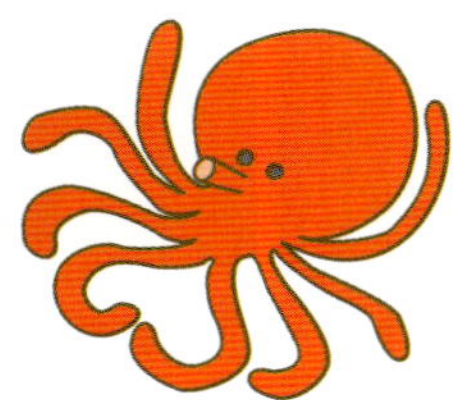

File name: MA_T27_08
Page 27

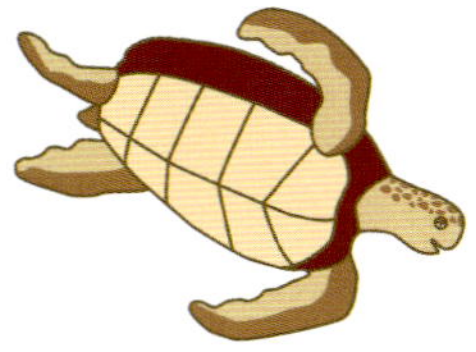

File name: MA_T27_09
Page 27

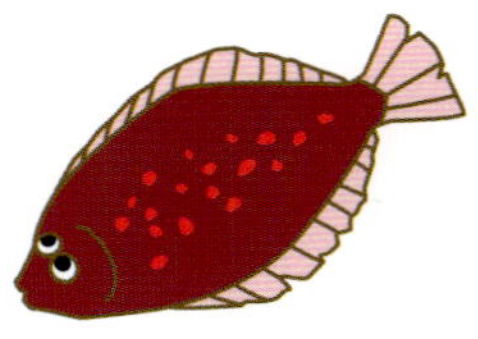

File name: MA_T27_10
Page 27

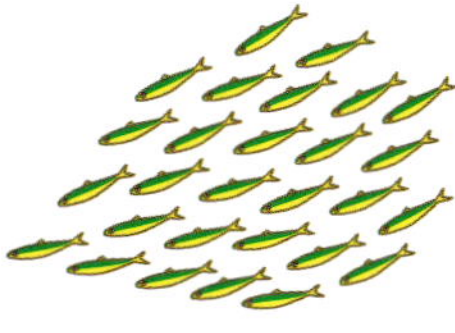

File name: MA_T27_11
Page 27

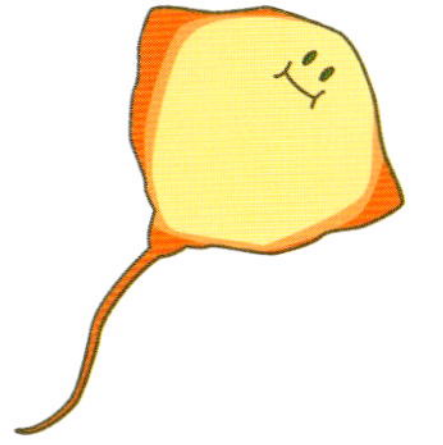

File name: MA_T27_12
Page 27

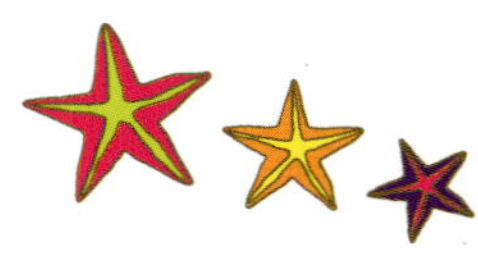

File name: MA_T27_13
Page 27

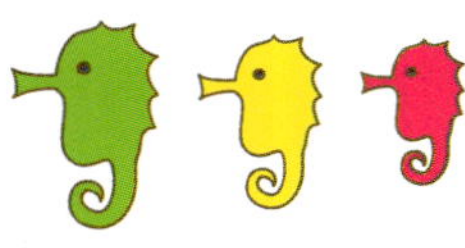

File name: MA_T27_14
Page 27

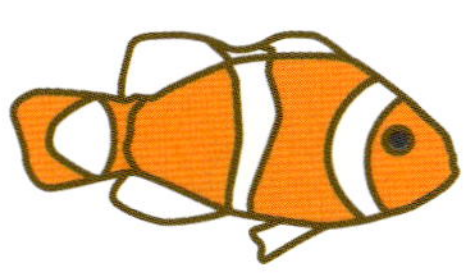

File name: MA_T27_15
Page 27

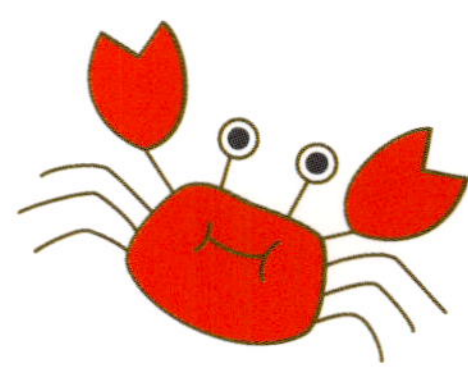

File name: MA_T27_16
Page 27

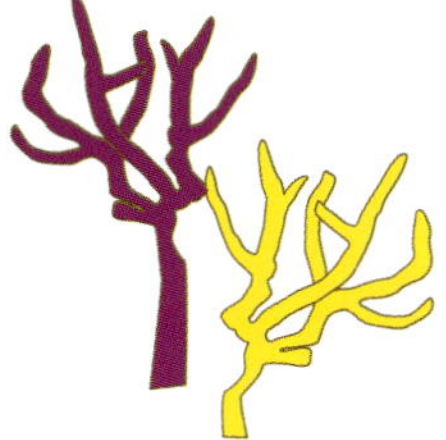

File name: MA_T27_17
Page 27

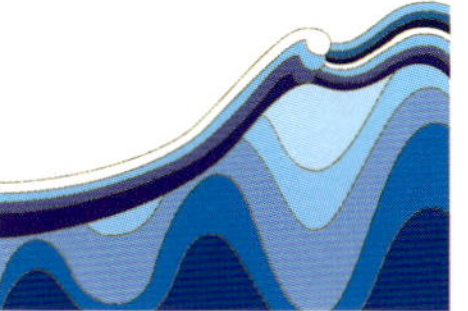

File name: MA_T27_18
Page 27

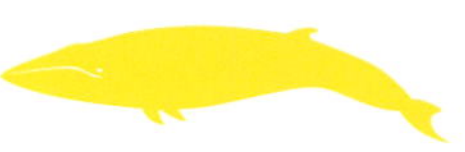

File name: MA_T28_01
Page 28

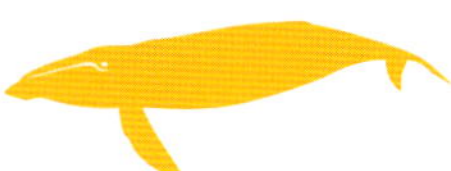

File name: MA_T28_02
Page 28

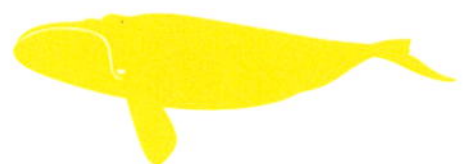

File name: MA_T28_03
Page 28

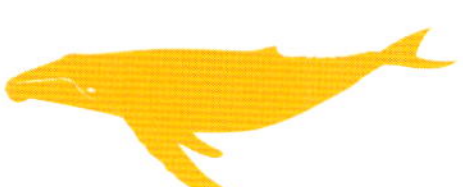

File name: MA_T28_04
Page 28

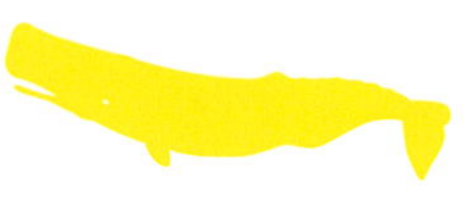

File name: MA_T28_05
Page 28

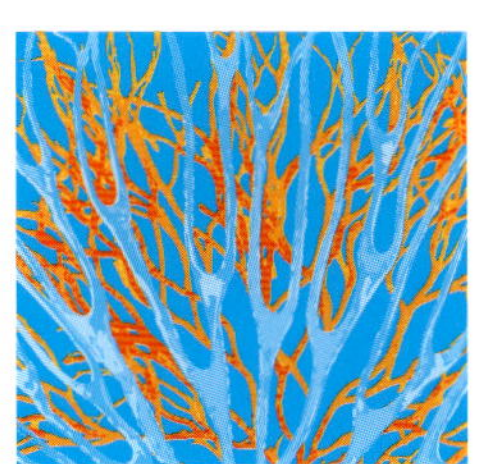

File name: MA_T28_06
Page 28

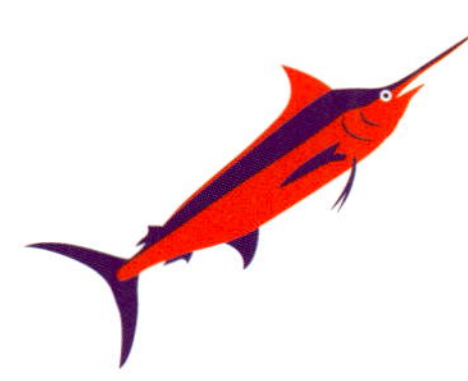

File name: MA_T29_01
Page 29

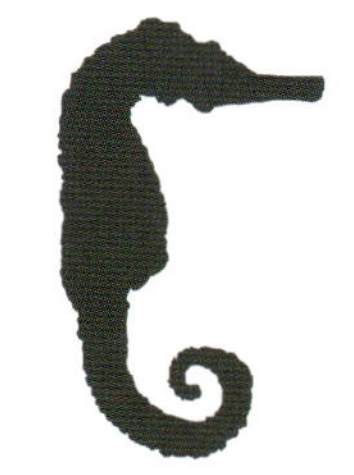

File name: MA_T30_01
Page 30

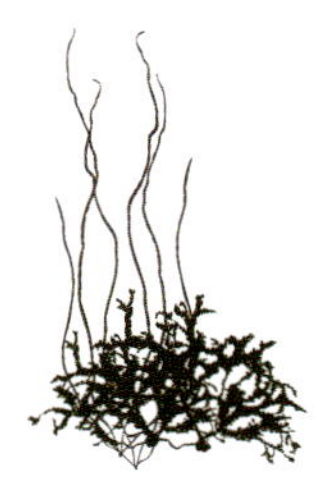

File name: MA_T30_02
Page 30

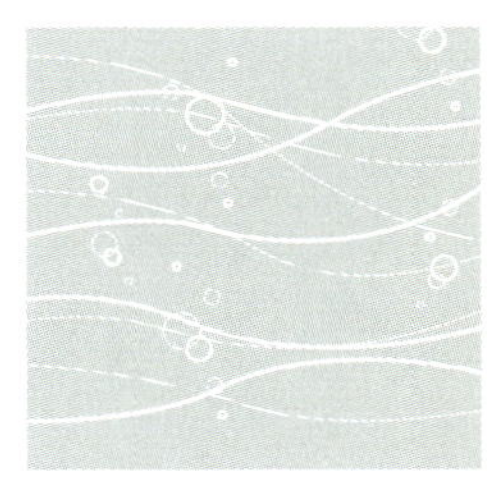

File name: MA_T30_03
Page 30

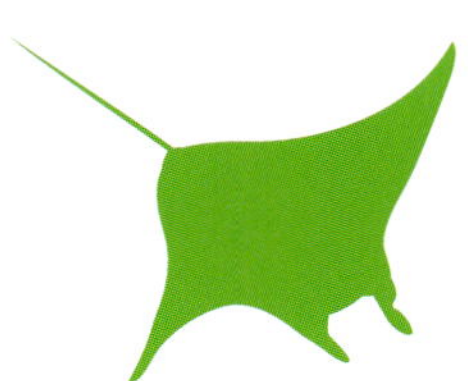

File name: MA_T31_01
Page 31

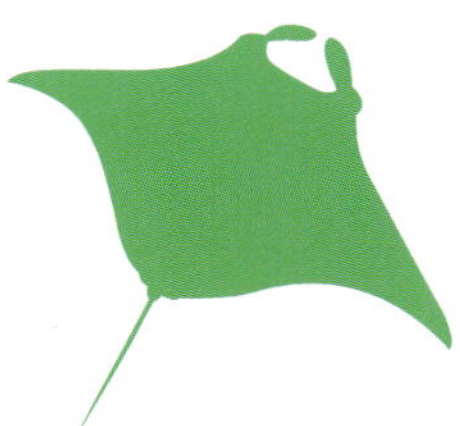

File name: MA_T31_02
Page 31

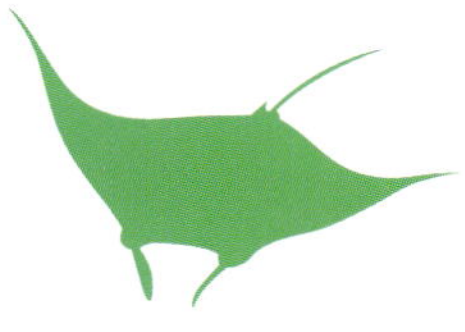

File name: MA_T31_03
Page 31

COMPONENTS

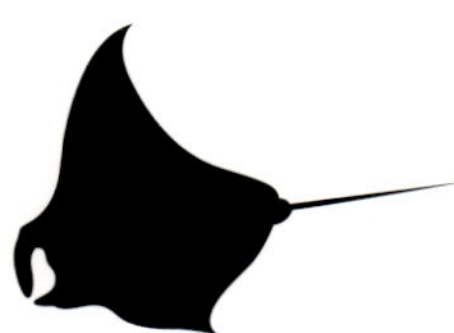

File name: MA_T31_04
Page 31

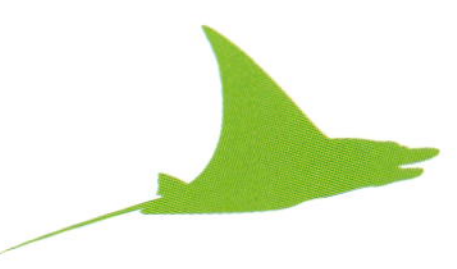

File name: MA_T31_05
Page 31

File name: MA_T32_01
Page 32

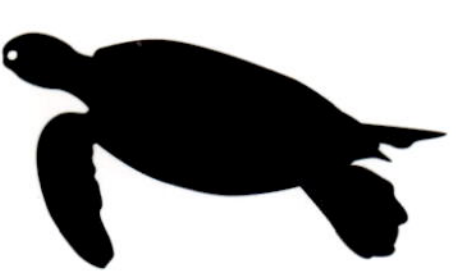

File name: MA_T32_02
Page 32

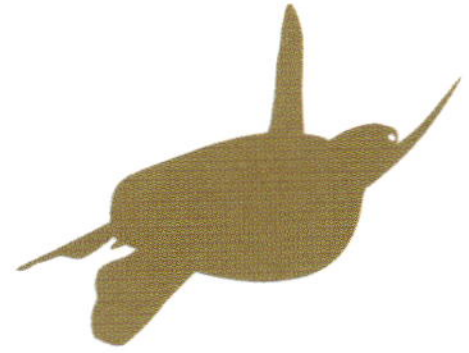

File name: MA_T32_03
Page 32

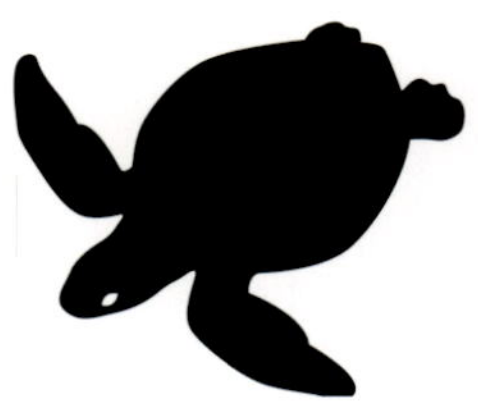

File name: MA_T32_04
Page 32

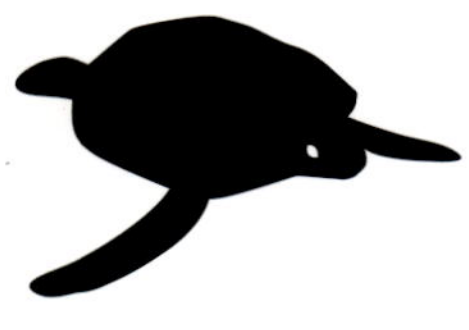

File name: MA_T32_05
Page 32

File name: MA_T33_01
Page 33

File name: MA_T33_02
Page 33

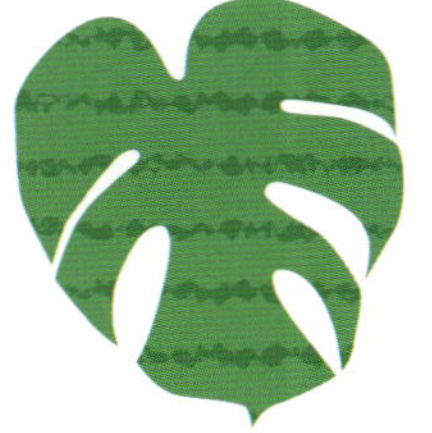

File name: MA_T33_03
Page 33

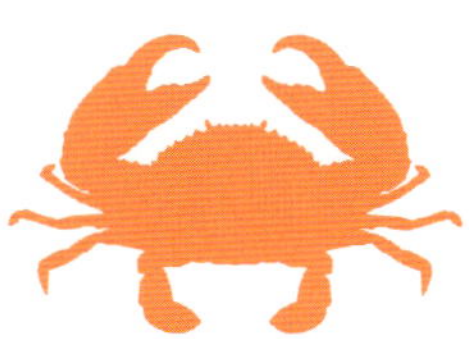

File name: MA_T34_01
Page 34

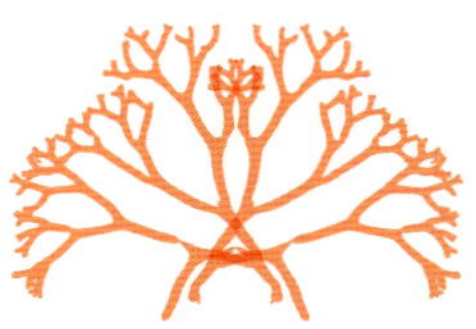

File name: MA_T34_02
Page 34

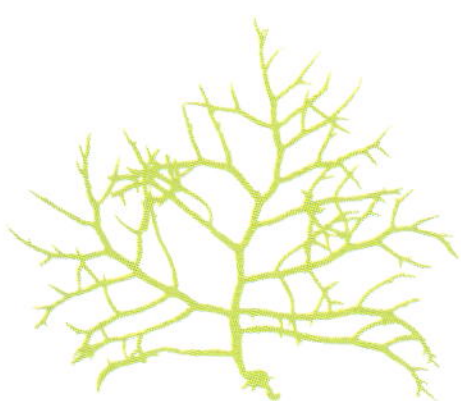

File name: MA_T34_03
Page 34

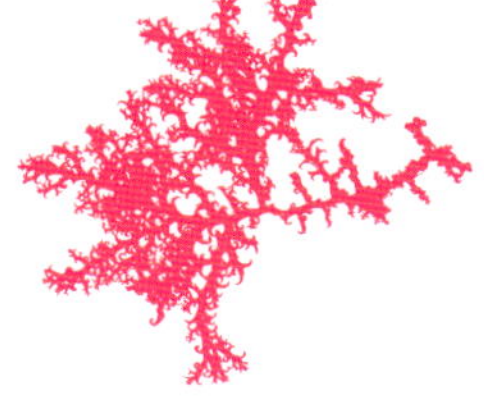

File name: MA_T34_04
Page 34

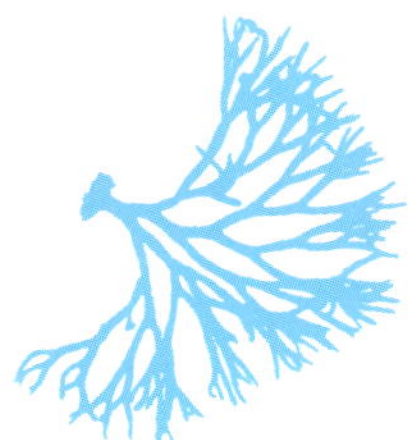

File name: MA_T34_05
Page 34

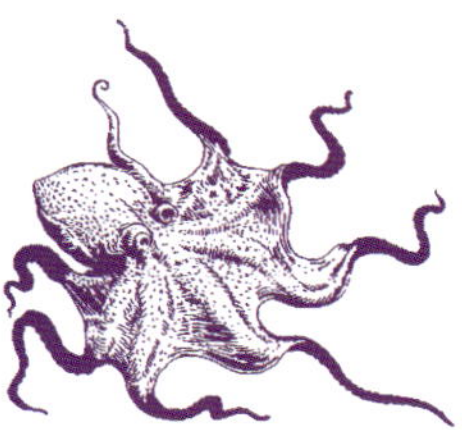

File name: MA_T34_06
Page 34

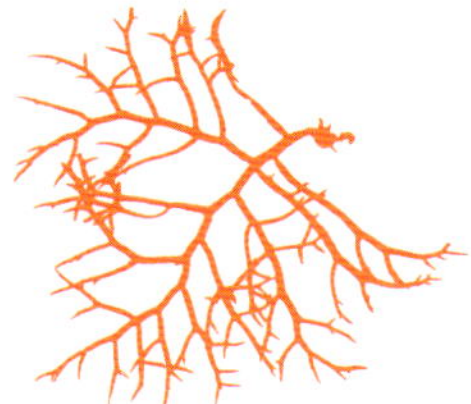

File name: MA_T34_07
Page 34

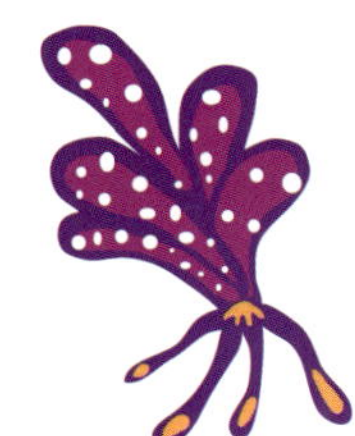

File name: MA_T35_01
Page 35

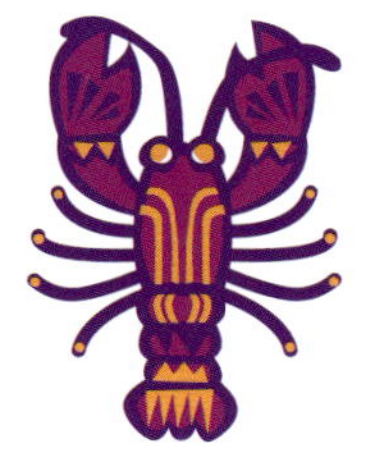

File name: MA_T35_02
Page 35

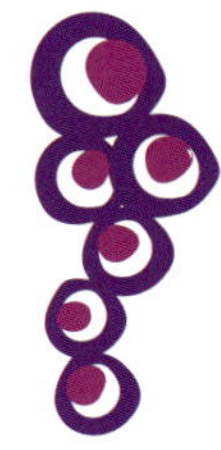

File name: MA_T35_03
Page 35

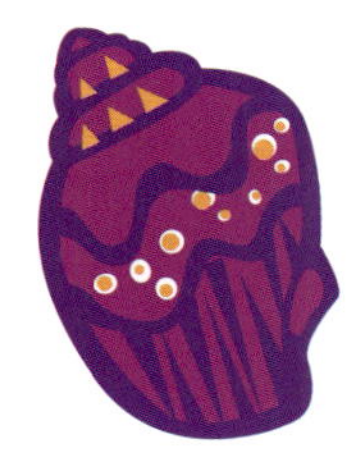

File name: MA_T35_04
Page 35

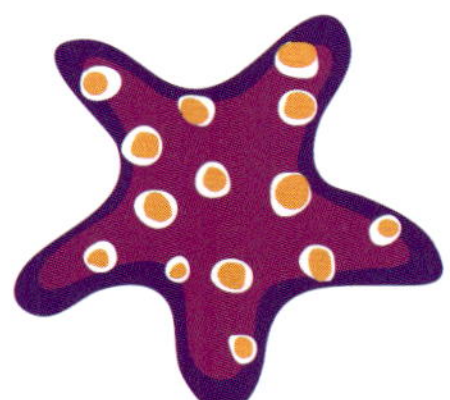

File name: MA_T35_05
Page 35

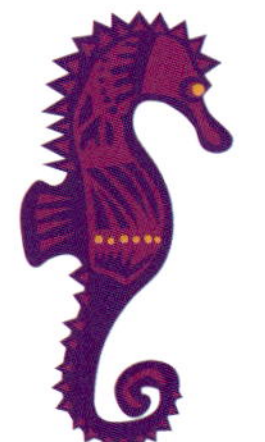

File name: MA_T35_06
Page 35

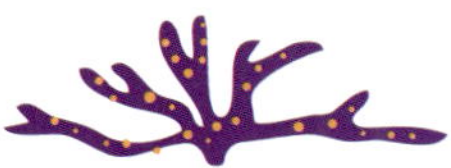

File name: MA_T35_07
Page 35

COMPONENTS

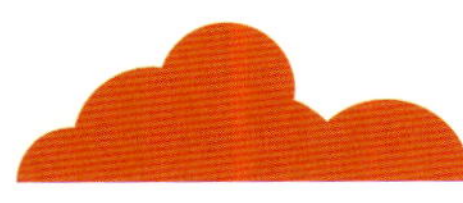

File name: MA_T36_01
Page 36

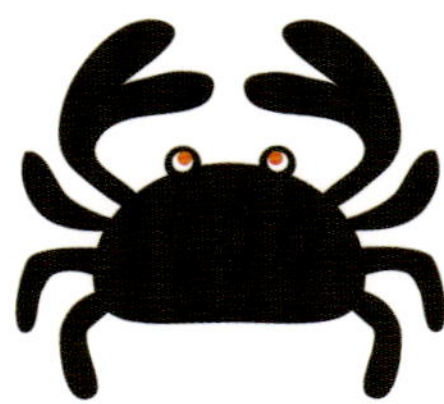

File name: MA_T36_02
Page 36

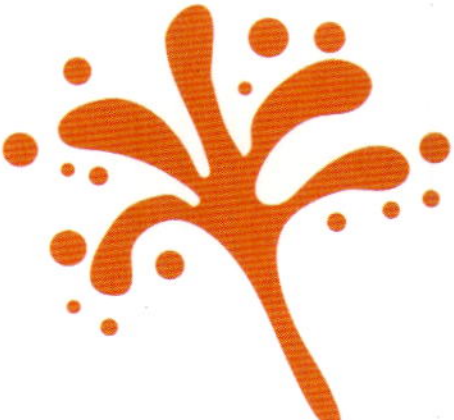

File name: MA_T36_03
Page 36

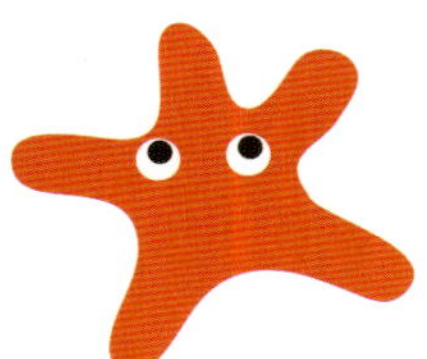

File name: MA_T36_04
Page 36

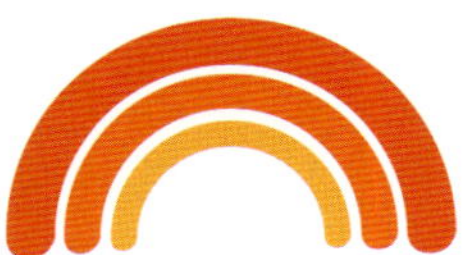

File name: MA_T36_05
Page 36

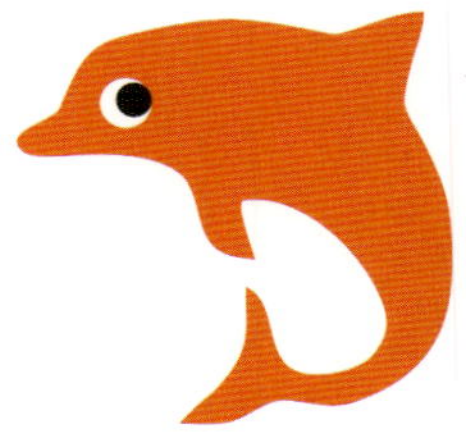

File name: MA_T36_06
Page 36

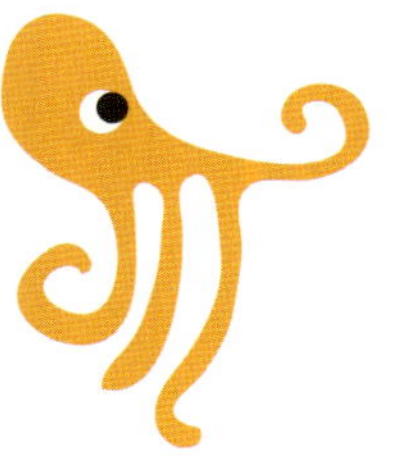

File name: MA_T36_07
Page 36

File name: MA_T36_08
Page 36

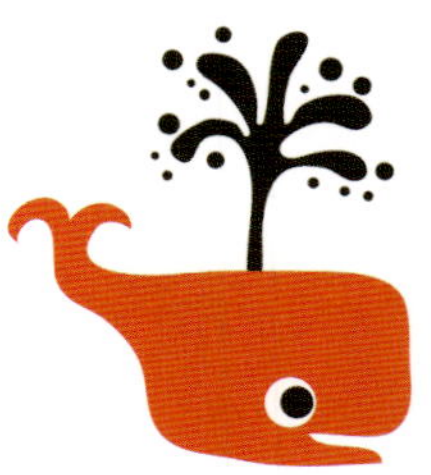

File name: MA_T36_09
Page 36

File name: MA_T36_10
Page 36

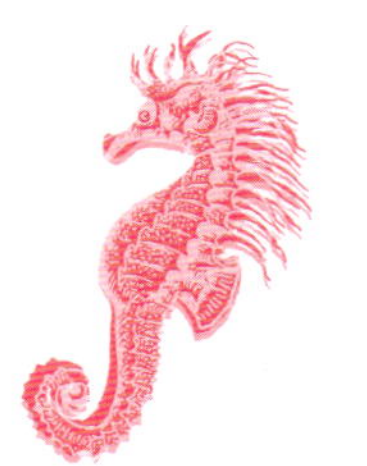

File name: MA_T37_01
Page 37

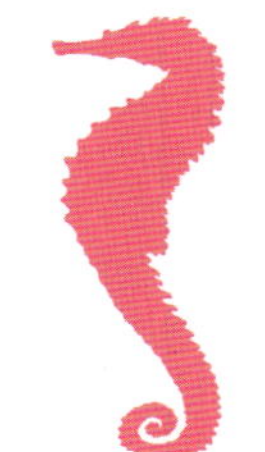

File name: MA_T37_02
Page 37

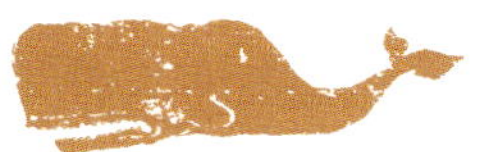

File name: MA_T38_01
Page 38

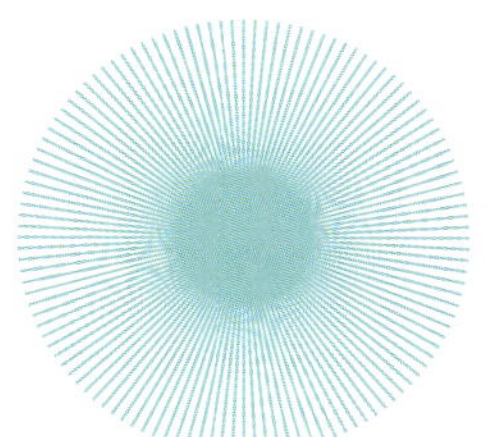

File name: MA_T38_02
Page 38

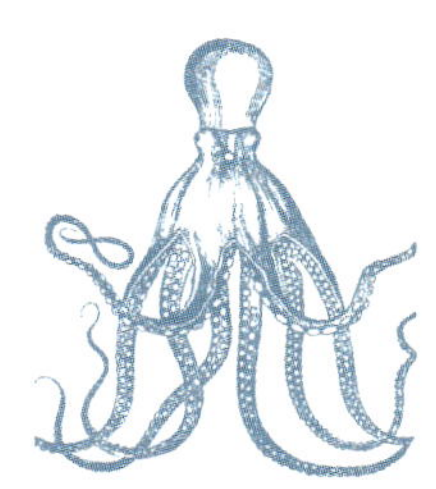

File name: MA_T39_01
Page 39

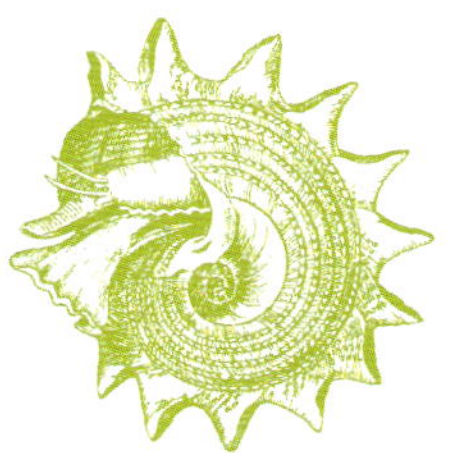

File name: MA_T39_02
Page 39

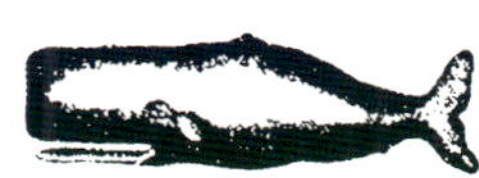

File name: MA_T39_03
Page 39

File name: MA_T40_01
Page 40

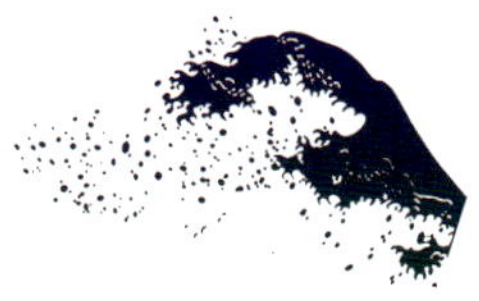

File name: MA_T40_02
Page 40

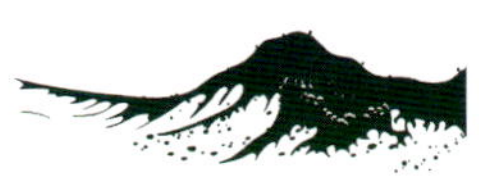

File name: MA_T40_03
Page 40

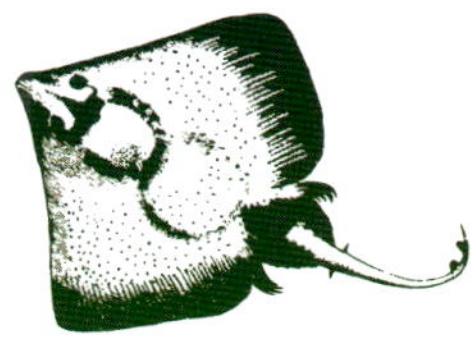

File name: MA_T40_04
Page 40

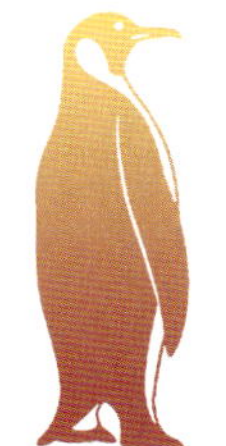

File name: MA_T41_01
Page 41

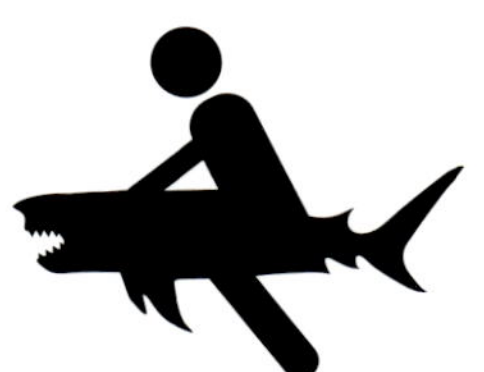

File name: MA_T42_01
Page 42

File name: MA_T42_02
Page 42

COMPONENTS

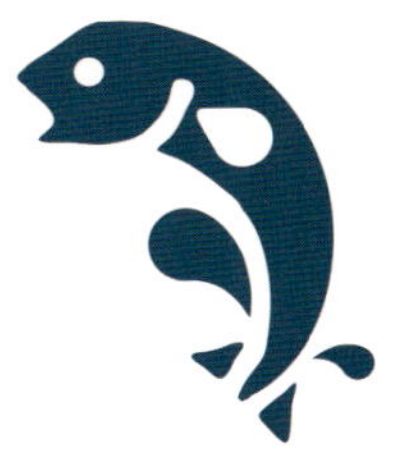

File name: MA_T43_01
Page 43

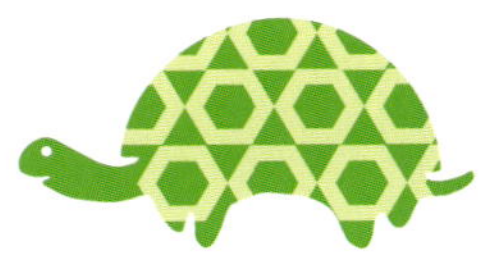

File name: MA_T44_01
Page 44

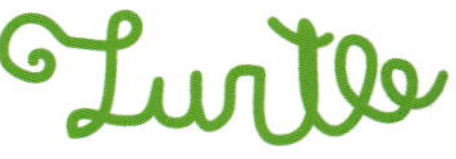

File name: MA_T44_02
Page 44

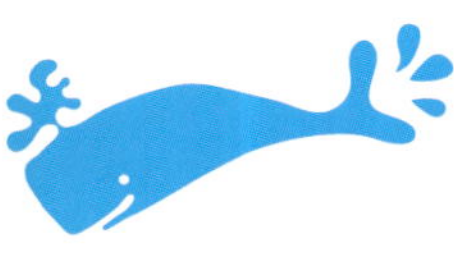

File name: MA_T45_01
Page 45

SAVE
THE WHALE

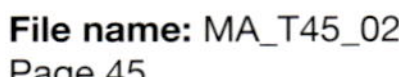

File name: MA_T45_02
Page 45

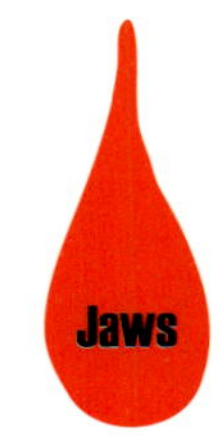

File name: MA_T46_01
Page 46

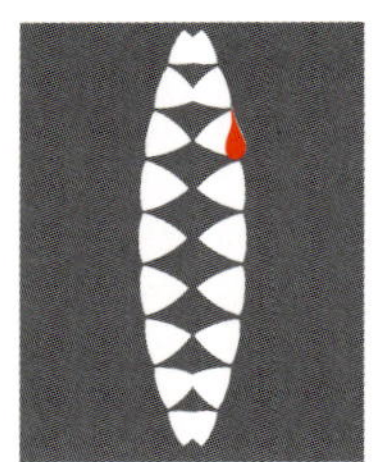

File name: MA_T46_02
Page 46

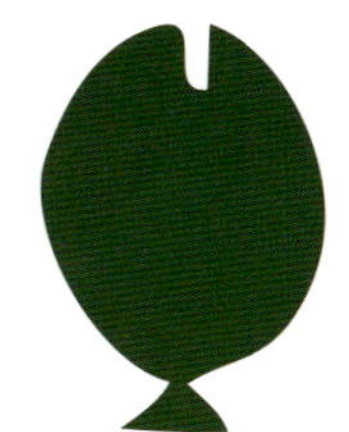

File name: MA_T47_01
Page 47

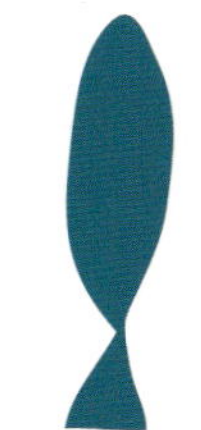

File name: MA_T47_02
Page 47

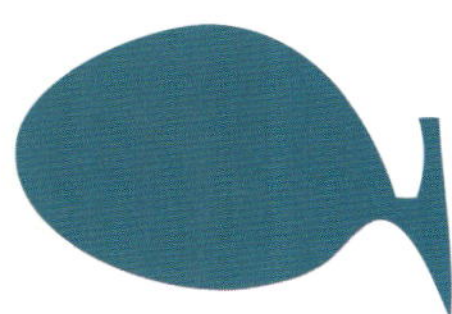

File name: MA_T47_03
Page 47

File name: MA_T47_04
Page 47

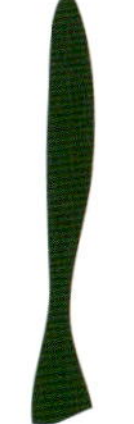

File name: MA_T47_05
Page 47

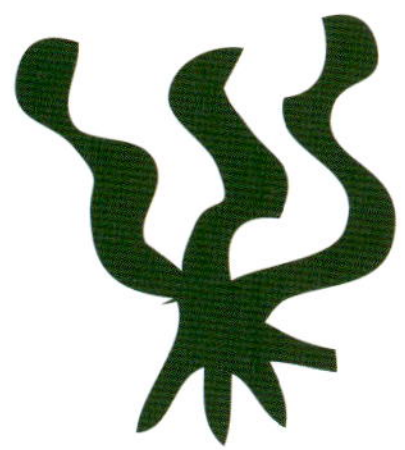

File name: MA_T47_06
Page 47

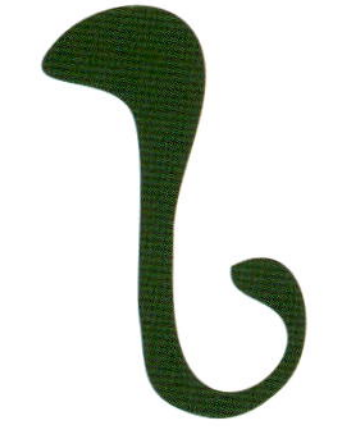

File name: MA_T47_07
Page 47

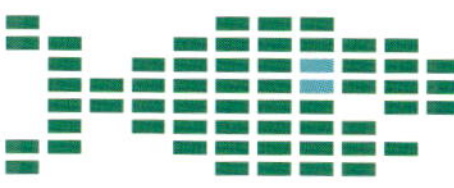

File name: MA_T48_01
Page 48

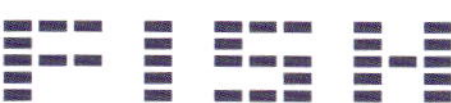

File name: MA_T48_02
Page 48

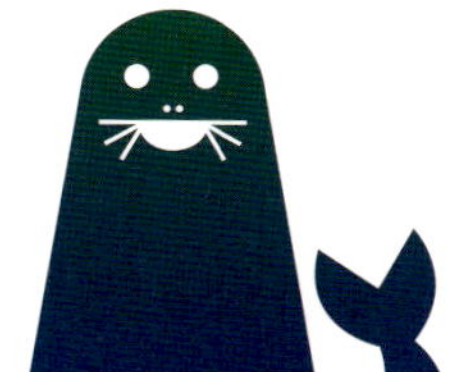

File name: MA_T49_01
Page 49

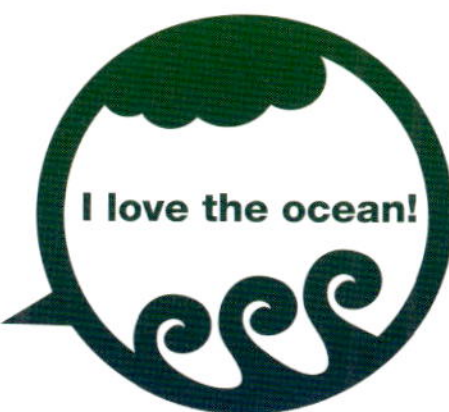

File name: MA_T49_02
Page 49

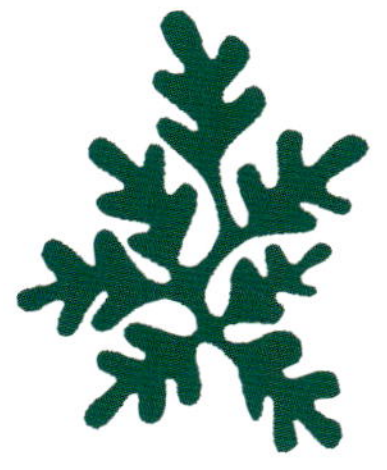

File name: MA_T50_01
Page 50

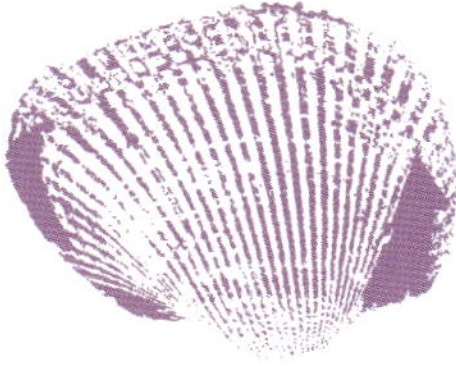

File name: MA_T50_02
Page 50

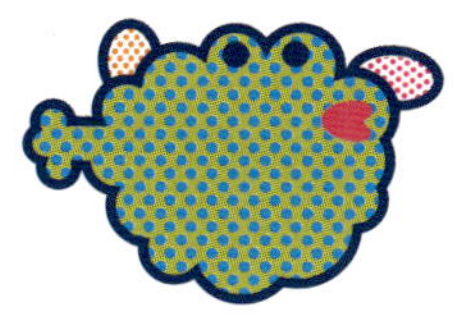

File name: MA_T51_01
Page 51

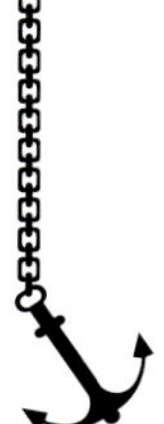

File name: MA_T51_02
Page 51

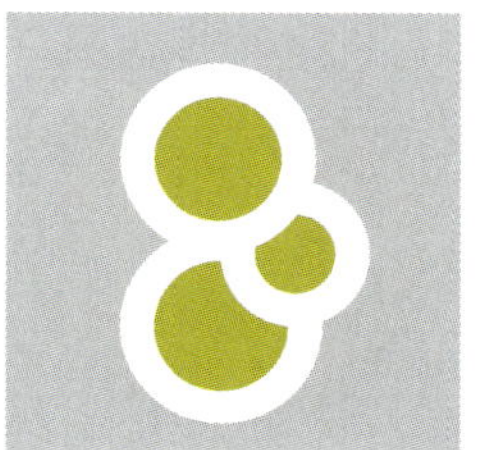

File name: MA_T51_03
Page 51

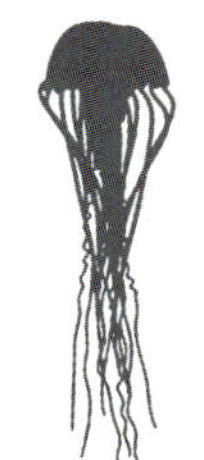

File name: MA_T52_01
Page 52

COMPONENTS

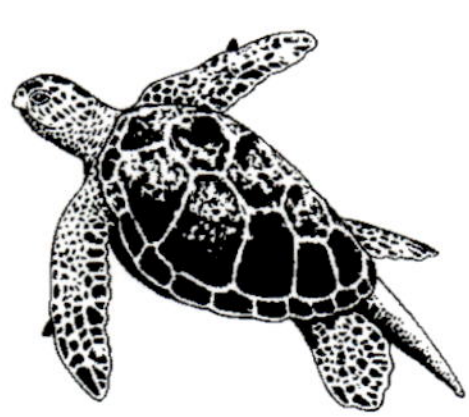

File name: MA_T52_02
Page 52

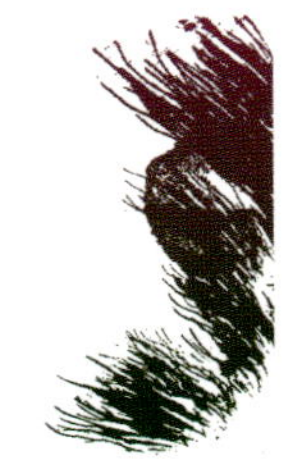

File name: MA_T52_03
Page 52

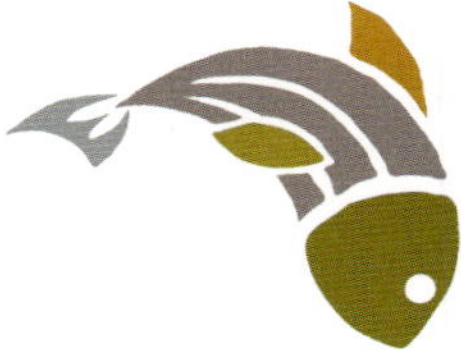

File name: MA_T53_01
Page 53

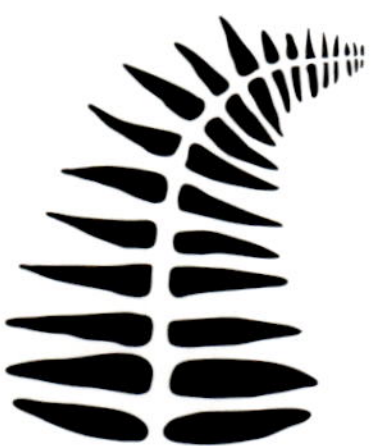

File name: MA_T54_01
Page 54

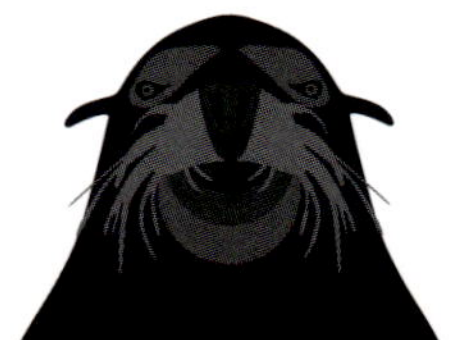

File name: MA_T55_01
Page 55

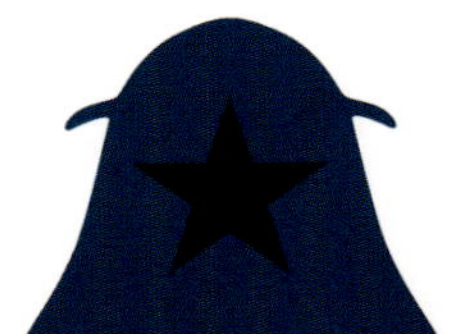

File name: MA_T55_02
Page 55

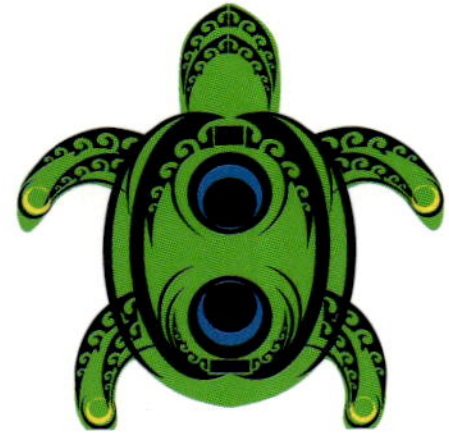

File name: MA_T56_01
Page 56

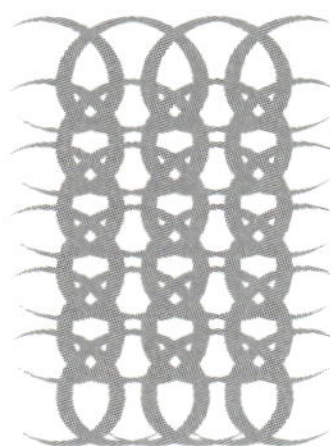

File name: MA_T56_02
Page 56

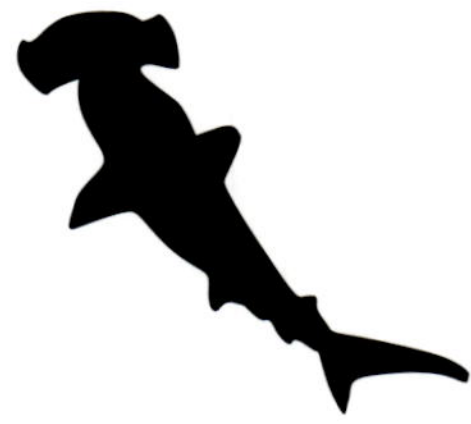

File name: MA_T57_01
Page 57

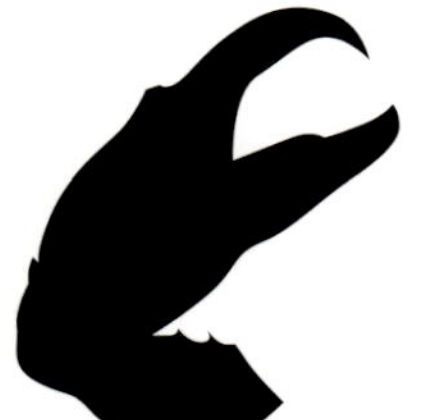

File name: MA_T57_02
Page 57

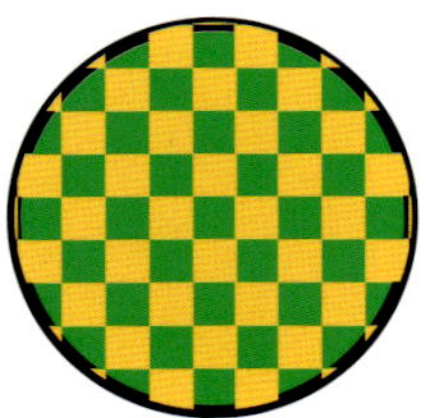

File name: MA_T57_03
Page 57

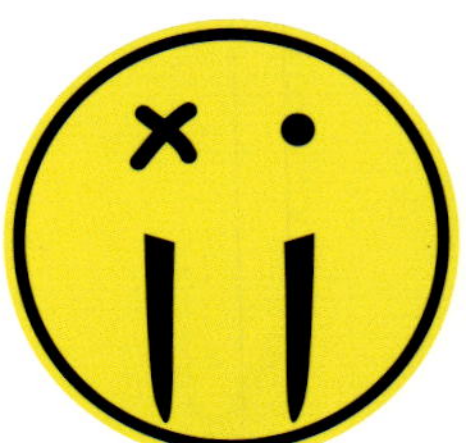

File name: MA_T58_01
Page 58

File name: MA_T59_01
Page 59

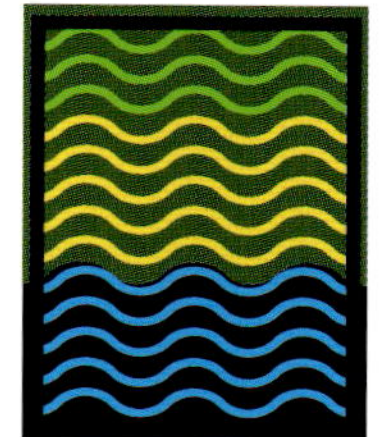

File name: MA_T59_02
Page 59

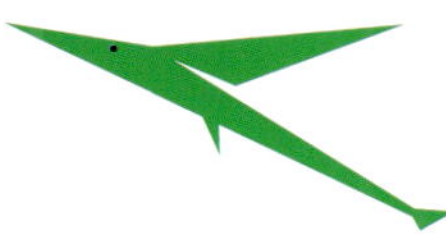

File name: MA_T60_01
Page 60

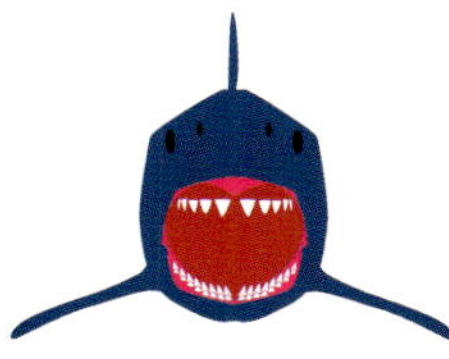

File name: MA_T61_01
Page 61

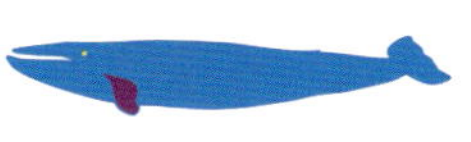

File name: MA_T62_01
Page 62

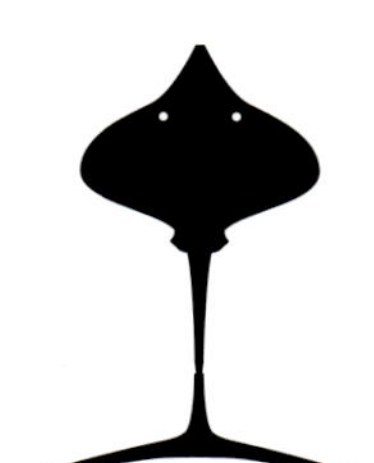

File name: MA_T63_01
Page 63

FLIPPER

File name: MA_T63_02
Page 63

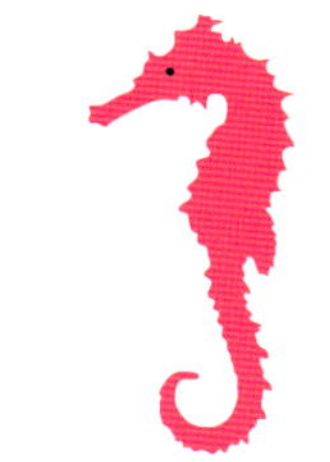

File name: MA_T64_01
Page 64

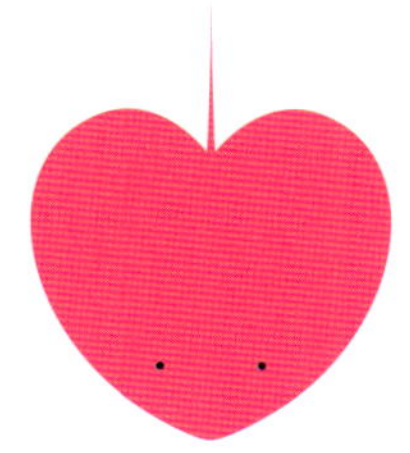

File name: MA_T64_02
Page 64

the ocean

File name: MA_T64_03
Page 64

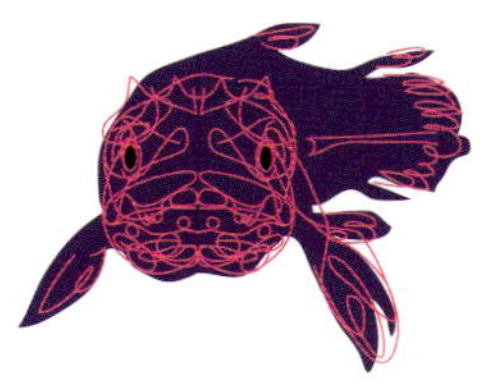

File name: MA_T65_01
Page 65

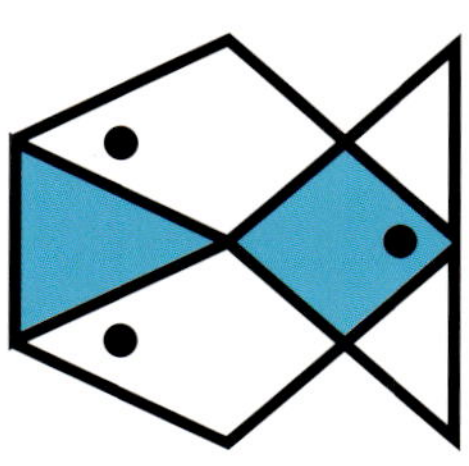

File name: MA_T66_01
Page 66

COMPONENTS

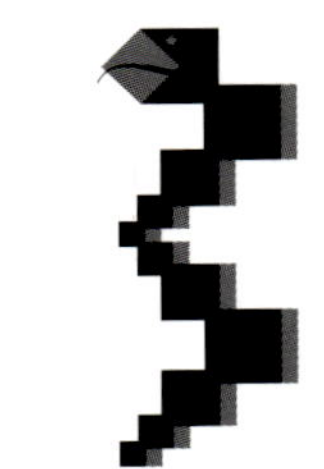

File name: MA_T67_01
Page 67

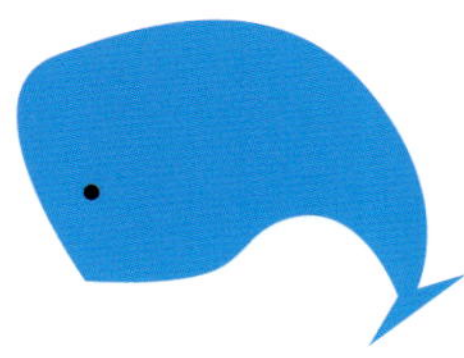

File name: MA_T68_01
Page 68

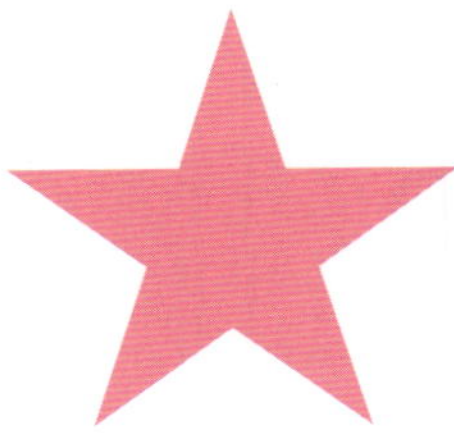

File name: MA_T68_02
Page 68

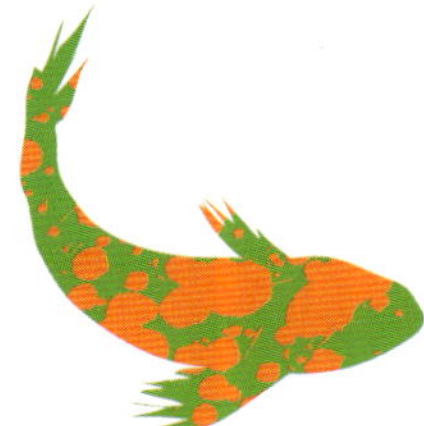

File name: MA_T69_01
Page 69

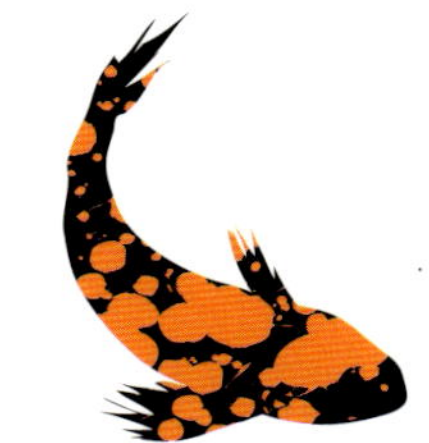

File name: MA_T69_02
Page 69

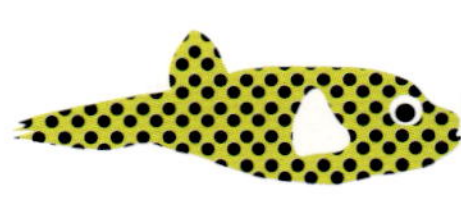

File name: MA_T70_01
Page 70

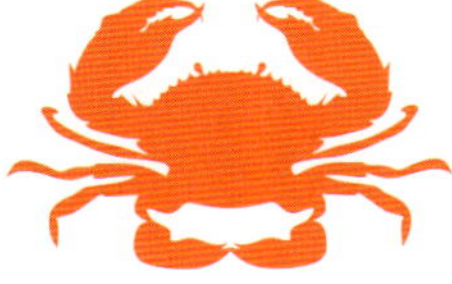

File name: MA_T71_01
Page 71

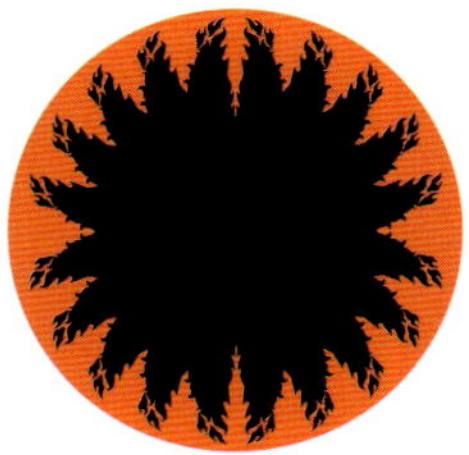

File name: MA_T71_02
Page 71

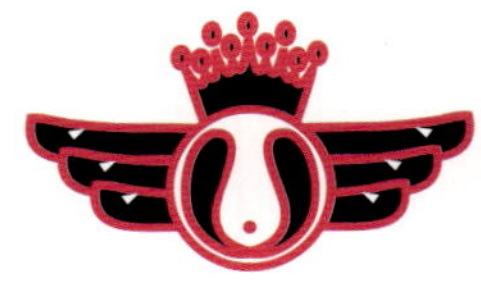

File name: MA_T72_01
Page 72

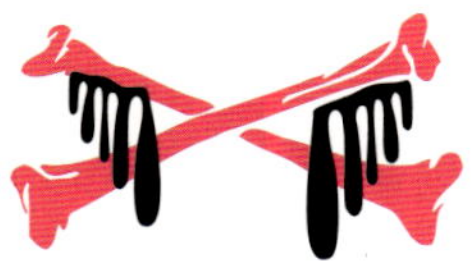

File name: MA_T72_02
Page 72

File name: MA_T72_03
Page 72

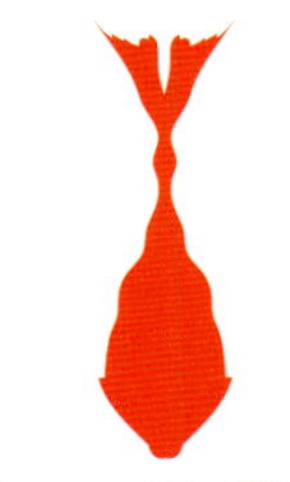

File name: MA_T73_01
Page 73

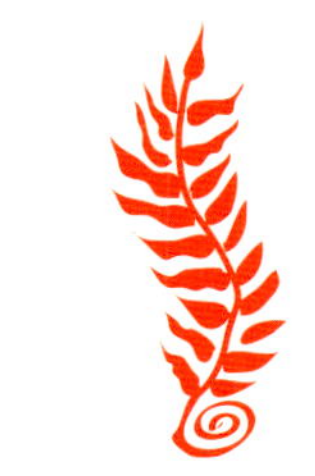

File name: MA_T73_02
Page 73

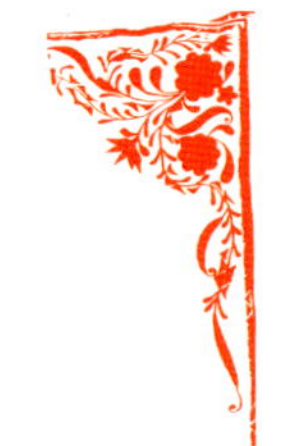

File name: MA_T73_03
Page 73

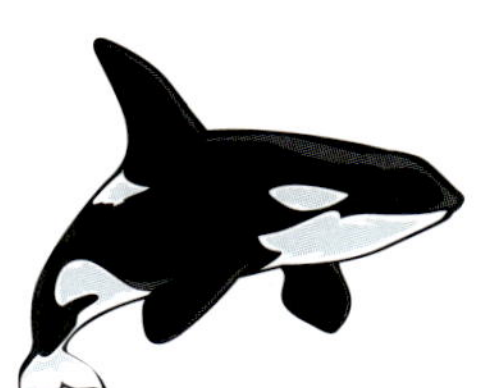

File name: MA_T74_01
Page 74

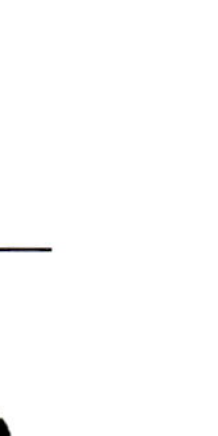

File name: MA_T74_02
Page 74

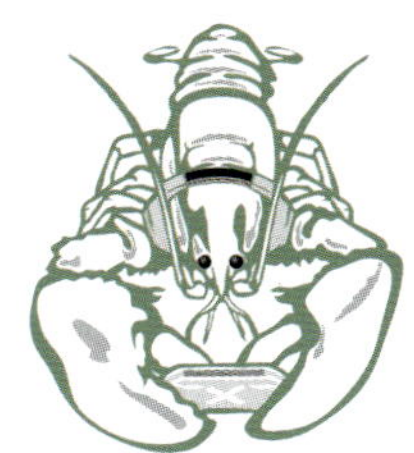

File name: MA_T75_01
Page 75

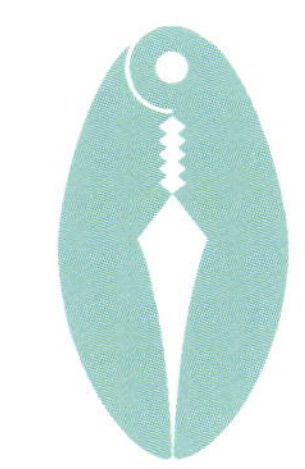

File name: MA_T75_02
Page 75

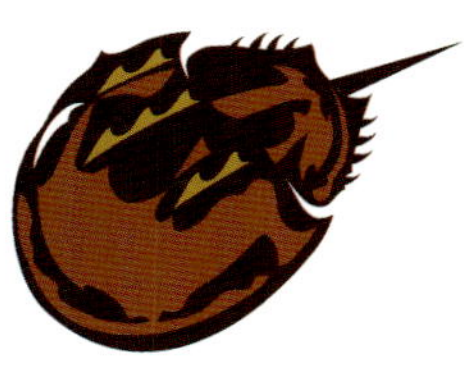

File name: MA_T76_01
Page 76

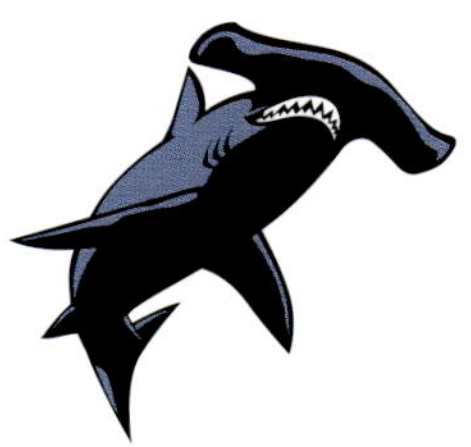

File name: MA_T77_01
Page 77

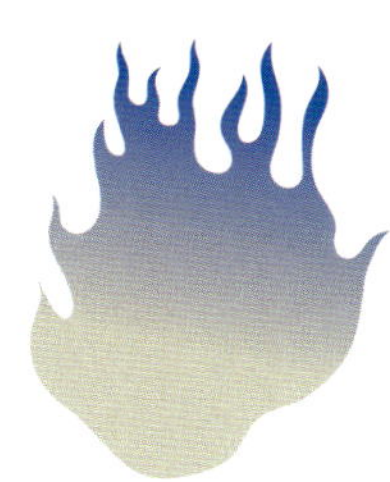

File name: MA_T77_02
Page 77

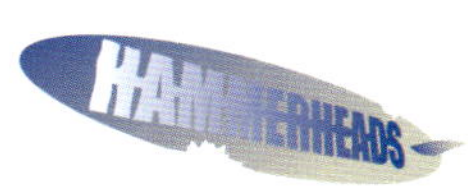

File name: MA_T77_03
Page 77

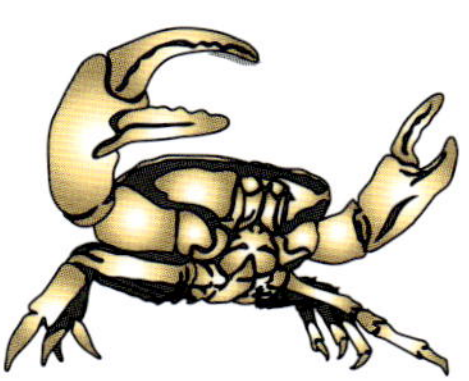

File name: MA_T78_01
Page 78

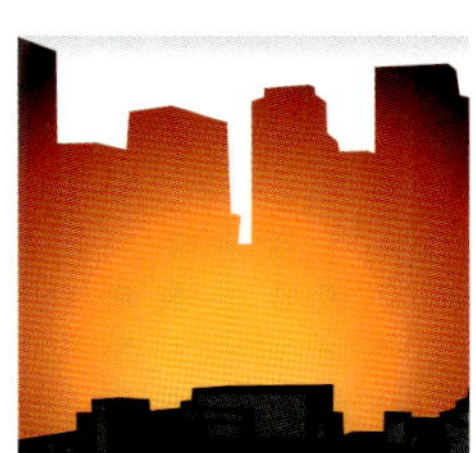

File name: MA_T78_02
Page 78

COMPONENTS

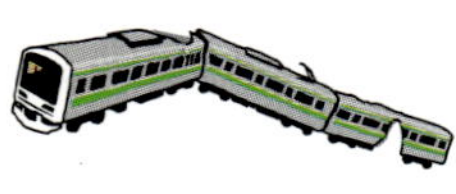

File name: MA_T78_03
Page 78

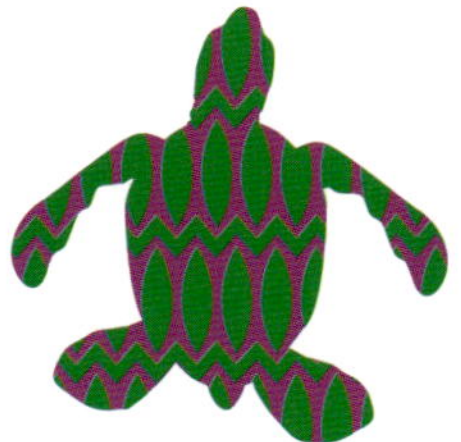

File name: MA_T79_01
Page 79

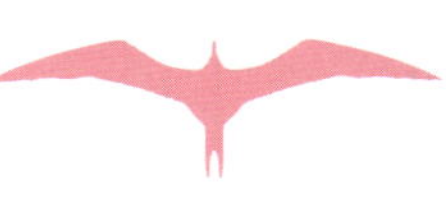

File name: MA_T79_02
Page 79

File name: MA_T79_03
Page 79

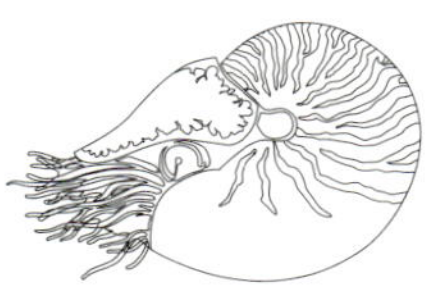

File name: MA_T80_01
Page 80

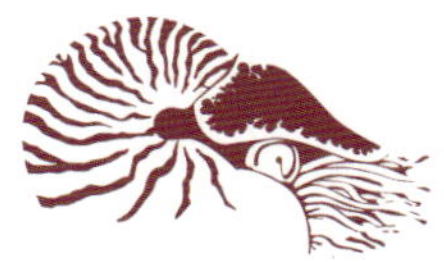

File name: MA_T80_02
Page 80

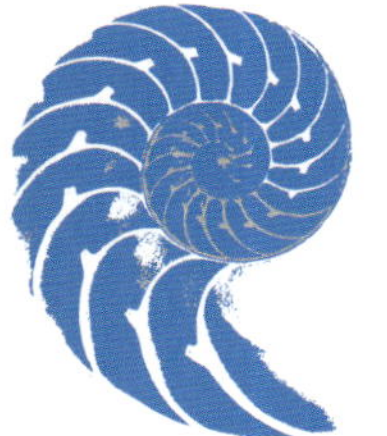

File name: MA_T80_03
Page 80

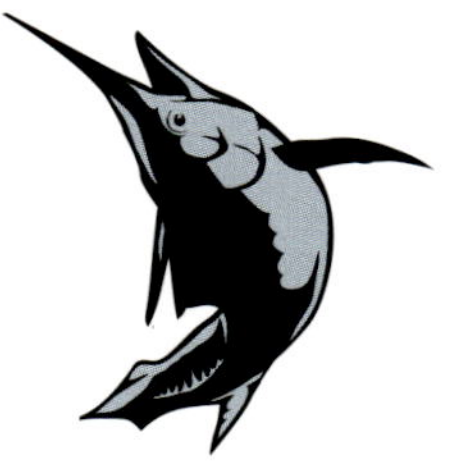

File name: MA_T81_01
Page 81

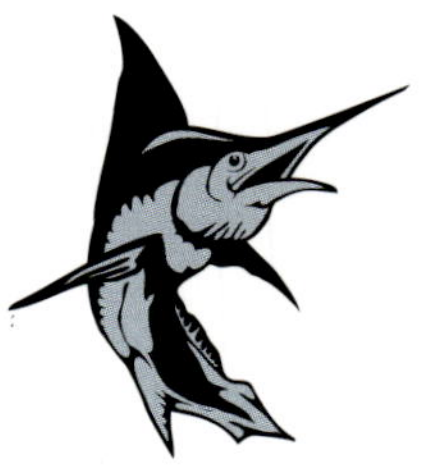

File name: MA_T81_02
Page 81

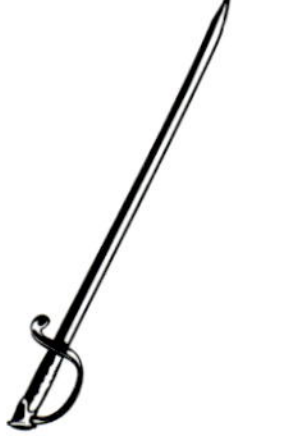

File name: MA_T81_03
Page 81

File name: MA_T81_04
Page 81

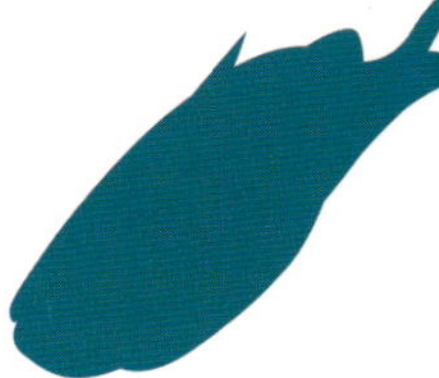

File name: MA_T82_01
Page 82

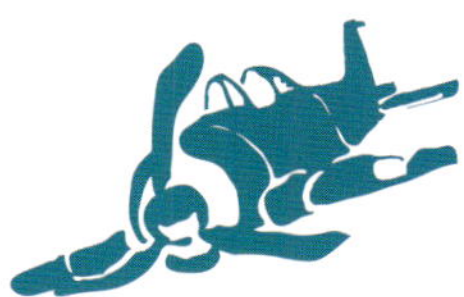

File name: MA_T82_01
Page 82

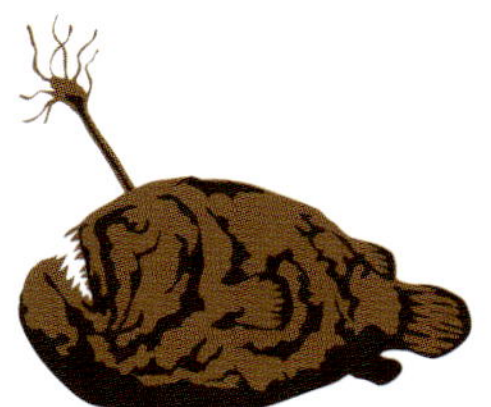

File name: MA_T83_01
Page 83

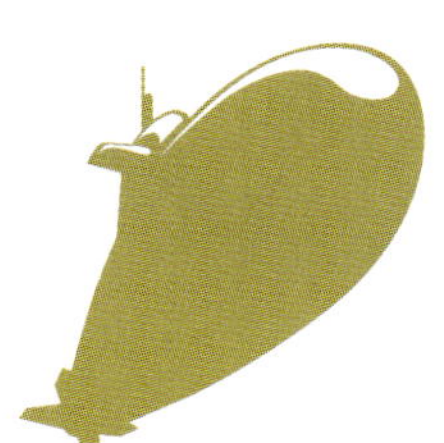

File name: MA_T83_02
Page 83

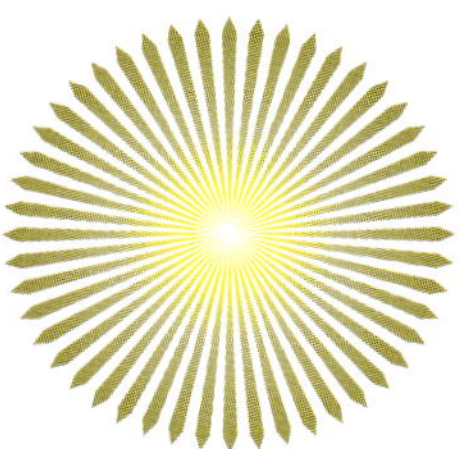

File name: MA_T83_03
Page 83

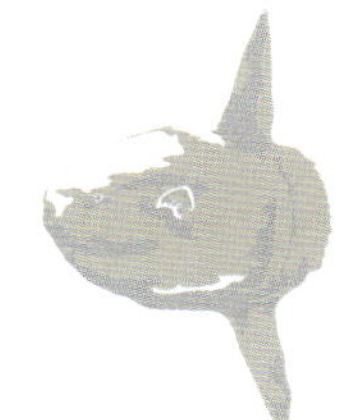

File name: MA_T84_01
Page 84

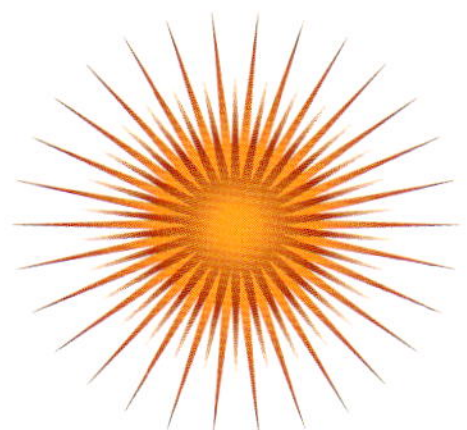

File name: MA_T84_02
Page 84

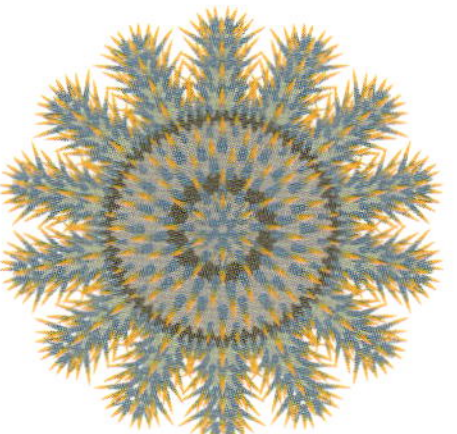

File name: MA_T85_01
Page 85

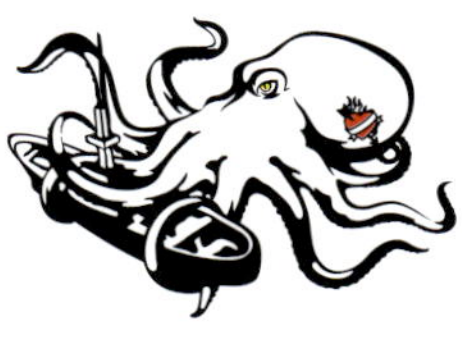

File name: MA_T86_01
Page 86

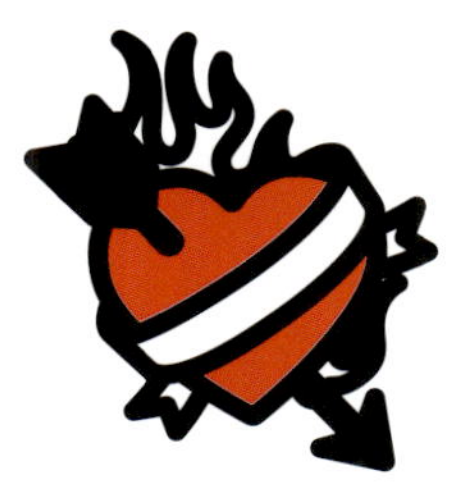

File name: MA_T86_02
Page 86

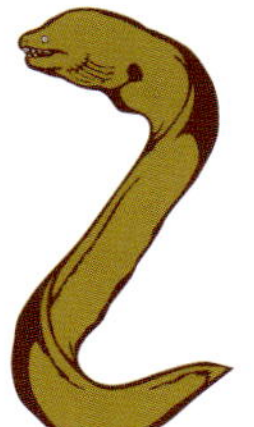

File name: MA_T87_01
Page 87

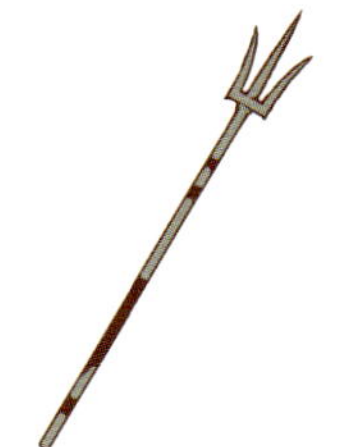

File name: MA_T87_02
Page 87

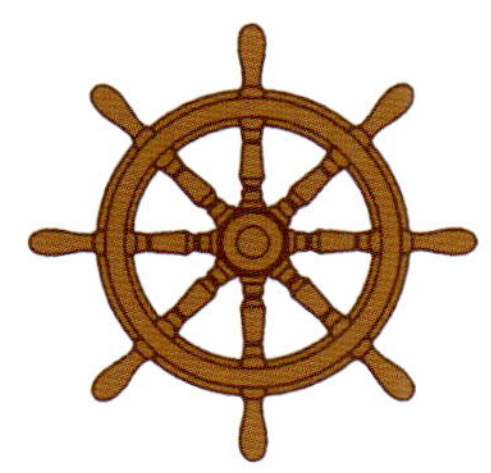

File name: MA_T87_03
Page 87

COMPONENTS

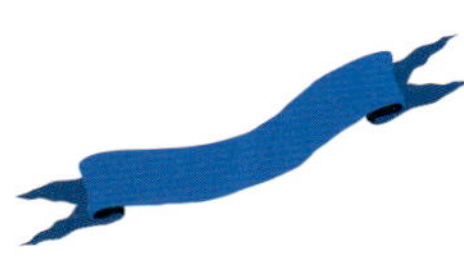

File name: MA_T87_04
Page 87

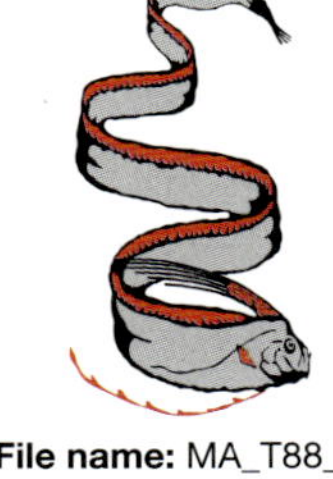

File name: MA_T88_01
Page 88

File name: MA_T88_02
Page 88

File name: MA_T88_03
Page 88

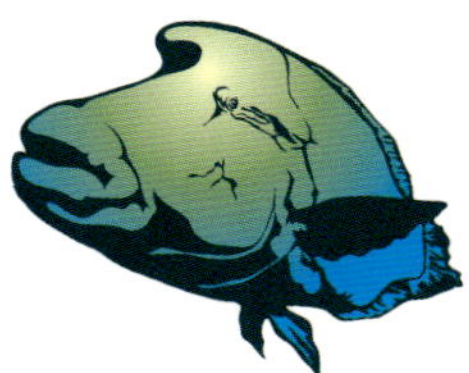

File name: MA_T89_01
Page 89

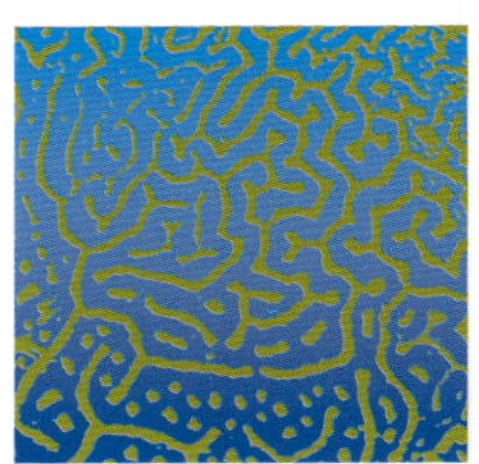

File name: MA_T89_02
Page 89

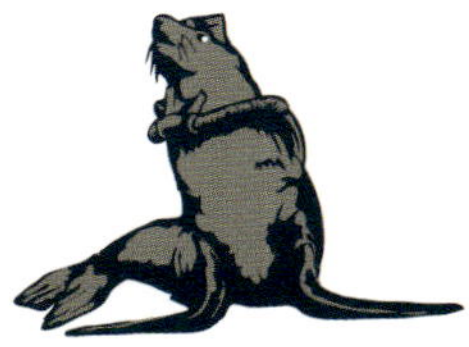

File name: MA_T90_01
Page 90

File name: MA_T90_02
Page 90

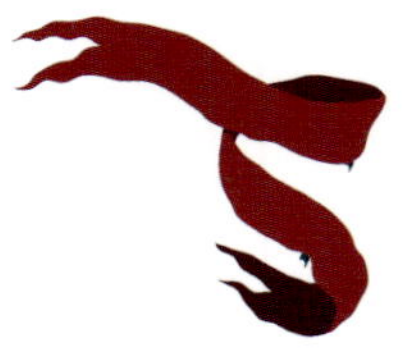

File name: MA_T90_03
Page 90

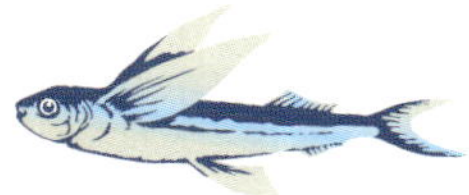

File name: MA_T91_01
Page 91

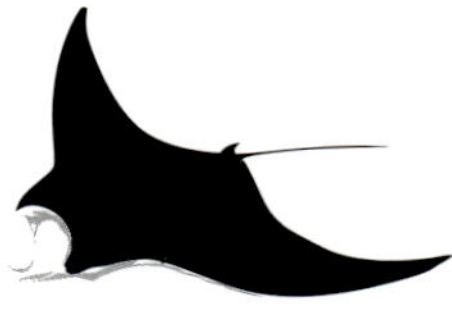

File name: MA_T92_01
Page 92

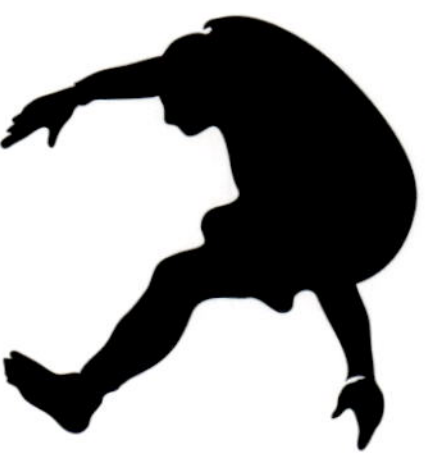

File name: MA_T92_02
Page 92

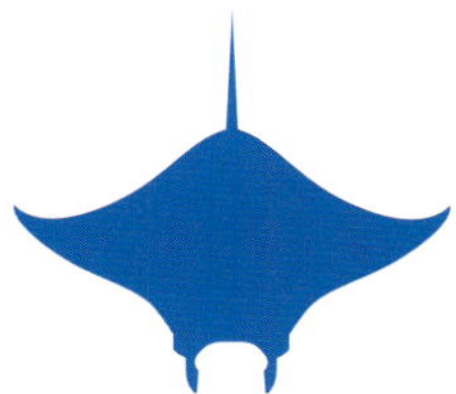

File name: MA_T92_03
Page 92

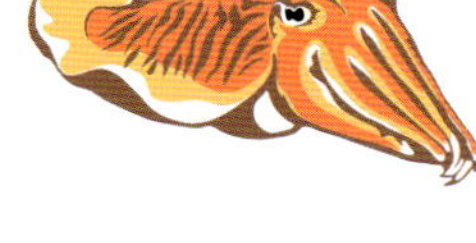

File name: MA_T93_01
Page 93

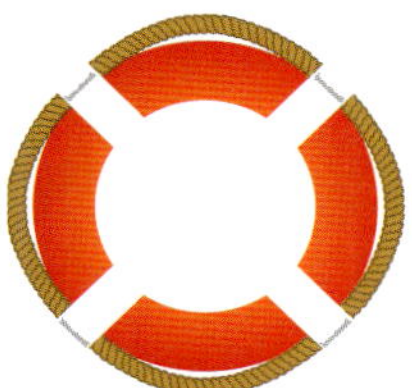

File name: MA_T93_02
Page 93

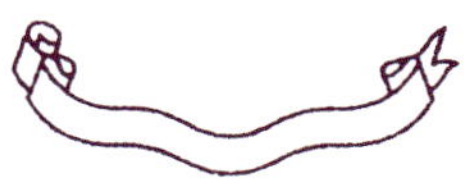

File name: MA_T93_03
Page 93

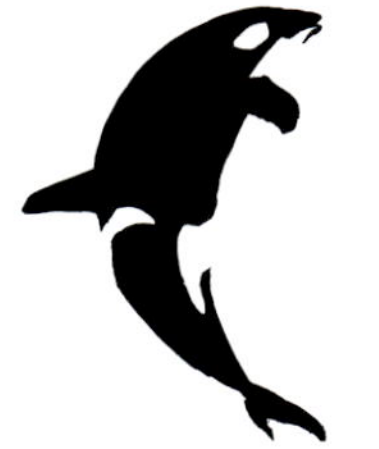

File name: MA_T94_01
Page 94

File name: MA_T94_02
Page 94

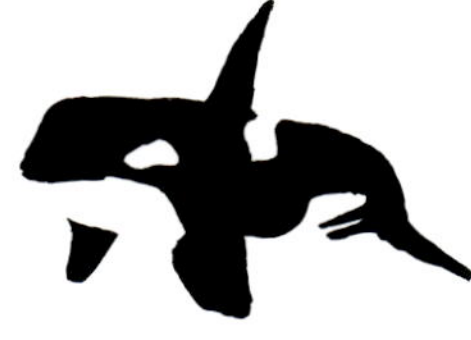

File name: MA_T95_01
Page 95

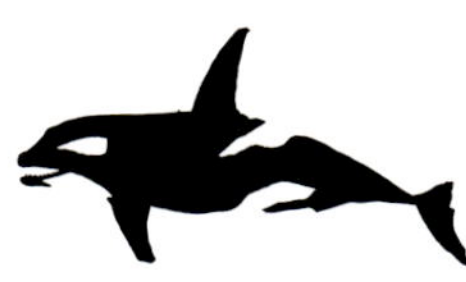

File name: MA_T95_02
Page 95

File name: MA_T95_03
Page 95

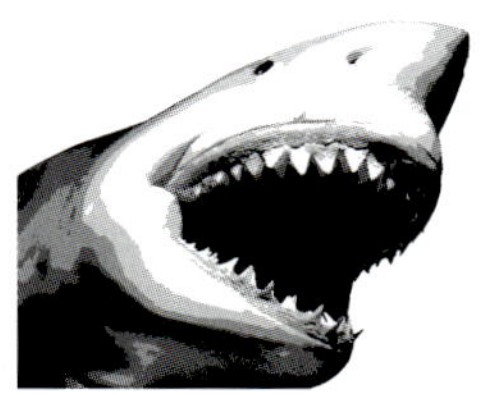

File name: MA_T96_01
Page 96

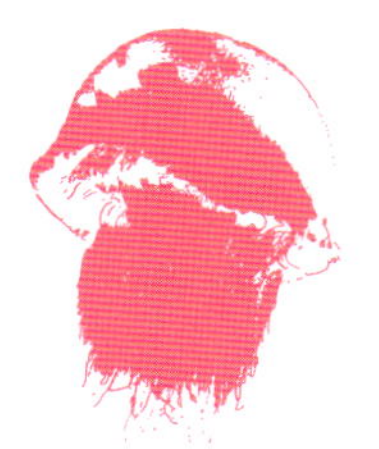

File name: MA_T97_01
Page 97

File name: MA_T97_02
Page 97

COMPONENTS

File name: MA_T98_01
Page 98

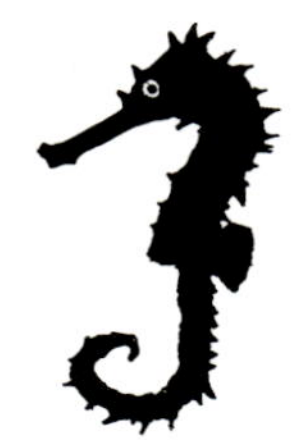

File name: MA_T98_02
Page 98

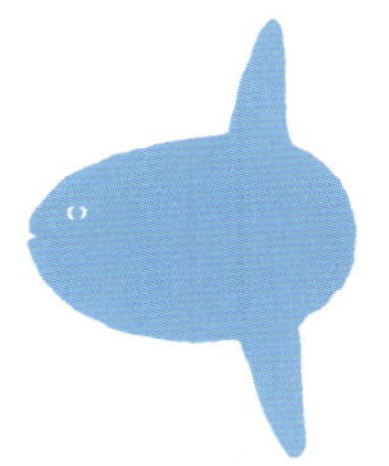

File name: MA_T98_03
Page 98

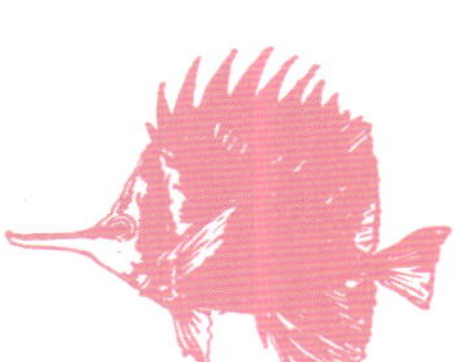

File name: MA_T99_01
Page 99

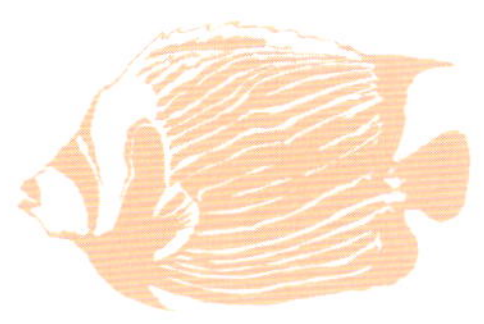

File name: MA_T99_02
Page 99

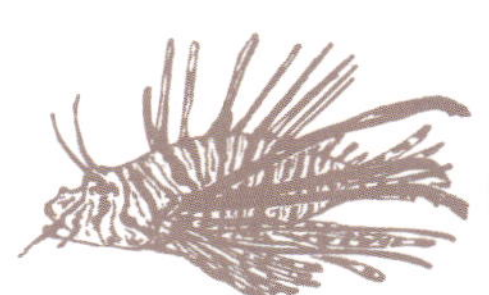

File name: MA_T99_03
Page 99

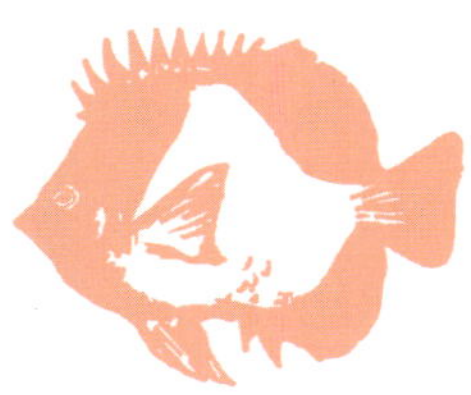

File name: MA_T99_04
Page 99

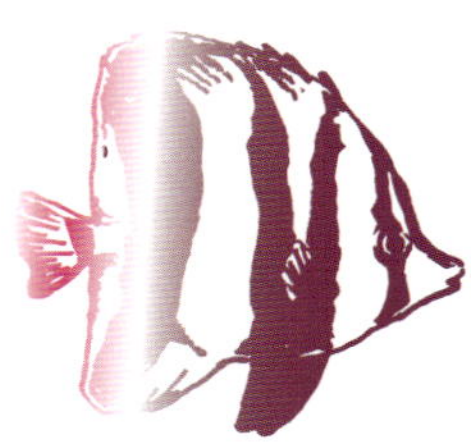

File name: MA_T100_01
Page 100

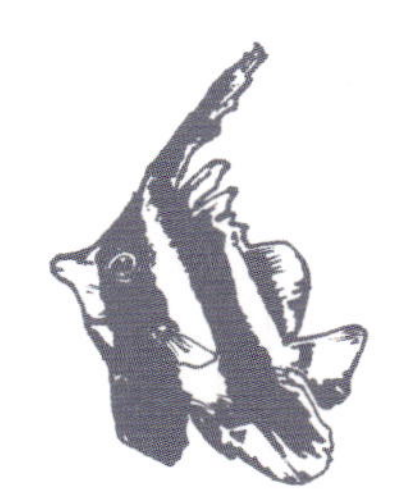

File name: MA_T101_01
Page 101

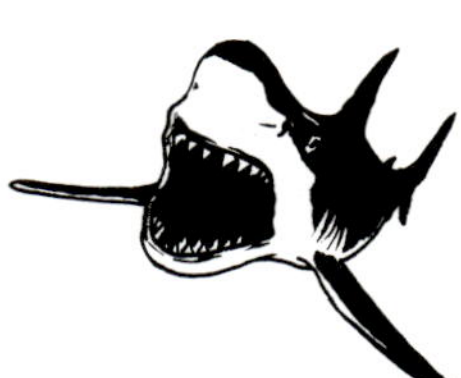

File name: MA_T102_01
Page 102

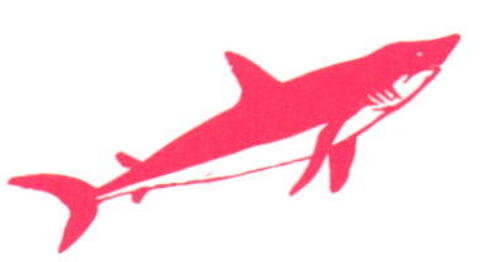

File name: MA_T102_02
Page 102

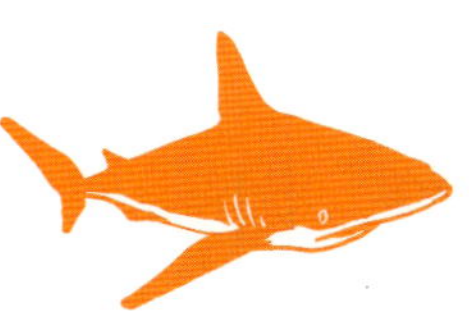

File name: MA_T102_03
Page 102

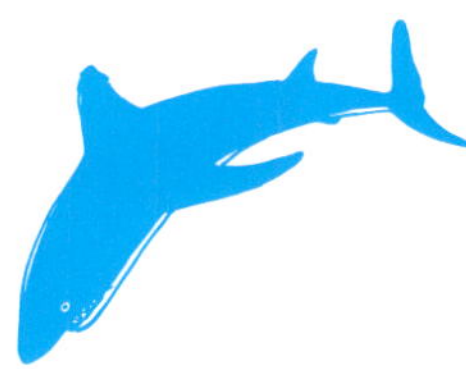

File name: MA_T102_04
Page 102

File name: MA_T103_01
Page 103

File name: MA_T103_02
Page 103

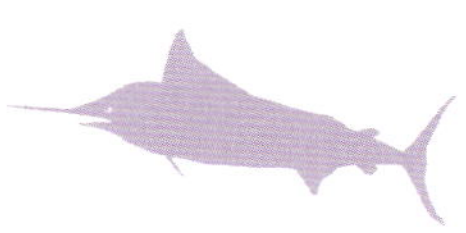

File name: MA_T104_01
Page 104

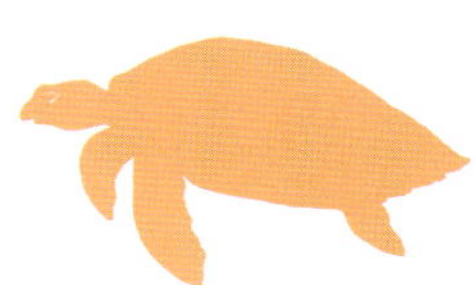

File name: MA_T104_02
Page 104

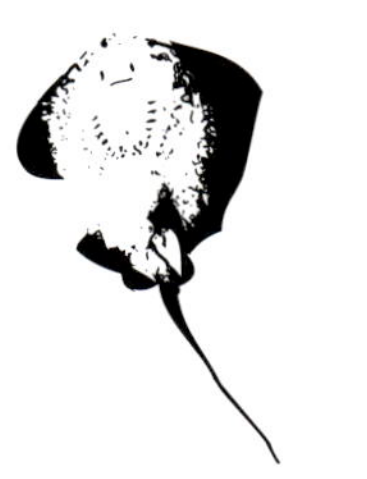

File name: MA_T105_01
Page 105

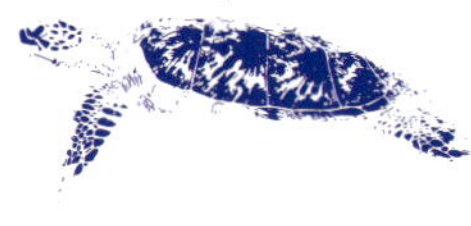

File name: MA_T105_02
Page 105

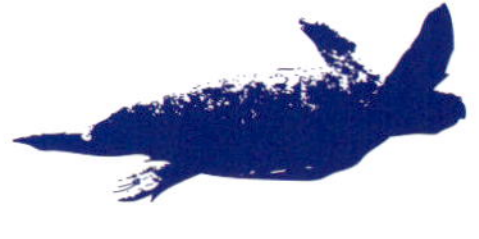

File name: MA_T105_03
Page 105

File name: MA_T105_04
Page 105

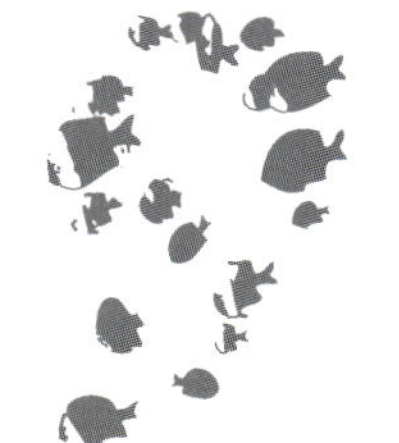

File name: MA_T105_05
Page 105

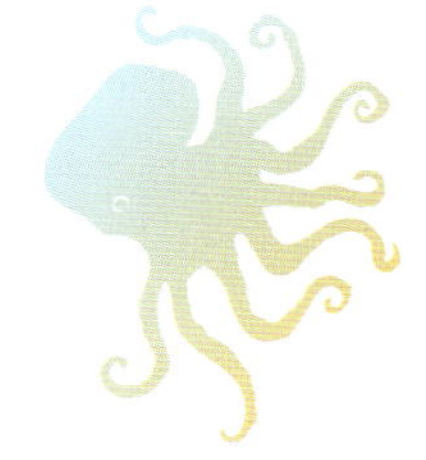

File name: MA_T106_01
Page 106

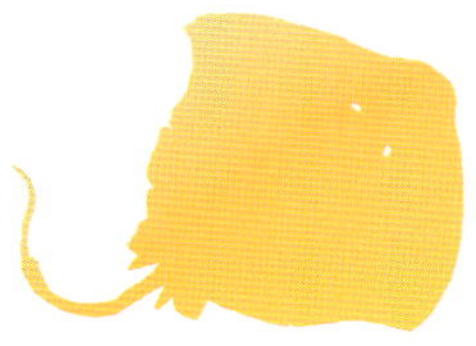

File name: MA_T106_02
Page 106

COMPONENTS

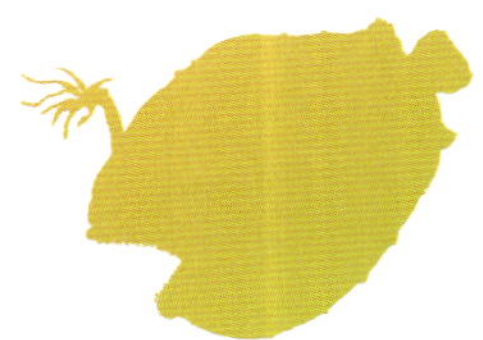

File name: MA_T106_03
Page 106

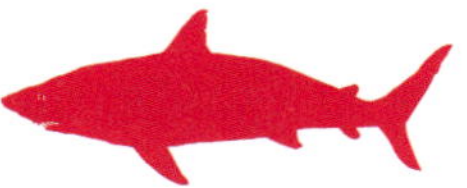

File name: MA_T107_01
Page 107

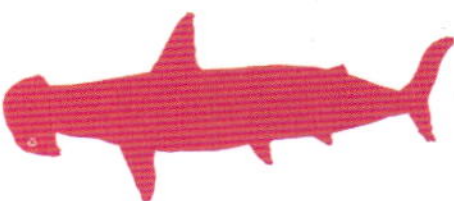

File name: MA_T107_02
Page 107

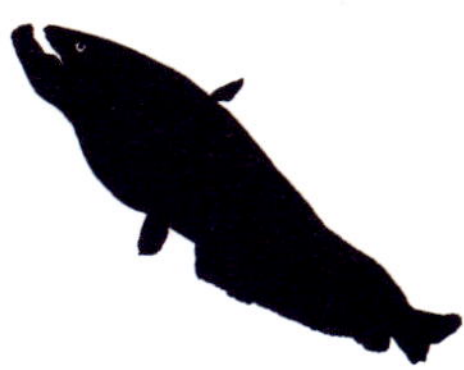

File name: MA_T108_01
Page 108

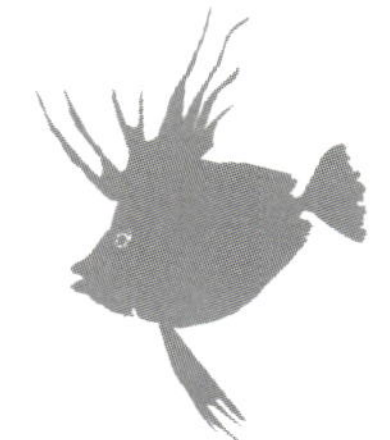

File name: MA_T109_01
Page 109

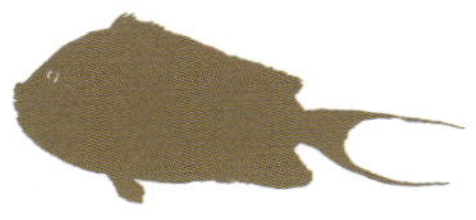

File name: MA_T109_02
Page 109

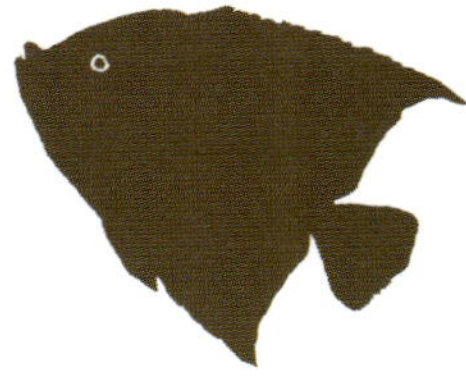

File name: MA_T109_03
Page 109

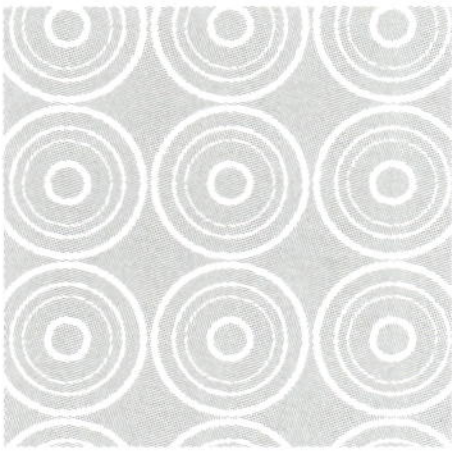

File name: MA_T109_04
Page 109

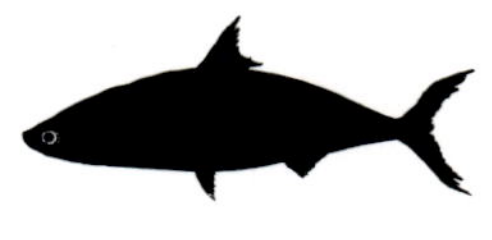

File name: MA_T110_01
Page 110

File name: MA_T110_02
Page 110

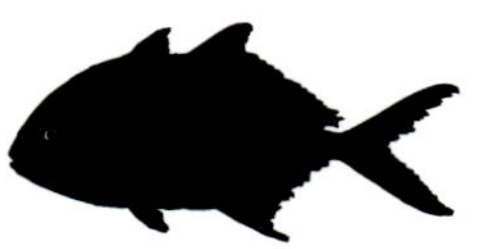

File name: MA_T110_03
Page 110

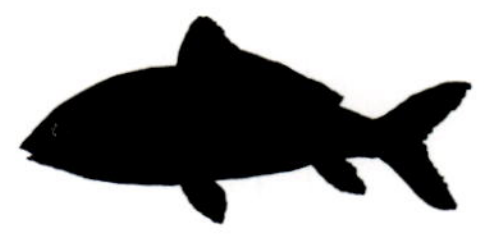

File name: MA_T110_04
Page 110

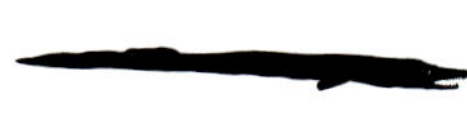

File name: MA_T110_05
Page 110

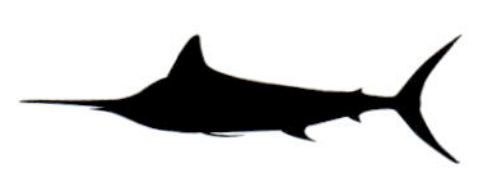

File name: MA_T111_01
Page 111

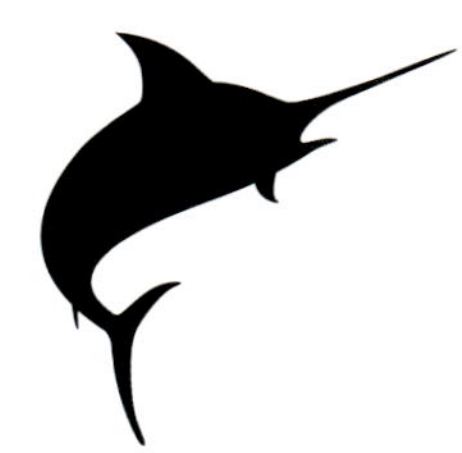

File name: MA_T111_02
Page 111

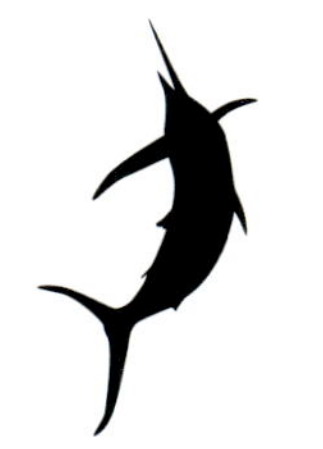

File name: MA_T111_03
Page 111

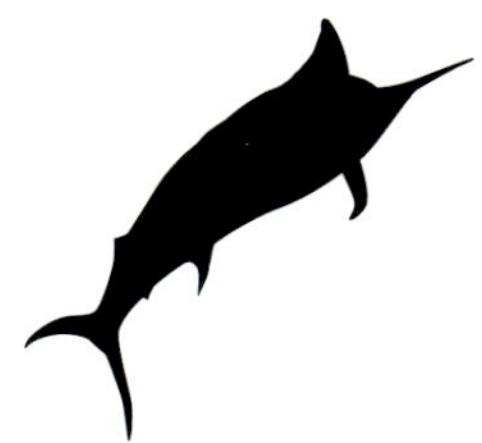

File name: MA_T111_04
Page 111

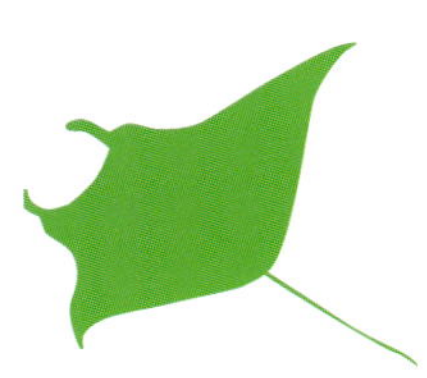

File name: MA_T112_01
Page 112

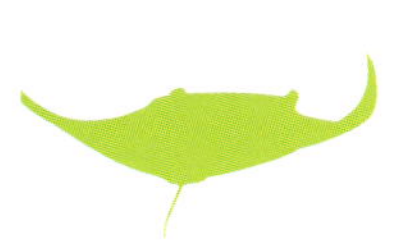

File name: MA_T112_02
Page 112

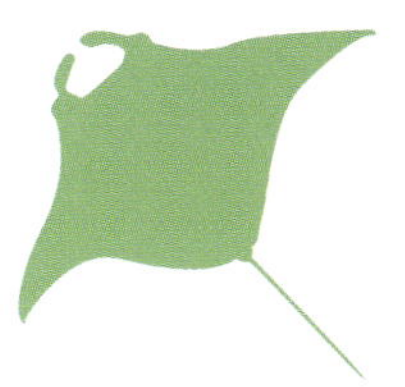

File name: MA_T112_03
Page 112

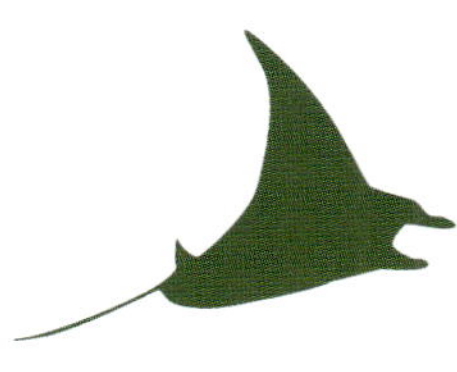

File name: MA_T112_04
Page 112

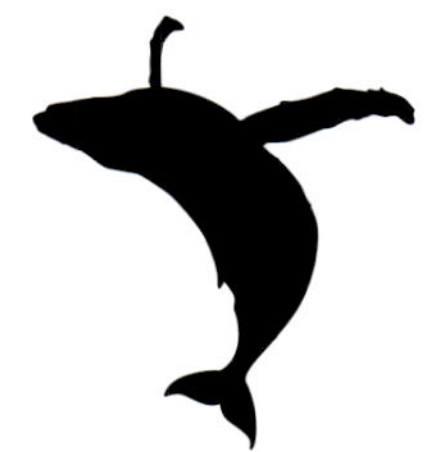

File name: MA_T113_01
Page 113

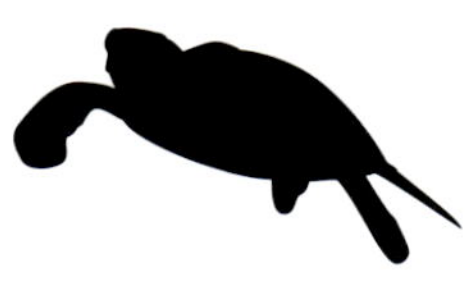

File name: MA_T113_02
Page 113

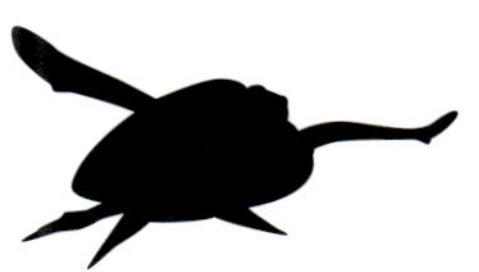

File name: MA_T113_03
Page 113

COMPONENTS

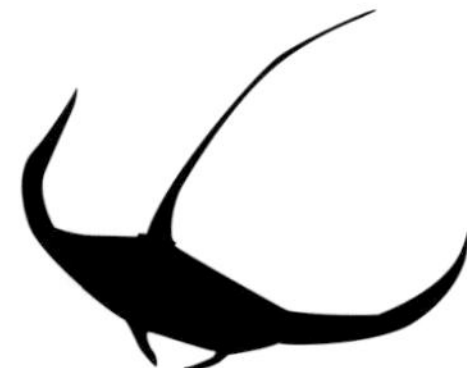

File name: MA_T113_04
Page 113

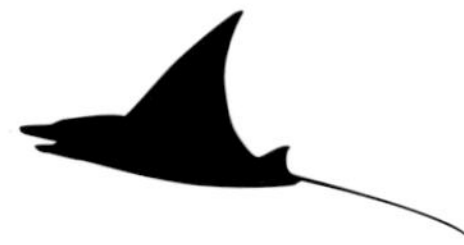

File name: MA_T113_05
Page 113

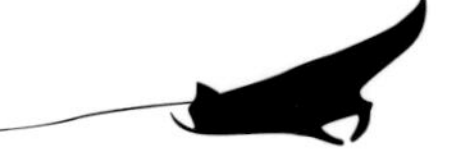

File name: MA_T113_06
Page 113

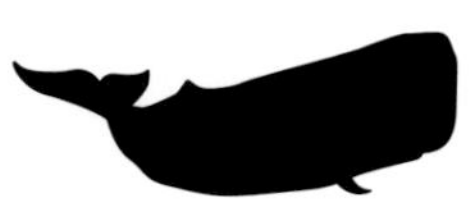

File name: MA_T113_07
Page 113

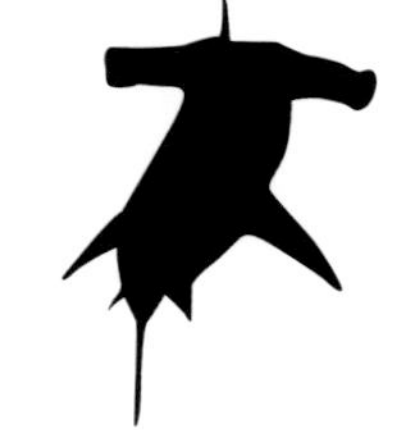

File name: MA_T113_08
Page 113

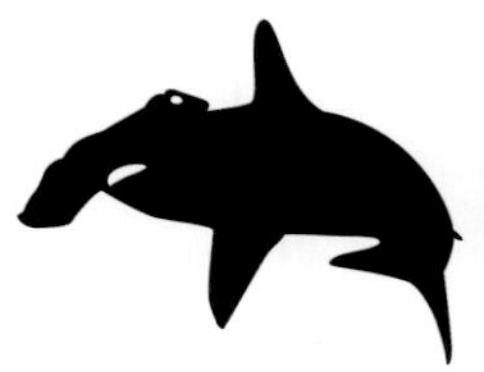

File name: MA_T113_09
Page 113

File name: MA_T113_10
Page 113

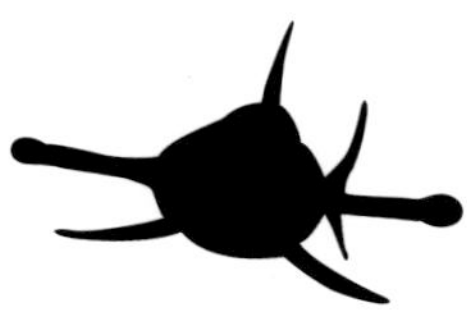

File name: MA_T113_11
Page 113

License Agreement for the CD-ROM Files

Licenser: ricorico

1. License
Licenser hereby grants a non-exclusive and non-transferable right and license to use the Templates and Components files in the CD-ROM (hereinafter referred to as "Files") to a customer who purchased the book Bones and Skulls (hereinafter referred to as "Book"), and who agreed to the terms and conditions of this Agreement (hereinafter referred to as "User").

The User may process, modify, and/or edit the Files included in the CD-ROM or distribute them as a single file or in combination with other materials on a printed matter as design material in the User's work, such as:

a. digital media, including websites.
b. graphics for shop interiors and signs.
c. leaflets, flyers, posters, direct mail, catalogues, pamphlets, and other tools for advertisement or sales promotion.
d. goods, clothes, greeting cards, business cards, and other articles for personal production and use. The files may be used for personal, professional, and commercial purposes, provided that the articles produced are not offered for sale. The User may not sell articles made with the Files even when of a personal nature. Please read the following Limitations carefully:

2. Limitations
The User is not licensed to do any of the following:

a. License, or otherwise by any means permit, any other person to use the Files.
b. Use the Files for commercial production of postcards, business cards, or any other articles, or sell any such articles made using the Files.
c. Provide downloading services using the Files (including greeting card services).
d. Use the Files in order to produce any software or any other objects for sale.
e. Acquire the copyright in any material in the Files or any objects created using the Files.
f. Use the Files to create obscene, scandalous, abusive or slanderous works.

3. Copyright and Other Intellectual Property
ricorico and its suppliers reserve the copyright and other intellectual property rights in the Files. When specifying the User of a product made using the Files, please also indicate "© 2010 ricorico".

4. Exclusion of Damages
In no event shall Rockport Publishers and ricorico be liable for any damages whatsoever (including but not limited to, damages for loss of profit or loss of the file contents) related to the use or inability to use the Files or use the materials in the Files.

5. Termination of this License Agreement
If the User breaches any of the articles in this Agreement, Rockport Publishers and ricorico have the right to withdraw the User's License granted on the basis hereof.

ABOUT THE AUTHOR

ricoricio *is a Tokyo-based book packaging company established in 2009. They have been actively producing books in the area of graphic design, photography, craft, pop culture, and manga, including two titles that they also authored.*